Books by Edward Hallowell

Driven to Distraction

Answers to Distraction

Finding the Heart of the Child

When You Worry About the Child You Love

Emotional and

Learning Problems

in Children

Edward Hallowell, M.D.

Simon & Schuster   New York

SIMON & SCHUSTER
Rockefeller Center
1230 Avenue of the Americas
New York, NY 10020

Designed by Karolina Harris

Manufactured in the United States of America

1 2 3 4 5 6 7 8 9 10

Library of Congress Cataloging-in-Publication Data
Hallowell, Edward
When you worry about the child you love : emotional and learning
problems in children / Edward Hallowell.
p.   cm.
Includes index.
1. Emotional problems of children—Physiological aspects.   2. Learning
disabilities—Physiological aspects.   3. Emotional problems of children—
Genetic aspects.   4. Learning disabilities—Genetic aspects.   I. Title.
RJ486.5.H24   1996
618.92′89—dc20   96-33857
CIP
ISBN 0-684-80090-X

This book is for my children, Lucy, Jack, and Tucker—and, even though their mother wanted me to leave the dedication just for the kids, it is also for my wife, Sue. With all my love.

Contents

Contents

When You Worry

About the Child

You Love

Introduction

....

A Parent's Worry Should Lead to Hope: What's in This Book

The worry we feel over our children is a special kind of pain. It hurts differently than other kinds of worry. It is a sweet agony every parent knows, made of love and fear, helplessness and faith all combined. It knows no end. Once you have your first child, you are never free of it for very long. It is often our first thought of the day and our last thought at night. There is no way to avoid this worry, but sometimes knowledge or a friendly voice can help. This book offers both.

When I was a fourth-year medical student at Tulane, I did a rotation in obstetrics at Charity, a sprawling, steamy New Orleans hospital, bustling with life in all its critical stages. The medical students did most of the normal deliveries at Charity because there were not enough full-fledged doctors to go around. I delivered thirty-seven babies there that August, and I got to know many mothers well as I sat with them hour after hour during labor. "You gotta be crazy to have kids," groaned one woman, who was having her fourth baby. As the pain subsided she added: "But you gotta be more crazy not to. You have kids?" she asked.

"No, not yet," I replied. "I hope to, though, someday." I wasn't even married at the time.

"Well, when you do, remember this: If you do right by 'em, that'll turn out to be the best thing you ever did in your whole life." I've turned her advice over in my mind many times since then. I think she was right. Raising kids *is* the best thing I have ever done—although not always the thing I've done best!

We parents love our children more than anything in the world. Being the father now of three children myself, I've learned the meaning of that love firsthand, and being a child psychiatrist, I have learned about it from many other parents' points of view. Love for our children makes us better than we ever were before, but that love challenges us as nothing else does. The love we feel for our children grows over us like a spell. It becomes part of who we are.

We stick with our children, if not physically at least psychologically, throughout life, and they stick with us. Your child teaches you about love as you never knew it could be. Just as the lady at Charity said, raising our kids is the best thing we ever do.

But like all love, a parent's love is complex, and so is what a child gives back. Sometimes our kids drive us crazy. They can be exasperating, frustrating, annoying, and demanding, sometimes all at once. And, of course, there is that never-ending worry. I have a sixty-five-year-old friend who runs a successful consulting business; his ninety-year-old mother still calls him up when it rains to remind him not to go outside without his rubbers. Our worry winds its way from cradle to grave: their cradle, our grave.

Most of us are good parents—at least, we're as good as we can be. We read all the time about "bad" parents, parents who abuse or neglect their children, but most parents, the ones we never read about, spend their days providing for their children and taking care of them as well as they can. Good parents—and this includes the *vast* majority of parents—stick up for their children at every turn, suffering inside at every slight and every disappointment.

I am a relative newcomer to parenthood. Ten years after my time at Charity my wife, Sue, gave birth to Lucy, our first child. That was July 16, 1989. Three years later, our first son, Jack, was born. Three years after Jack's birth we had Tucker, our third child and second son. So we are at the beginning of the great adventure. And what an adventure it is!

It is a good thing we have children. When we are growing up, we live for ourselves, and we are too young to know the deeper meanings of life. We are too busy living, just as our children are busy now. This is the great gift our children give us: They release us to love them more than we love ourselves. We will keep our children safe forever, as long as forever lasts for us.

But in keeping them safe, we all need help. When problems arise, as they always do, we parents start to wonder what we have done wrong and what we should be doing differently. Since there is no definitive manual on how to be a parent we look to whatever guidance is at hand: cultural folklore, grandparents' advice, newspaper articles and books, the practice of friends' parents, or the suggestions of professionals such as teachers, pediatricians, and various practitioners in the field of mental health. Fortunately, the collective wisdom of these advisers is usually reliable.

Sometimes, however, it is not. Sometimes the cause of the child's problem is hidden from the view even of our family elders and local experts. The past few decades have seen such a burst of growth in the sciences, particularly the sciences of child development and neurobiology, that many generally knowledgeable adults are still misinformed about invisible biological causes of emotional problems in children. What is common knowledge to scientists and physicians has not yet made its way to the average parent or the general public.

This means that many parents and their children suffer unnecessarily. The children do not get the right diagnosis because the right diagnosis, which is medical, lies buried under the wrong diagnosis, which is, more often than not, moral. "Bad" might be the diagnosis, for example, applied to child and parent alike. Or "spoiled," or "lazy," or "manipulative," or "incorrigible," or even "evil." There is a long list of moral diagnoses, and they can totally eclipse the light of the correct, medical diagnosis.

The purpose of this book is to end that eclipse. Parents need to know that many causes of childhood emotional problems are beyond their control and their children's. When a child is disruptive or unhappy or unable to fit in, it is not always the parents' fault, the child's fault, or anybody's fault. Parents and their children need help to find illuminating answers, instead of obscuring judgments, so that they can get past blame to proper treatment.

Sometimes the problem is simply a matter of fit between parent and child. Stella Chess and Alexander Thomas, two pioneers in temperament research, emphasized the importance of examining the "goodness of fit" between parent and child. If the fit is off— if, for example, a rambunctious, outgoing child is born to a quiet, introverted parent—the problems that can ensue should reflect poorly on no one; rather, there is simply a difficult fit. Instead of blame, the parent needs help in learning how to deal with the child's basic nature.

Beyond inborn temperament, there are a number of other childhood conditions that may have a strong base in biology. Some syndromes are common, like shyness or depression; some are less common but not rare, like attention deficit disorder and obsessive-compulsive disorder; some are much more common than most people realize, like Tourette syndrome, a disorder that produces involuntary tics, and trichotillomania, the compulsion to pull out one's own hair. All these conditions originate in the biological makeup of the child, not in parental mistakes or in the child's immediate environment.

Biology contributes to all behavior and personality. Not only severe pathological syndromes but also many mild emotional problems or common maladaptive tendencies may stem from genetics. In our culture we look immediately to the environment

—parents, school, friends, neighborhood—to explain a child's problems, while often ignoring the biological blueprint the child was born with.

Almost weekly we parents read or watch reports in the media about new information on the brain. For example, the February 19, 1996, cover of *Newsweek* magazine ran the headline, "Your Child's Brain," followed by the sub-headline, "How Kids Are Wired for Music, Math, & Emotions." The article reported on the exciting developments from neurobiology over the past decades that stress the formative value of positive experiences in early childhood for optimal brain development. In other words, we are learning that it matters *at the cellular, neuronal level* what kind of early experience a child has. By the age of ten or fifteen, many of the neuronal connections have been made, connections that will last a lifetime. Before those connections close for good, childhood provides crucial windows of opportunity for the parent, teacher, or other adult or peer to enrich the child's brain by interacting with the child, reading to him or her, singing, smiling, and playing with the child. What we do with our children actually can change how our children's brains get wired.

Only a few days before the *Newsweek* piece came out *The New York Times* ran a report of an article about how behavioral therapy can alter brain chemistry, in other words, how experience can alter basic brain makeup. The report was of a study of children who had obsessive-compulsive disorder, a condition marked by repetitive, ritualistic behavior. Both the *Newsweek* and *Times* reports mark outposts on the great frontier neuroscientists are currently exploring: the human brain.

As parents, all this information can be daunting. We need a roadmap, a guide to help us figure out how to use the data. We hear of so many new developments—diet, new methods of teaching, medications that can help the brain, individual learning styles—that it can be hard to know what to do with them. Life was easier when we were kids and mom just said, "Go out and play." But, at the same time, there was a lot our moms didn't know, information that is potentially of great value to our children, information we want to be able to evaluate critically and use properly. The new information is exciting—that experience can shape our brain's basic, biological functioning—but it also raises the question, What can we do about it? How can we shape experience to best manage our brains, and more compellingly for us parents, how can or should we shape our children's experience to help them best manage their brains? These are the questions this book answers.

We have learned from the physiologists and the neuroscientists that many aspects of *normal* behavior are cousin to more well-defined pathological syndromes. For example, a child who is meticulous and detail-oriented may share parts of the genetic makeup of a child who has full-blown obsessive-compulsive disorder. Or a child who is sad more often than his or her peers may have brain chemistry somewhat like that of a child whom we would diagnose as clinically depressed.

It is daunting how many different forces impinge simultaneously upon your child, from the unseen (genetics, past history, God and chance) to the seen (friends, teachers, TV). So much is happening all at once that we have trouble seeing it all simultaneously. I envision an enormous web of interconnected factors, all influencing each other, all touching your child. It is impossible to tease out exactly which is doing what to whom and when, because all the forces are also affecting each other most of the time. This is what makes understanding human behavior so complicated.

The web might include the following forces:
Your child, plus:

1. Mom and Dad
2. Siblings
3. Extended family
4. Neighborhood, community
5. Popular culture and the media

6. The "parent's advice bank," which includes all advice—from grandparents, in-laws, magazines, books, friends, pediatricians, psychiatrists and other mental health professionals, teachers, newspapers, TV, clergy and church, respected others, and those people who give you advice whether you want it or not.
7. School and teachers
8. Close friends of your child
9. Peers of your child (including nonfriends)
10. Genes, biological factors, family history
11. God, chance, fate

How do we begin to sort out these diverse influences as we try to understand and help our children? Is there a way to break down the inner lives of our children into categories without oversimplifying or missing too much? Put more practically, what do parents, teachers, and others concerned with children really need to know about what's in that web that they might not know already?

To answer that question, this book organizes children's emotional and learning problems into four categories: Mad, Sad, Afraid, and Confused. Anger, sadness, and fear are three basic emotions that can lead to problems or to healthy adjustment, depending upon the intensity of the emotions and the control the child has over them. "Confusion" is the summarizing word I use to cover problems with learning, from attentional problems to reading problems to any difficulty in gaining knowledge.

Anger, sadness, fear, and confusion can range from mild to moderate to severe. All children feel mild sadness at times, but extended periods of severe sadness we call depression. All children feel anger now and then, but the chronically angry child we may diagnose with a conduct disorder. All children struggle to pay attention now and then, but the constantly inattentive child may have attention deficit disorder.

We can imagine each of these spectra—Mad, Sad, Afraid, and

Confused—expanding like a cone or megaphone. And most of the diagnosable disorders of childhood can be organized logically in one of these four cone-shaped clusters. At the small end of the megaphone we see the normal, uncomplicated expression of a particular feeling. The irritated child says, "I'm angry," or the confused child says, "I don't get it." At the open end of the Mad megaphone the first child is screaming, "I'm going to kill you!," while at the open end of the Confused megaphone, the child is sitting in a classroom completely unaware of what is being taught day after day. The farther out the megaphone you go, the louder, or more problematic, the emotion can be. As anger, sadness, fear, or confusion are amplified, they can become more difficult to manage, for child and parent alike.

Often children develop their symptoms in an attempt to make themselves heard. Sometimes they must increase the amplitude of a symptom in order to make a point, send a message, or just get some adult's attention. They need to make someone hear. If a whisper doesn't work, they speak. If speaking doesn't work, they shout. If shouting doesn't work, they scream. The image of the megaphone aptly emphasizes this point.

Can the groups ever overlap? Yes, they can. When a child has a condition that lies at the wide end of two or more of the megaphones, that child is in more serious difficulty than the child who has only one. Some children even have problems at the extreme end of all four; these children are beset by extreme anger, sadness, fear, and confusion. Such a child needs intensive help, but with proper diagnosis, he can indeed find a new life for himself and his family. For example, the child who has a conduct disorder, plus major depression, plus intense fears resulting from past trauma, plus severe dyslexia is obviously at much greater risk of getting into serious trouble in life than the child who suffers from only one of these conditions. But there is hope. *There is always hope.* With appropriate help, these children can do well. Without help, however, they may get into serious trouble through drugs, violence, crime, or even suicide.

If you are the parent of such a child, my best suggestion is this: *Never worry alone.* Get help. Get it from a friend, another parent, your pediatrician, a teacher, or a minister or other clergyperson. Do not let the sun set on an unshared worry. The worst disasters occur when a problem is being ignored, denied, or fretted over by a parent who's alone, with no place to go and no one to worry with or ask for help.

As parents, we all need help. We need help in figuring out where our children are compared to others, what "normal" actually is, and how abnormal "abnormal" needs to be to justify our worrying about it or seeking professional advice.

When You Worry About the Child You Love points out how hidden biological elements shape the emotional life of children, and how if we understand those elements the pain of unnecessary blame can give way to insight and understanding. I never ignore or dismiss environmental or "nurture" factors; the thesis of this book weaves nature into nurture in order to stitch out the true fabric of a child's life. This book does not just rehash childhood disorders. Instead it looks through a lens that is new to most parents, a lens made of the most current knowledge we have about children and what happens to them as they grow up.

Too often parents (and teachers and others who deal with children) do not know about the biologic or genetic basis of their children's behavior, so they blame themselves or the child unnecessarily and fail to give the child the treatment he or she needs. In order for the child and the parent to obtain the proper help, it is essential that the underlying causes of behavior and emotion be recognized. Otherwise, child and parent alike risk spending years in a fruitless, demoralizing process of exhortation, struggle, and blame.

For example, consider the problem of bed-wetting. For decades it was widely assumed that a child who wet his bed was upset about something. He may have been angry or worried. He may have been seeking relief by unconsciously "relieving" himself into his bed. Some authorities cautioned that bed-wetting was an act of defiance. Many parents therefore punished their children for wetting the bed, assuming that it was done on purpose. Many also blamed themselves for being unable to help their child gain better control, or they blamed the child, or both. Many children who wet the bed suffered ridicule at the hands of friends and peers, often having to give up the fun and social training of sleepovers or overnight camp. Bed-wetting became an emotional ordeal in which children felt shame and blame.

Parents and children both suffered all manner of emotional problems in the wake of the problem of bed-wetting. An innocuous symptom to begin with, the condition grew pernicious as it took on elaborate psychological meanings.

However, as doctors began to look more closely at bed-wetting they began to find different patterns. In one pattern, called primary bed-wetting or enuresis, the child never really gained bladder control at night. He was never fully trained, and so had no prolonged "dry" periods. This pattern accounts for 75 percent of all bed-wetting.

Furthermore, doctors noticed that primary bed-wetting tended to run in families. If you found out when the parent stopped bed-wetting, you could confidently predict the child would stop at the same age.

Then in 1995 the clinical evidence doctors had been observing was confirmed. Dr. Hans Eiberg and his colleagues in the department of genetics at the University of Copenhagen discovered a gene linked to bed-wetting, specifically to primary bed-wetting. The report was published in the July issue of the journal *Nature Genetics* and made front-page news. *The New York Times* ran an account of Dr. Eiberg's discovery on page one of the July 1, 1995, issue. Dr. Eiberg told the *Times:* "This may make it easier for children. The families [in our study] were very relieved to learn it was genetic, and so beyond the control of parent or child."

"Beyond the control of parent or child." The more we learn from science the more we discover hidden biological factors influencing what we had thought was solely the province of discipline and will. This is what made the genetics of bed-wetting front-page news: It's not always your fault.

Willpower and discipline will always matter. They may matter more than any other qualities in determining success and moral decency in life. However, we should not use them like cudgels, bringing them out whenever we don't know what else to use. If we can't figure out the cause of a problem we should not automatically attribute it to lack of willpower or discipline.

By applying current knowledge to old problems, from poor school performance to social shyness to wetting the bed, we can rethink many of those problems in more helpful ways. We can reduce some of the unfair humiliation we have subjected children to for centuries simply by using the knowledge we now have.

This book endorses a balanced view. The conditions discussed here cannot be treated properly without recognizing the importance of nurture—upbringing, environment, the quality of a parent's love. Nor can they be treated without taking into account the child's genetic makeup and inborn temperament: the work of nature. The key is to balance nurture with nature. *Both* affect the fate of the child.

Most of the specific examples in this book reflect situations in which parents are unaware of the biological influence upon their child's behavior. If, for example, your child has obsessive-compulsive disorder and you do not know that this is a treatable medical condition, you may not get him or her the appropriate help.

While none of the syndromes discussed can be totally cured, they can all be dramatically helped. In general, I am a therapeutic optimist. I think most problems in childhood can be helped. I think where there is no cure there is palliation. I believe that most of the time an unhappy child can get happier, a sick child can get better, and a parent who is pinioned by guilt and blame can be set free from those emotional bonds.

HOW TO USE THIS BOOK

This book is organized so that it may be read from beginning to end, or may be dipped into according to the interest of the reader.

Chapter 1 introduces a number of treatable emotional and/or learning problems that have a genetic or other biological basis. These are problems that parents, teachers, and other caretakers deal with every day, but they may not know that the symptoms constitute a recognized, treatable medical condition. The chapter emphasizes practical understanding and the importance of up-to-date information, an emphasis that runs throughout the book. What is causing your child's problem? Is it biological? Is it in the genes? Could it be due to something the average person might not know about? The chapter gives many specific examples of conditions most parents do not know enough about.

Chapter 2 takes up the question of genetics and the biological basis of emotional and learning problems in children. It lists the main conditions for which we now have solid evidence of a genetic basis, and it considers the interaction between nature and nurture.

Chapter 3 gives some concrete advice, "Twenty-five Practical Tips on Managing Emotion and Learning." These tips are useful for children of all ages.

The next chapters get more specific. Chapters 4 through 8 present in greater detail the conditions associated with the states of anger, sadness, fear, and confusion. Chapters 4 and 5 look at the group of conditions I subsume under the heading "Confused." Chapter 4 is about various problems in learning, while Chapter 5 is about attention deficit disorder. If your child is having difficulty in school, these are the chapters for you. But they are not just about children who have problems in learning; they are about learning styles in general. Learning is hard for us all, at times. Chapters 4 and 5 look at the common reasons for that, as well as at what can be done to make learning less difficult.

Chapters 6, 7, and 8 look at the categories of Mad, Sad, and Afraid. Most emotional problems in childhood relate to one or more of those three feeling states. Elvin Semrad, one of the great teachers of psychiatry in Boston in this century, observed that everyone is either "mad, sad, or afraid," and I add "confused." Many of us are all four! But sometimes one of those basic emotions runs out of control. If your child is overly aggressive, combative, or disobedient, or has trouble controlling anger, you should read Chapter 6, "Mad." If your child is overly serious or seems depressed, read Chapter 7, "Sad." And if your child is particularly shy, skittish, or fearful, read Chapter 8, "Afraid."

Chapter 9 examines four less common problems in childhood —problems that are common enough to deserve mention, however, because they are so often misunderstood or improperly diagnosed. The first is social remoteness. Some children are socially extremely awkward or withdrawn. Parents often waste a lot of time trying to figure out what they or some teacher did wrong, when this condition is no one's fault. These children may have a disorder called Asperger's syndrome, or they may have what is called pervasive developmental disorder—intimidating terms, but important to know about because they suggest a positive approach for treatment. The second problem Chapter 9 takes up is trichotillomania, or repetitive pulling out of one's own hair. Bizarre as this may sound, the problem is much more common— and more treatable—than most people think. The third problem discussed in Chapter 9 is Tourette syndrome. The child with Tourette syndrome is beset by involuntary muscle twitches, or motor tics, as well as verbal outbursts, or vocal tics. In days gone by these children were made fun of or punished; now, they can get treatment that works. Chapter 9 concludes with a description of fetal alcohol syndrome and fetal alcohol effect, both the result of maternal alcohol use during pregnancy. These conditions are often mistaken for something else, because the symptoms are so varied. Obviously, the best treatment is to prevent alcohol reaching the developing baby in the first place; unfortunately, many mothers are simply unaware of the risks involved in drinking during pregnancy.

Chapter 10 is about medication. This subject is given a chapter of its own because so many parents, teachers, children, and even clinicians express deep reservations over the use of medication to treat emotional and learning problems in children. When should medication be used? What is medication good for, and what is it not good for? What are the common side effects? What are the psychological implications of giving a child medication? These are the questions Chapter 10 takes up.

Chapter 11 offers some suggestions for where to find help.

The book concludes with an afterword, which addresses some of the hopes and fears we all have regarding our children. By the end of the book, parents should be ready to stop blaming themselves or their children and feel hopeful in taking responsibility effectively and with confidence.

Chapter 1

....

Treatable Conditions Parents Should Learn to Recognize: Examples and Solutions

Never worry alone.
—*Thomas Gutheil, M.D.*

Sometimes what you don't know as a parent can hurt you and your child. Children can have many symptoms that we typically dismiss as attitude problems or evidence of low intelligence, but that up-to-date knowledge would tell us are *treatable* medical or psychiatric conditions, based in the biology of the brain, not in moral fiber or bad character. These conditions are *not anyone's fault*. They are not the result of inadequate parenting or poor teaching or lack of character on the part of the child. They are medical problems, in need of accurate diagnosis and rational treatment. The good news is that treatment usually helps. The bad news is that many parents, teachers, and even physicians have never heard of many of the diagnoses—Asperger's syndrome, for example (see Chapter 9)—or their treatments. Sometimes even if they have heard of them they do not know that they can occur in children—as in the case of manic-depressive illness. And sometimes, even if they have heard of them and know they can occur in children, they do not think of them—hearing impairment or poor vision, for example.

Here is a sampling of some common symptoms occurring in

children which are often regarded as moral failings or evidence of low intelligence on the part of the child. Each set of symptoms is followed by an example, a "snapshot," of a child from real life. Then a possible medical or psychiatric explanation is given, a diagnosis which is based in biology, not character, failure, or fault. Next comes a brief description of the remedies you might try at home, as well as of the kind of professional treatment currently available for each condition. Most of the diagnoses mentioned in this list will be discussed more fully elsewhere in this book, so after each item I state which chapter gives more information about the condition.

As you read through these examples, you may find a resemblance to your own child. If you do, there will be more information in the chapters that follow. In addition, you might consider getting help from a professional. Many pediatricians can screen for behavioral, learning, or emotional problems by taking a history or using a simple instrument called the Pediatric Symptom Checklist. You do not necessarily need to consult a mental health professional right away; rather, you can start with the person you probably know best, your pediatrician.

You should also be aware of what conditions cause children to be considered at high risk. These are children who have a family history of emotional or learning problems, children who are currently having problems in school, children who are undergoing chronic stress (for example, from extreme parental conflict, separation or divorce), children who have been hospitalized often, and children who are victims of abuse or neglect.

Early intervention—or, ideally, prevention—is key. Good prenatal care can prevent damage to the central nervous system, damage that may first manifest itself as an emotional or learning problem. For example, alcohol ingestion during pregnancy can harm the developing nervous system. Proper immunizations can prevent infections that also can damage the developing brain, either in utero or during the child's early years. In addition, making sure that your child is not exposed to environmental hazards can prevent significant damage to the developing brain and nervous system. For example, lead paint poses a serious environmental hazard to toddlers.

Knowledge provides the best protection of all.

✳

Symptoms: The child continually breaks rules, bullies others and gets into fistfights often, steals frequently, skips school regularly.

Snapshot: Eddie is twelve years old, going on twenty. "He's becoming a thug," his mother says desperately. "I don't know what to do." Eddie's behavior is becoming increasingly uncontrollable. He shows no respect for rules or authority, and his parents wonder if he is getting involved with a gang.

Possible diagnosis: Conduct disorder. This is not just the latest term for "bad boy" (or "bad girl"). It is a condition that can be diagnosed and treated. In addition, it is one of the childhood disorders for which we have solid evidence of a genetic basis. As long as parent and child are stuck in the "bad boy" paradigm, not much progress will be made. However, the diagnosis and subsequent treatment of conduct disorder, although never easy, usually result in marked improvement. The key here is to move the parents and child out of attack-and-blame mode and into diagnosis-and-rational-treatment mode.

At-home remedies: Use structure. What is structure? Rules, regulations, schedules, supervision; predictable, consistent rewards and consequences. As the child defies rules, set up consequences and contingency plans to deal with the behavior. Such contingency plans might range from a graduated set of rewards and punishments to which the family strictly adheres, to family therapy and intensive social coaching and modeling, even to hospitalization. Use contracts and negotiation instead of spur-of-the-moment crisis intervention.

Professional treatment: Treatment involves a combination of parent education, child counseling, family support, and medication, as well as hospitalization at times. The earlier these children get help the better for everyone, and the better the prognosis. (For more on conduct disorder, see Chapter 6.)

⁎

Symptoms: Disobedience, disrespectfulness, obstreperousness, deceitfulness.

Snapshot: Andy is a seven-year-old terror. He fights with other kids often, disobeys teachers as well as his parents regularly, seems unaffected by any kind of punishment, and is "more stubborn than a pack of mules," according to his mom, who is at her wits' end. "He's in a constant battle with me, and he's winning," she says hopelessly.

Possible diagnosis: Oppositional defiant disorder. This is often a precursor of conduct disorder. It is like conduct disorder, but milder. Oppositional defiant disorder (or ODD) includes symptoms of disobedience, defiance, angry outbursts, obnoxious behavior, and a resentful attitude, but is less intense than conduct disorder, and does not include the symptoms of flagrant rule-breaking and cruelty to others that we see in conduct disorder. Since all children are oppositional or defiant at times, the diagnosis of ODD depends on the child's displaying such behavior for an extended period (six months or more) and with an intensity that is greater than that of his peers.

At-home remedies: The treatment for ODD is similar to that for conduct disorder. The family must come together around a plan of increased structure, supervision, rules, contingency plans, and rewards and punishments. This plan must be followed consistently and without interruption over a long period of time. ODD does not go away overnight. The child must feel there is an authoritative presence in his life, a presence which he comes to respect and finally internalize. One reaches this goal not through

physical punishment but through the consistent and fair impos-
ing of rules, limits, and rewards.

Professional treatment: Family education and contract-making, individual counseling, family therapy, social coaching and group
therapy, and sometimes medication all can be useful. (For more
on ODD, see Chapter 6.)

❄

Symptom: Rage attacks.

Snapshot: Penny, an eight-year-old girl, is cooperative and well-
behaved most of the time. Sometimes, however, she flies into a
rage for no apparent reason, attacking friends, parents, visitors,
whoever is within her reach. She gives no explanation, only that
she felt "upset."

Possible diagnosis: Some rage attacks are due to a form of epilepsy, or seizure disorder, called temporal lobe epilepsy (TLE).
Sometimes the source of the seizure activity is too deep in the
brain to be detected even by the brain-wave measure, or EEG.

At-home remedies: This condition requires professional evaluation.

Professional treatment: If your child has persistent rage attacks,
you should consult a neurologist to see if an undetected seizure
disorder might be the cause. Even if the seizure activity does not
show up on an EEG, your neurologist might prescribe a trial
of antiseizure medication. Such medication can be dramatically
effective. (For more on seizure disorders, see Chapter 6.)

❄

Symptom: The child blurts out remarks without raising hand or
waiting turn, interrupts frequently, can't sit still, changes subject
abruptly, is easily distracted.

Snapshot: Timmy is a second-grader who has been a handful
ever since his parents can remember. His first baby-sitter set the
tone when she told his parents, "You have a very labor-intensive

child." That was when he was six months old; the labor has become more intensive the older Timmy has grown. Unable to sit still in a classroom for more than a minute, never keeping his place in any line, always interrupting whoever is talking, never raising his hand, frequently blurting out inappropriate remarks, Timmy is wearing everyone out at school—and at home.

Possible diagnosis: Not so long ago the only "diagnosis" to be considered would have been "rude child." However, we now know that these symptoms, along with a constellation of others that will be discussed in Chapter 5, are part of the syndrome called attention deficit hyperactivity disorder, or ADHD. Not every child who has these symptoms has ADHD, but it is worth checking out the possibility with a professional. To miss the diagnosis of ADHD, and assume that your child has a discipline problem instead can be as harmful as missing a diagnosis of nearsightedness.

At-home remedies: There are a wide range of at-home and at-school remedies for the child with ADHD. Exercise, for example is extremely important. These children (and adults) need to exercise as much as possible, twice a day at least. A regular sleep schedule makes a big difference. Breaking large tasks down into small tasks helps keep them from being overwhelmed. All forms of structure—lists, reminders, schedules, predictable consequences for specific actions—help them stay in a routine. These children need prompt and frequent feedback to keep them on task. They also need *lots* of encouragement and positive stroking because they tend to accumulate a great deal of negative feedback as their day progresses.

Professional treatment: First of all, you need a professional to make an accurate diagnosis. The person you consult may be a child psychiatrist, psychologist, pediatrician, neurologist, family practitioner, or other professional trained in the field of learning disabilities and ADHD. You also want to make sure the professional you see can look for other conditions that may accompany ADHD, such as dyslexia, depression, post-traumatic stress disorder, manic-depressive illness, anxiety disorders, or substance abuse. ADHD is usually accompanied by something else. Once the diagnosis has been made, the professional will oversee a treatment plan that should include education, structure, psychotherapy and/or coaching, and often medication. (For more on this, see Chapter 5.)

※

Symptom: The child daydreams a great deal, is very quiet, sits in the back of the class lost in thought, is highly imaginative, and underachieves academically

Snapshot: Laura is a bright sixth-grader whose parents are waiting for her to "get motivated" and begin to get marks commensurate with her obviously high intelligence. Laura says that she already *is* motivated, but that she often has trouble paying attention in class and that school is "boring."

Possible diagnosis: Attention deficit disorder *without* hyperactivity. Many parents, teachers, and even doctors are unaware that a child may qualify for the diagnosis of ADD even though she shows no signs whatever of being hyperactive and is highly intelligent. Indeed, children who have ADD without hyperactivity may be unusually serene in their behavior and may test very high on standard IQ tests. However, they have great difficulty paying attention, are easily distracted, and tend to daydream whenever they can.

At-home remedies: The key is to make the diagnosis. Once you know that the problem is neurological—rather than a lack of effort on the part of the child—you can redirect your own efforts toward supplying the additional structure and organizational aids these children need.

Professional treatment: If you suspect ADD, with or without hyperactivity, you should consult a professional to be sure of the diagnosis. Once the diagnosis is made, treatment may include medication, which must be prescribed by a physician, in addition to the additional structure mentioned above. (For more on ADD, see Chapter 5.)

❊

Symptoms: The child acts up a great deal, has a poor memory, does not seem to understand as much as he should of what is said to him, and looks a little "funny," with a small head, drooping eyelids, low-set ears, and a small chin.

Snapshot: Blake is a second-grader in an expensive private school. His parents can't understand why he is doing so poorly as a student. He forgets assignments, can't organize himself, has trouble finding the right words for what he wants to say, and often misbehaves for no apparent reason. His mother has a long-standing habit of drinking three or four cocktails every day before dinner.

Possible diagnosis: Fetal alcohol effect, or FAE. Both fetal alcohol syndrome (FAS), which is the more severe version of this condition, and fetal alcohol effect result from a mother's drinking too much alcohol during pregnancy. The symptoms include the "funny-looking" appearance described above and problems with conduct, memory, attention, and word-finding. We do not know what the minimum amount of alcohol is that can lead to FAS or FAE, but certainly three or four drinks per day can do it. Estimates are that at least 15 percent of American women drink enough alcohol during pregnancy to produce FAS or FAE in their offspring.

At-home remedy: The key here is prevention. It is advisable to keep one's alcohol intake during pregnancy as low as possible. An occasional glass of wine probably will do no harm, but daily drinking might.

Professional treatment: The most important step is to make the diagnosis, and then treat the parent as well as the child. In addition to getting help with her possible drinking problem, the mother may need help with her feelings of guilt; few mothers intentionally cause these problems in their children. It can come as a shock to learn that the child's problems stem from alcohol ingestion during pregnancy. Treatment of the child often resembles the treatment for attention deficit disorder, with an emphasis on structure, encouragement, and sometimes stimulant medication. (For more on FAS and FAE, see Chapter 9.)

✳

Symptom: Chronic anxiety.

Snapshot: Ellen is a friendly eleven-year-old girl who, for no apparent reason, is anxious most of the time. She frets over her school performance constantly, even though she gets excellent grades. She is always worried—much more worried than her peers—about how she will do in any activity. She almost always excels, and yet she fears failure at every turn. Her parents bend over backward not to put pressure on her; in fact, her mom says she wishes Ellen would just relax instead of feeling so anxious about doing well. Ellen's parents wonder if they have "unconsciously" pressured her into feeling so anxious.

Possible diagnosis: Overanxious disorder of childhood. Ellen's parents shouldn't blame themselves; the chances are one or both of them would know it if they were putting enough pressure on Ellen to create these symptoms. Some children simply impose upon themselves unbelievably high standards, and then they become terrified of falling short. They feel insecure within themselves, even though they come from secure families. Such generalized anxiety is part of overanxious disorder of childhood. Sometimes children with this disorder feel anxious even in the absence of strong performance anxiety. They simply carry anxiety with them everywhere, as if it were mixed into their blood. This condition should be distinguished from anxiety related to a specific cause, such as post-traumatic stress disorder; from separation anxiety (homesickness or refusal to go to school, for example); from fear of heights or snakes or other specific places or items; and from anxiety induced by substance abuse.

At-home remedy: These children need a great deal of reassurance. Even though reassurance never seems sufficient, give it anyway; these children need it even if they appear to ignore it. Make it clear that you love them for who they are, not for the grades they get or how well they play the violin or skate or pitch a baseball.

Professional treatment: Sometimes psychotherapy can be very helpful for anxious children. A skilled psychotherapist can pinpoint some of the causes of the anxiety and address them with the child. Also, various medications can help. (For more on over-anxiety in childhood, see Chapter 8.)

❊

Symptom: Episodic bouts of extreme anxiety.

Snapshot: Harry is a well-liked but rather shy twelfth-grader who gets extremely anxious all of a sudden now and then. At a loss to explain why, he reports that these bouts of anxiety come on abruptly, without warning, and are accompanied by severe physical symptoms: sweating, a racing heart, trembling, shortness of breath, and dizziness. He has no idea what is going on, and he feels very frightened.

Possible Diagnosis: Panic attacks. Unlike the chronic anxiety described in the previous example, panic attacks occur *as attacks* —suddenly—and pass in a matter of minutes. Although more common in adults, panic attacks do occur in children. They are extremely upsetting, often terrifying. Out of the blue the sufferer is hit with all the symptoms and sensations of panic—*and he or she has no idea why.* This feeling of helplessness only intensifies the fear, which adds to the cascade of panicky feelings.

At-home remedies: Give reassurances during the attack. Keep the child safe. Try placing a paper bag over his or her head to counteract the effects of hyperventilation, which usually happens during panic attacks. If you breathe fast, or hyperventilate, you blow off too much carbon dioxide, which can lead to a change in the acid/base balance in your blood. A paper bag forces you to breathe back in some of the carbon dioxide you have blown off, thus correcting the acid/base problem and reducing the subjective feeling of terror.

Professional Treatment: A number of medications, especially tricyclic antidepressants such as imipramine (Tofranil), have been found to be useful in staving off panic attacks. (For more on anxiety, see Chapter 8.)

✣

Symptoms: The child has frightening dreams, exhibits avoidant behavior, startles very easily, has difficulty with concentration, and is excessively cautious and vigilant.

Snapshot: Sally is a five-year-old girl who complains of frequent nightmares, the content of which she cannot recall. She avoids certain people and situations without giving any explanation why. In addition, she is excessively vigilant, watching everything, fearful of danger around every corner.

Possible Diagnosis: Post-traumatic stress disorder (PTSD). There is a classic triad of symptoms that suggest PTSD: *reexperiencing* the trauma, which in a child may appear as nightmares she cannot recall; *avoiding* any person or scene reminiscent of the trauma; and *hypervigilance,* suspicion, and fear of danger everywhere.

At-home remedy: Most important, recognize the symptoms as possibly signifying recent trauma. Often little children are too frightened to tell you that someone has abused them or that they have witnessed a scene that traumatized them. Instead they dream about the event—but keep the dreams to themselves for fear of what might happen if they talk about them—and their nervous systems wire up to stave off future attacks by sending out danger signals all the time. Parents need to intervene by reading the implied message in these symptoms.

Professional treatment: The extent to which professional treatment is needed varies according to the child and the nature of the trauma. Sometimes the family is able to handle the matter and very little outside support is needed. Usually, however, professional intervention is called for. Trauma to a child upsets everyone. To help you and your child deal with feelings about the trauma and with actual dangers, and then move on successfully, you need to consult a clinician experienced in helping children and adults. (For more on PTSD, see Chapter 8.)

❊

Symptom: Forgetfulness.

Snapshot: Jimmy, a third-grader, is an absent-minded professor before his time. He forgets everything, from his lunch box in the morning, to his raincoat when he leaves school, to every other word his teacher speaks, to most things his mom tells him. His parents have been ascribing his forgetfulness to the fact that he's a child and thus not interested in all the details grown-ups want him to attend to. However, the symptom is beginning to interfere significantly with his performance at school.

Possible diagnosis: This very common childhood symptom can have many causes, and certainly not all of them are biologically based or medically treatable. However, many are. Lead poisoning, for example, may lead to forgetfulness. A seizure disorder found in children, petit mal epilepsy, can also result in moments of forgetfulness; for this reason petit mal seizures are also called absence episodes. Certain learning disabilities derive in part from inborn faults in short-term memory or in active working memory. "Active working memory" refers to the amount of data you can retain in your mind at any one moment, data that you can use on the spot in solving a problem, writing a sentence, following a direction, and so on. Some "forgetful" children have reduced memory banks and so appear to be less intelligent than they truly are.

At-home remedies: Try to "forget-proof" Jimmy's world as much as you can. Make lists of what he is supposed to do each morning. Post one in his bedroom, one in the bathroom, one in the kitchen, and one on the wall on his way out the front door. Ask his teacher to give him a checklist to post on his desk at school and have him review that list before he leaves school every day.

Provide him with daily schedules and routines, so that he knows what to expect each day. Professional evaluation is also necessary when the symptom of forgetfulness persists.

Professional treatment: The key here is to make the right diagnosis. Start by having your pediatrician rule out medical causes, such as lead poisoning. Then he or she will refer you to a psychologist for testing. Good neuropsychological testing can usually determine what is going on, and treatment will depend upon the diagnosis. (For more on the possible causes of forgetfulness, see Chapters 4 and 5.)

Symptom: Insists upon doing things her own way, according to odd patterns or superstitions.

Snapshot: Harriet is a hyperorganized fifth-grader who is so meticulous that her parents are starting to worry. In addition, she is developing strange rituals and patterns of behavior that she says she cannot resist—for example, she must count to three before entering a new room. One day Harriet told her mom, "I'm worried I'm going to have to count higher pretty soon."

Possible diagnosis Obsessive-compulsive disorder (OCD). Children who have OCD develop many unusual rituals, such as feeling compelled to wash their hands often or count to one hundred before leaving a room or make sure all their sheets of paper are perfectly aligned before starting their homework. They may also be bothered by repeated unbidden thoughts—often unpleasant thoughts of damage or destruction, or thoughts of sexual or religious nature. The child can't control these thoughts.

OCD is not due to corruption within the child, as once was thought, but rather to a change in the neurochemistry of the brain. Medication usually is the best treatment.

At-home remedy: Don't make fun of the behavior. Let your child explain it to you. Then give reassurances that her world is safe. Sometimes children with OCD are really scared. Try to help them resist the rituals if they can, by encouraging them and reassuring them that the ritual is not in fact necessary for their safety.

Professional treatment: Various medications have been found to be effective in treating OCD, particularly clomipramine (Anafranil), a tricyclic antidepressant, and fluoxetine (Prozac), a different kind of antidepressant. (For more on OCD, see Chapter 8.)

❊

Symptoms: The child is unusually shy and has trouble fitting in socially.

Snapshot: Tom is a sweet, quiet five-year-old whose parents are terribly concerned that he may be too withdrawn. Both extremely outgoing themselves, Mom and Dad can't believe that Tommy could be happy when he's so shy.

Possible diagnosis: Shyness based on genetic makeup. In this instance it is important not to overdiagnose, not to read more into the condition than there is—simply a temperament, a state we call being shy. As with certain other traits that children can be born with and that parents sometimes want to change (as left-handedness used to be, for example), it is not a good idea to try to eradicate shyness in your child. Rather, help your child live happily being who he or she is.

At-home remedy: Accept Tom as he is. Try not to make him feel different or bad because of being shy.

Professional treatment: None is needed usually. However, if the shyness is severe enough to create major problems, various kinds of psychotherapy and sometimes medication can help. (For more on shyness, see Chapter 8.)

❊

Symptom: The child gets grades that are lower than his or her ability would predict.

Snapshot: The first few years of school posed no great problem, although Ann did not glide by easily. But now she is struggling with the material presented in the fourth grade, and the work is really stopping her in her tracks. In conversation Ann seems quite bright, but her written work clearly lags behind that of her peers.

Possible diagnosis: Before you decide that your child is simply lazy, check out these medical possibilities: poor vision or hearing; a reading disability (dyslexia); a math disability; attention deficit disorder; central auditory processing disorder; depression. Of course, many other factors can contribute to academic under-achievement, including laziness and lack of interest, but if you do not think of the medical possibilities mentioned here, you will not find them.

At-home remedy: None should be attempted until the diagnosis is made.

Professional treatment: Ann really needs a professional evaluation. The treatment will depend upon what the evaluation turns up. Ann should not be dismissed as simply a slow child. (For more on learning difficulties, see Chapters 4 and 5.)

❋

Symptoms: The child "freaks out" a lot or throws tantrums.

Snapshot: Billy is a ninth-grader who has started to lose his temper with alarming frequency, becoming irate at the drop of a hat. In addition, his energy level seems to be escalating, so much so that he cannot stay quiet in class, and he has a tendency to stay up all night for days at a time. His mother cannot understand where he gets all that energy.

Possible diagnosis: Bipolar disorder, also called manic-depressive illness. This condition, which we are finding occurs much more commonly in children than we used to think, can lead to frequent tantrums, mood swings, irritability, a "passionate" temperament, high levels of energy, and an effect of being on the go all the time.

At-home remedy: Observe Billy for other signs of bipolar disorder: grandiose or "big-shot" thoughts or behavior; flight of ideas, which is a rapid changing of topics with only the barest connection between them; easy distractibility; irritability; sleeplessness and loss of appetite; substance abuse; search for high stimulation such as loud music, intense conversations or arguments, fast driving, or sudden romance. Also watch for the other side of the cycle: the peaking of the energized phase, leading into a slow, depressed period. If you observe this pattern, get a professional to intervene.

Professional treatment: A number of medications, such as lithium, carbamazepine (Tegretol), and divalproex sodium (Depakote), are effective in stabilizing the mood swings of bipolar disorder and reducing the condition's other symptoms. (For more on bipolar disorder, see chapter 6.)

⁜

Symptom: The child frequently asks that questions or explanations be repeated.

Snapshot: Eugene sits in the front row in first grade. He drives his teacher nuts because he doesn't pay attention. He is forever behind the rest of the class, and he frequently asks that explanations just given be repeated.

Possible diagnosis: Hearing loss. Often it is assumed that children who constantly ask that questions or explanations be repeated are "slow." However, be sure to check out the possibility that they may have an undiagnosed hearing impairment. If someone does not think of this it will not get diagnosed.

At-home and professional remedy: The key here, of course, is for someone—parent, teacher, or pediatrician—to think of the possibility of hearing loss so that proper remediation may be set up.

⁜

Symptoms: The child makes frequent social mistakes, as if oblivious to social cues, particularly in new situations; he or she has academic difficulties in certain areas.

Snapshot: Although Davy, a socially isolated fifth-grader, can recognize words with ease and decode them, his reading comprehension is poor. He uses words well in conversation, although he does not pick up on the nonverbal cues that are so important in getting along with others. As for school, math is starting to present great difficulties. Davie "forgets to remember" what he is supposed to do in solving a problem. For example, although he knows how to "carry" and "borrow," he forgets to go into his memory bank and bring out the skill when he needs it. So his performance is starting to fall way behind.

Possible diagnosis: Social awkwardness coupled with an academic profile like Davy's may be a tip-off to a "nonverbal learning disability" (NLD). Children with this condition talk well, showing good verbal skills, but have difficulty using and interpreting nonverbal language, such as physical gestures, body language, facial expressions, and tone of voice. The typical academic profile of a child with NLD shows, on the positive side, good ability to decode words, spell, write, and memorize—but, on the negative side, major problems with reading comprehension, abstract reasoning, math, and science.

Children with NLD also have difficulty picking up on social cues, because of various kinds of information-processing problems in their brains. They can process things they hear well, and they rely on rote memorization to learn, but problem-solving is difficult for them. While their vision is fine, their analysis of visual information is impaired. They also have difficulty assimilating new concepts or reasoning in the abstract. They can read, but as they grow older their comprehension deteriorates. Math and science become extremely difficult as demands for abstract reasoning increase in the upper grades. Children with NLD can memorize, but they have difficulty using what they commit to memory. Often these children are called "out of it" or receive some other negative social label, when what they really need is good psychological testing to define their cognitive assets and vulnerabilities so they can get proper help.

At-home and professional treatment: There is no "cure" for NLD, but once the diagnosis has been made, individual tutoring as well as social skills training can help the child develop to the best of his or her abilities. Additionally, the diagnosis itself is therapeutic in that it guides expectations appropriately. (For more on NLD, see Chapter 4.)

Symptoms: The child offends others with socially inappropriate behavior, as if unaware of the impact the behavior has on them, and seems unable to show empathy or make meaningful contact with peers or adults.

Snapshot: Allan is a first-grader who stands apart from his peers due to his apparent lack of interest or even awareness of what is going on around him. He seems to be lost in a world of his own. The other children have become used to him, and they ignore him. When the teacher attempts to draw him into a social situation he looks nonplussed and confused.

Possible diagnosis: There is a condition called pervasive developmental disorder (PDD), which is similar to autism. Children with PDD simply do not relate to others. They seem cut off emotionally. They are not sad or anxious or upset; rather, they just have an unmistakable remoteness about them.

At-home remedy: Unlike the shy child, who just needs acceptance, the child with PDD needs help in learning how to socialize. While he also needs love and acceptance, of course, he needs to be taught how to relate to others. This can actually be rehearsed at home.

Professional treatment: PDD is a condition that requires the involvement of a professional. Children with PDD sometimes benefit from medication, sometimes an antidepressant, sometimes a stimulant, sometimes an antianxiety agent, and sometimes an antipsychotic medication. More important, they can benefit greatly from a skilled psychotherapist as well as from group psychotherapy. (For more on PDD, see Chapter 9.)

Symptom: The child is socially very withdrawn, can't relate to others, and seems sullen, but gets good grades and is intelligent.

Snapshot: Donnie can't make friends. He doesn't even seem interested in making friends. He likes to do things most second-graders find boring, such as watching clocks tick or counting tiles on the floor. He is able to relate to his family, but virtually no one else.

Possible diagnosis: The diagnosis may be Asperger's syndrome, a kind of pervasive developmental disorder in which intellectual capabilities are not impaired but social development is, especially away from home. The treatment is the same as for PDD, described above. (For more on Asperger's syndrome, see Chapter 9.)

Symptom: The child can't stop talking.

Snapshot: Susie is a seventh-grader who never shuts her mouth, or so it seems. Gregarious, friendly, and warm Susie has many friends, but she irritates all of them at times with her constant chatter. Where one sentence will do, she uses eight. It is a family joke that if Susie opens her mouth at breakfast to describe a movie or an outing the night before, everyone else can finish eating before she finishes her story. A constant comment from her English teacher on Susie's otherwise good writing is "Try to be more concise!"

Possible diagnosis: Frontal lobe syndrome. In some children (and adults), the frontal lobe of the brain is "wired" in such a way that they do not inhibit what comes in or goes out as much as other people do. People with frontal lobe syndrome seem to talk end-lessly, never quite coming to the point. It is important to know that this is not a kind of selfishness or a moral flaw, but rather a relative lack of inhibition due to the wiring of the frontal lobes of the brain.

At-home remedy: Try to help Susie get to the point. Instead of letting her talk on and on, interrupt her gently and say, "Okay, Susie, now try to tell us about it in five sentences or less." Make a game out of it. Her English teacher, by the way, could do the same thing: make a game out of helping her to revise and pare what she has already written.

Professional treatment: There is basically none needed. Sometimes people with frontal lobe syndromes are helped by stimulant medication, but this is usually not necessary. At-home treatments like those mentioned should be enough. (For more on learning variations see Chapter 4.)

✢

Symptom: The child insists on taking everything apart.

Snapshot: Albert is a lively four-year-old who is into everything. He picks up, or tries to pick up, everything he sees. Anything he has in his hands he tries to take apart or somehow dismantle. He loves gadgets, appliances, TVs, VCRs, telephones—anything he can get his hands on or into. Unfortunately, he does not always leave these instruments as he found them.

Possible diagnosis: Kinesthetic learning style. There are three main styles of learning: auditory, visual, and tactile or kinesthetic. We all use all three, but in most of us one predominates. The kinesthetic learner learns best by feel, so he naturally likes to take things apart.

At-home remedy: Obviously, you need to "Albert-proof" your house. But in addition to the obvious inconvenience Albert creates, remember the positive side: As kinesthetic learners grow older they quickly become adept and handy. Albert may end up fixing all the things he is breaking now.

Professional treatment: None is needed.

✢

Symptoms: The child is emotionally intense and unpredictably rageful; he or she flip-flops from loving to hating the same person easily, has great difficulty with regulating moods, has a poorly defined sense of self and chronic feelings of emptiness, and is sometimes self-injurious.

Snapshot: Karen is a lovely but moody college freshman, who is having extreme difficulty adjusting to life away from home. Desperately searching for affection wherever she can find it, she finds sexual partners everywhere, but a stable relationship nowhere. She has started drinking heavily, and is using cocaine whenever it is offered to her. One morning, when she woke up with a new partner, she felt overwhelmed with despair and ran to the bathroom, where she found a razor and cut her wrists. The young man found her in time to save her.

Possible diagnosis: This alarming set of symptoms, not extraordinarily rare among adolescents, may be a prelude to a syndrome called borderline personality disorder (BPD). Usually this condition is not diagnosed in children under eighteen, because the symptoms of normal adolescence can mimic it at times and because personality in general fluctuates so much before the age of eighteen. (However, if a child under eighteen has intense symptoms that persist for a year or more, the diagnosis of borderline personality disorder may be made.) Girls with borderline personality disorder (it is more common in girls, by a ratio of three to one), like boys with conduct disorder (which is much more common in boys), are usually dismissed as "bad" and in need of punishment or other moral remediation. However, punishment is not what these young people really need. They need accurate diagnosis and treatment.

At-home treatment: What the young person needs more than anything is a stable, caring relationship. This may be with a parent, a boyfriend, even a friend or a therapist.

Professional treatment: Treatment of borderline personality disorder, like treatment of conduct disorder, can be difficult and tiring for all involved. However, there is rational treatment available. So we can avoid punishment and chaotic struggling, which are what take place when there is no diagnosis or rational plan for treatment. The treatment usually involves intensive psychotherapy, medication, at times brief hospitalization, and family counseling. (For more on borderline personality disorder, see Chapter 6.)

*

Symptoms: The child is anxious and irritable, sometimes trembles, tends to feel hot even in cool places, has angry outbursts, and misbehaves a lot.

Snapshot: Diane has changed over the past six months. She has become high-strung, irritable, fidgety, and annoying. In addition she has lost weight, feels hot most of the time, and feels her heart racing.

Possible diagnosis: Diane may have hyperthyroidism, a condition affecting the thyroid gland, which is located in the neck and controls the body's metabolic rate. Symptoms of hyperthyroidism may be mistaken for psychological problems, as people who suffer from the condition may behave erratically.

At-home treatment: This condition requires a diagnosis by a physician.

Professional treatment: The treatment depends upon what is causing the hyperthyroidism. Medication, and sometimes surgery, take care of hyperthyroidism effectively.

*

Symptoms: A sudden drop in grades; sudden weight loss; development of a negative attitude.

Snapshot: Marie has done well in school until this year, the tenth grade, when, for no apparent reason, her grades have plummeted. Asked if the material is too difficult, she replies sarcastically, "Obviously." Refusing help from parents and teachers, Marie seems to be cutting herself off to a dangerous degree.

Possible diagnosis: Suddenly falling grades may be a sign of depression. So, too, can weight loss or a change in attitude signify depression. Whereas it used to be thought that children couldn't get depressed, we now know they can and do. We currently recognize depression as a very important and potentially dangerous problem in childhood. In the past decade the suicide rate has doubled among children ten to fourteen years old. Depression is therefore very real, and potentially lethal. Any change in behavior or performance may signify the onset of depression in children. The first thing to do is simply ask, "Are you sad about something?"

In older children one might also consider the possibility of drug abuse, which in turn may represent the child's attempt to self-medicate an underlying depression. (Of course, a drop in grades, or other change in behavior, may be a sign of something totally different—such as falling in love.)

At-home treatment: Listen, support, talk. Don't deny what your child is feeling. It can be difficult to hear, but if your daughter tells you that she is really sad, listen to her and believe her. Make contact, and keep contact. This matters more than anything else. Offer support, but do not feel you must make the bad feelings go away. Just help her bear them by hearing them, believing them, staying with them, and not leaving the scene.

Professional treatment: If depression persists, professional intervention may help. Although antidepressant medication has not been demonstrated to be as effective in children as it is in adults, the combination of medication and psychotherapy has been found useful in children. (For more on depression, see Chapter 7.)

Symptoms: The child is overly serious and sad.

Snapshot: Hugh's nickname is Eeyore, after the character in the Winnie-the-Pooh stories, because he is so serious and slow of speech. He has always been this way, just as his father was (and is). Now in the fifth grade, Hugh is consistently serious.

Possible diagnosis: Unlike Marie's depression in the preceding example, this seriousness is Hugh's normal state; he is constitutionally melancholy. How do you distinguish clinical depression from constitutional melancholy? The way to tell the two apart is that clinical depression appears as something new, a change from a previous state, whereas one's constitution is a constant. A child *develops* depression, but he is *born* with his temperament. If your child has been happy-go-lucky, but then becomes unusually sad or serious, think of clinical depression as a possible diagnosis. On the other hand, if he has always been serious, even morose at times, this may just be how he is put together. *Do not feel you have done anything wrong.*

At-home remedy: Enjoy Hugh for who he is.

Professional treatment: None is needed. For more on sadness in children, see Chapter 7.)

Symptoms: The child constantly trips over himself or herself, drops things, doesn't concentrate on physical activities, is a klutz.

Snapshot: Shauna has been clumsy ever since she was born, or so it seems to her mom. When she runs, she trips. When she picks up a glass, she drops it. When she ties a bow, it turns into a tangle. She loves sports, and she plays on enthusiasm alone, for the coordination just isn't there.

Possible diagnosis: If the onset of these symptoms is sudden, if they are not consistent with how the child has been for most of her life, you should have her checked out by a neurologist, because various kinds of neurological problems may lead to difficulty with coordination and gait. However, if your child has always been like Shauna and is slow to develop athletically, instead of calling her a klutz we can apply a more neurologically correct term and say she has "developmental coordination disorder." This may seem like a euphemism, but the fact is that children develop motor skills differently, and it is damaging to hang humiliating labels like "klutz" or "spaz" on them.

At-home remedy: Support your child's enthusiasms and help her or him not feel ashamed. Most children will more or less catch up.

Professional treatment: None is needed (unless the onset of the symptoms is sudden, as mentioned above).

✳

Symptom: The child pulls out his or her own hair as a nervous habit.

Snapshot: Candace is a college sophomore who has developed the annoying habit of pulling out her own hair. She is embarrassed because she is developing a bald spot on her scalp, but she finds herself unable to stop.

Possible diagnosis: This problem is called trichotillomania, and it is not as uncommon as was once thought. The person with trichotillomania feels a compulsion, a sort of itch, that he or she can scratch only by pulling out hair.

At-home remedy: It is best to consult a professional.

Professional treatment: Behavioral therapy, cognitive therapy, and medication have all been shown to be helpful. (For more on trichotillomania, see Chapter 9.)

✳

Symptom: "Whatever I say to him just doesn't sink in."

Snapshot: Brian sits in the front row in fourth grade; his teacher placed him there in exasperation because he didn't retain anything that was said to him. "Brian, you simply have got to learn to listen to what I say so that it sinks in," she told him.

Possible diagnosis: This common symptom has for centuries been taken as evidence of stupidity, laziness, stubbornness, or all three. However, there are some distinct medical possibilities, including what is called a receptive language disorder. This condition is also called central auditory processing disorder. This means the child has difficulty processing what he receives via language. The condition is diagnosed by psychological testing, and can be helped with certain kinds of tutoring. A child with a receptive language disorder may also have an "expressive language disorder," in which he cannot find the right words for what he is trying to say, even though he has an adequate vocabulary.

Whether the condition is called a central auditory processing disorder (CAPD), a receptive language disorder, or some other term depends usually on the background of the evaluator. Speech-language pathologists tend to diagnose children who cannot make best use of what they hear with CAPD, whereas medical doctors tend to diagnose the same set of symptoms as a receptive language disorder, an attention deficit disorder, or some other learning problem. This can be confusing for the parents and child. The best way I know of to resolve the confusion is to stay focused on the target symptoms. What are the actual symptoms that are bothering the child? As long as treatment is directed at those target symptoms, it doesn't really matter what diagnostic label is applied.

It is interesting that the core symptom of having trouble processing language can lead to a wide array of other symptoms such as problems with memory, easy distractibility, disorganization, poor social skills, and low self-esteem. Language is such an important cognitive function that any problem with it can ramify out in many directions. Hence the child with the language problem may be diagnosed with ADD, or receptive language disorder, or even depression or an anxiety disorder. Effective treatment must get at the core symptom of difficulty with language, however.

At-home remedy: At home and at school, it is important to make sure these children do not get lost. Having them sit in the front row makes sense (as long as it is not presented as a punishment), as do repeating instructions, asking them if they follow what you're saying, giving written instructions whenever possible, and asking for frequent feedback.

Professional treatment: The treatment may be simple tutoring, to help the child keep up, or you may need a much more elaborate treatment plan, implemented and supervised by a speech-language pathologist, a reading specialist, a child psychiatrist, or a pediatric neurologist. And make sure the language functioning is carefully evaluated before treatment begins. (For more on central auditory processing disorder, see Chapter 4.)

Symptom: The child falls asleep in class.

Snapshot: Marvin has been getting into trouble in high school because he has fallen asleep in a number of classes. The principal has sent a note home to his parents advising them of the problem and suggesting that Marvin might not be getting to bed early enough.

Possible diagnosis: There is a sleep disorder called narcolepsy in which the individual has what amount to "sleep attacks." He or she falls asleep suddenly, without wanting to, but the sleep is irresistible. This is another one of those conditions that sounds like an excuse if you do not have it yourself. However, narcolepsy is a real, brain-based disorder. Of course, not every child who falls asleep in class has narcolepsy; most just didn't get enough sleep the night before. However, if your child frequently falls asleep without wanting to, consider seeing a doctor to check out the possibility of narcolepsy or some other sleep disorder.

At-home remedy: Make sure your child gets enough sleep and exercise.

Professional treatment: If the problem persists, there is medication (methylphenidate, or Ritalin) that will help. This is the same medication used to treat attention deficit disorder; narcolepsy and ADD may be related genetically.

Symptoms: The child is withdrawn, tired, and suspicious, even paranoid.

Snapshot: For the past few months Rob has been looking unusually tired and run-down. When asked about it, he simply says school is hard. However, his teacher, who also notices that Rob has a definite worn-out look most of the time, says the work shouldn't be hard for him. Rob is only in the sixth grade, but the teacher wonders if he might be using drugs.

Possible diagnosis: These symptoms may indicate a problem with substance abuse. Children of almost any age may develop a problem with drugs and alcohol. It is never too early to consider the possibility. If you are concerned, ask the child. Also ask older siblings what they think.

At-home remedy: Obviously, you must set the right example by not abusing drugs yourself. In addition, try to create an atmosphere at home in which drug use can be talked about, not in hushed tones, but openly. The absolutely best policy for all children is abstinence. However, once your child is past a certain age—and that age is getting lower all the time—it is likely that he or she will experiment. You want to make sure you have prepared him with plenty of information.

Professional treatment: Don't wait for the problem to become severe before you involve a professional. Remember, drug use can be a signal of other emotional problems as well.

Symptom: The child can't do math.

Snapshot: Jill is discouraged by the fact that she is having such a hard time with sixth-grade math. She has done poorly in math all through school, but she had resolved to beat the problem this year, and yet she doesn't seem to be able to.

Possible diagnosis: Jill may have a specific mathematics disorder. This is a condition you are born with. Some children do not catch on to math well, because of the makeup of their brains. On the other hand, beware of social influences here. Many girls are conditioned not to perform well with numbers. They feel they *shouldn't* do well. Psychological testing can help you tell the difference.

At-home remedy: Encourage excellence in mathematics in boys *and* girls. But also be aware of the fact that some kids, on a genetic basis, have a math learning disability.

Professional treatment: Tutoring may be helpful. (For more on learning difficulties, see Chapter 4.)

✳

Symptoms: The child grimaces and twitches inappropriately in class, and sometimes grunts and even swears for no reason.

Snapshot: Nancy is a sixth-grader who has developed the habit of blinking her eyes a lot. Sometimes she also squinches up her nose and smacks her lips. She clears her throat often and makes coughing noises even when she really doesn't need to cough. Nancy is a very bright girl, particularly creative, who can get angry very quickly.

Possible diagnosis: This child may have what is called Tourette syndrome, a disorder defined by the symptoms of involuntary muscle movements, or "motor tics," and involuntary utterances or noises, "vocal tics." This combination of motor tics and vocal tics was first described by Gilles de la Tourette in 1885. Still, in 1995 most people have never heard of it, and a child who has it is usually "diagnosed" as rude or obnoxious. Obviously, the symptoms of Tourette syndrome can get a child into a lot of trouble. Once the correct diagnosis is made, medical treatment is highly effective in controlling both the motor and vocal tics.

Although defined by the presence of tics, Tourette syndrome may include a wide range of other symptoms. Some are beneficial, such as creativity; some are potentially bothersome, such as irritability, mood instability, and an inconsistent attention span.

At-home remedies: Tourette syndrome requires professional attention.

Professional treatment: A combination of medication, education, psychotherapy, and social interventions can help Tourette syndrome children dramatically. The medications do a good job in controlling the tics, while the rest of the treatment plan addresses other parts of the condition that may be present. (For more on Tourette syndrome, see Chapter 9.)

Symptom: Slow to read.

Snapshot: Mark is now in the fourth grade. Although he readily learned to talk, learning to read was a real problem for him. He attended a school where phonics was never taught; rather, students learned to read at their own pace, by what is called the whole language method. This did not work well for Mark. He was puzzled by words. They never emerged from the realm of hieroglyphics, as they did for other children learning to read by whole language. After much struggle, Mark can read a little, but he is well below grade level. An intelligent boy, he is very frustrated by his inability to read well.

Possible diagnosis: Dyslexia. Dyslexia is a difficulty in learning to read or spell one's native language. It is the most common learning disability, affecting 5 percent to 30 percent of children, depending upon which study you read. About four times as many boys as girls are affected.

At-home remedy: All home approaches that promote reading in general will help the dyslexic child. These include reading aloud (regardless of your child's age), limiting the amount of TV, video, and computer games your child watches or plays, playing word games, developing a sense of the sounds of words, playing games that involve spelling and sounding out words, and reading silently to oneself.

Professional treatment: An Orton-Gillingham tutor—you can find one through the Orton Dyslexia Society—is a good starting point. (For more on dyslexia, see Chapter 4.)

Most of the conditions I've described are quite common (for example, depression, ADD, and dyslexia), while some are relatively rare (for example, trichotillomania and Asperger's syndrome). All, however, have a biological basis and cause emotional and/or learning problems in children. To be treated properly, they must be recognized and correctly diagnosed. Since many parents are unaware of the range of these conditions, the following chapters will explore them in greater depth.

Chapter 2

Genetics: A Biological Basis of Problems in Emotion and Learning

As we learn more and more about the brain, we learn more and more, too, about hidden causes of emotional problems in children. We now must learn to recognize the signs of these problems so that we don't treat them simply as diseases of the will, moral failings on our children's part, or parental failings of our own.

Dr. Joseph Coyle, head of the psychiatry department at Harvard Medical School and a child psychiatrist and parent himself, once said to me, "One of the biggest misconceptions most people have about difficulties in children is that they believe adults can have mental disorders, but children can only have emotional problems. There is an overemphasis on the purely psychological explanation of children's issues."

By no means does Dr. Coyle suggest that psychological explanations are irrelevant, just that since Freud we have tended to exclude the biological component in assessing what is going on with our children. We invoke a double standard, one for adults, another for children. Grown-ups can be mentally disturbed, but in most people's lexicons, children cannot. In a way this is good, because in our culture mental disorders unfortunately bear a stigma that we do not want to inflict upon children. However, to overlook the biological factor in children does not make sense. We need to remove the stigma from both childhood and adult emotional problems and get rid of the slew of really vulgar and inflammatory words we use to describe emotional distress.

All people can feel out of sorts emotionally, and we can also all get very sick emotionally. Any one of us can. The brain is an organ in the body, and so is the mind. Indeed, they are the same. We might call "it" the mind-brain. It can get sick, and it can get better, too.

Especially in our children, we should think of the brain, the mind, and behavior as all of a piece, and not overlook, as we so often do, the biological influence on that entity. It is unlikely a parent will wonder, "What is going on in Johnny's brain now?" while Johnny is attacking his little sister. But in calmer moments we should reflect on this question of what is going on in Johnny's brain. It will give us a better idea of how to deal with him effectively.

This book stresses the balance between biology and experience. As a parent, you always need to consider *both*. For example, your child may do poorly in school because he is mad at you. On the other hand, he may do poorly in school because he has inherited a learning disability from someone in your family tree. Often you won't know for sure which is true, but there are certain patterns you should be aware of, certain questions you should ask, certain facts from your family history you should know in order to interpret your children's behavior accurately.

In reading through the following ten points, bear in mind that this list is not exhaustive, but rather suggestive of what you should look for to see if your child's problems may stem from his or her constitutional, genetic makeup.

TEN INDICATIONS THAT YOUR CHILD'S PROBLEM MAY BE BASED IN GENETICS OR OTHER BIOLOGICAL FACTORS

1. Someone in your family has (or had) the problem your child has, or a similar problem, trait, or tendency.

2. The problem—or the explanation you have been given—doesn't make sense to you. Something just doesn't add up. You feel that a key point is being missed by everybody.

3. There is a major change in your child's behavior or emotional tone. For example, your happy child becomes a sad child over the space of a few weeks or months; or your high-achieving child becomes an underachiever; or your outgoing child becomes a shy one.

4. Your child's problem seems more or less the same regardless of setting. Problems that derive from the environment tend to change depending on the environment. Biologically based problems are less dependent on the setting.

5. Your child can give no logical explanation for what is going on. When asked why he or she is feeling a certain way or behaving differently than usual, your child responds honestly, "I don't know."

6. Your child is taking medication for some medical problem unrelated to mood or behavior. This point, although perhaps obvious can easily be overlooked. Medications often have side effects that influence mood and behavior.

7. Your child's eating habits or sleep patterns have changed. Changes here are an important clue to depression, substance abuse, eating disorders, and certain medical problems like hyperthyroidism or hypothyroidism.

8. The season has changed. Some children's moods are dramatically influenced by seasonal changes. There is a condition called seasonal affective disorder (abbreviated, appropriately enough to SAD) in which the sufferer gets depressed in winter,

when there is little daylight. Special lights are available to treat this condition.

9. Your child has many physical complaints. Physical complaints may signify an underlying emotional problem.

10. Your child gets sick or is injured more often than formerly.

It is worthwhile to look at each of these factors in more detail. While some of the points may appear obvious, the significance of others can be misunderstood quite easily.

1. The family history. Family history is the most important factor of all in terms of predicting the genetic makeup of your offspring. An old rule of thumb in all fields of medicine is that the best predictor of what will happen in the future is what has happened in the past. Many emotional problems, many conduct problems, and many learning problems have a strong genetic component.

We are just discovering the exact numbers, but it is now widely agreed that genetics strongly contributes to how children behave and feel and learn. New discoveries come out all the time. Bed-wetting, as I mentioned in the introduction, is a good example of a condition that for years had been attributed to psychological conflict but that we now know is, in most instances, genetically transmitted. Scientists are hot on the trail of the gene, or combination of genes, behind numerous other conditions. All behavior and all personality are in some way genetically influenced, and to a greater degree than most of us take into account.

We now have strong evidence of the heritability of a number of common and not-so-common childhood psychiatric disorders. These include not only bed-wetting but also dyslexia, attention deficit disorder, conduct disorder, obsessive-compulsive disorder, depression, autism, schizophrenia, and Tourette syndrome.

The more we learn about genetics, the more clear it becomes that the gene is a contributor, not an absolute determinant. Our genes influence what we are, but they can be expressed in different shades and hues, depending upon the "lighting"—the environment. Rather than considering the gene as a simple on/off switch for a given human quality, we now think more in terms of genetic vulnerabilities, variable genetic expression, and complete or incomplete "penetrance" of a gene.

When we say a gene "penetrates" incompletely, we mean that the quality the gene carries is expressed in the real person only partially, or incompletely. Most genes are like this. They are not on/off switches, but rather hidden ingredients of the ultimate composition. One good analogy is the mixing of colors. In the color green we see neither the pure blue nor the pure yellow but a mixture of the two. We might say the yellow penetrates incompletely into the visible color green. Another analogy comes from cooking. In making a soup of complex flavor we might add many spices. No single spice will "penetrate" distinctly onto the taster's tongue when he samples the final soup, but rather a hint of each spice will combine to create the soup's own unique flavor. The cook may sprinkle pure cayenne pepper into the soup; however, the taster will not feel the burn of pure cayenne but a subtle expression of it instead.

So it is with the "soup" of human personality and behavior. Genes combine in various ways. They are not the simple on/off switches we sometimes imagine them to be. Even identical twins, who have *exactly* the same genes, are not all exactly alike. In fact, it is very rare for any condition to be passed 100 percent of the time to both identical twins. Let's say, for example, that one member of a pair of identical twins has autism, or obsessive-compulsive disorder, or depression, or some other complex emotional problem. What is the chance that the other member of the pair of twins will have the same condition? It is not 100 percent. In fact, it is much less than 100 percent. We know the conditions mentioned are passed down in families; that is to say, they are genetically influenced. But if the genetic influence were a simple on/off switch, then both members of pairs of identical twins would develop the condition 100 percent of the time, and this rarely happens. Studies of twins have given us a fascinating glimpse at the interface of nature and nurture. It seems the gene can establish a *vulnerability* in the child which life experience and other factors such as luck, God, and fate then shape into what happens in the individual's lifetime.

This only makes sense. If there were a one-to-one correspondence between a single gene and each human attribute, there would not be nearly enough space on the chromosome for all the genes we would need. There are a finite number of genes, but a nearly infinite number of human qualities. The genes provide the base from which all human qualities derive, but experience, free will, chance, and the grace of God create the ultimate shape.

What is the practical significance of genetics for a parent? Even if your child never has a diagnosable mental illness—and most children never will—by knowing your family history you will be able to look for mild versions of the more serious conditions. These mild versions, called subclinical conditions, are less severe than diagnosable conditions, but they cause problems nonetheless.

For example, your child may not have diagnosable obsessive-compulsive disorder, but he or she may be inordinately fussy and picky. This may be a subclinical expression of the full-blown condition.

Often the gene that can produce a full-blown condition, found far back in the family tree, is incompletely expressed in later generations: Your grandfather may have been almost illiterate because of a severe case of dyslexia, while in your child this gene finds expression in a mild reading problem. Such incomplete or partial expression of a gene may be the basis of what we think of as family temperament or style: The Joneses are an aggressive clan, while the Johnsons have always been quiet types. Variety within each family dilutes such generalizations, but there is some truth to them.

Without doubt, genes can be expressed in differing degrees. The incomplete expression of the gene for a full-blown syndrome may underlie much of one's basic personality. By looking at the extreme examples in your family tree, you may get a feel for the more subtle expressions of those extremes down the line.

For example, a boy named Tyrone was brought to see me recently by his parents because they were worn out. The boy, all six and a half proud years of him, wasn't the least bit worn out. That was the problem. Tyrone was exhausting his parents. This child threw fits. He was perfectly normal most of the time, but now and then he would tantrum. He had done this for as long as Mom and Dad could remember. "I'm an unpredictable volcano," Tyrone told me, apparently echoing the statement of some adult.

Mom and Dad had tried everything they could think of to control Tyrone. They had consulted with the usual expanding circle of experts, starting with their own parents, then moving on to neighbors, teachers, their baby-sitter, friends of neighbors, parents of friends, friends of parents, their own pediatrician, other pediatricians, a psychologist, a psychiatrist, two social workers, and their minister. They had collected a huge amount of advice, almost all of it good but almost none of it helpful. They had tried time-outs, they had tried a special time-out technique called "one, two, three magic," they had tried behavioral charts with prizes and punishments written in, they had tried spanking, they had tried throwing cold water on Tyrone when he threw a tantrum (this advice came from Mom's mom), they had tried different diets and sleeping arrangements (including one that put Tyrone outdoors), they had tried bribes and grounding, and they had thought of changing schools. The psychiatrist they saw referred Tyrone and his family to me.

The key to Tyrone's problem lay in the family history. Although neither Mom nor Dad had a psychiatric illness, one of Tyrone's grandfathers did. He had what we now call bipolar disorder, or manic-depressive illness. Tyrone's granddad was just like Tyrone: Now and then he "threw fits." When he was a child these fits manifested as temper tantrums. When he was an adult they blew up into what psychiatrists now call manic episodes, but in Granddad's day were simply referred to as "going crazy." It was part of the family lore that every few months Granddad would go 'round the bend. He would start screaming and drinking and spending money and going to town for women and in general just making a big mess out of his life and everyone else's. Some family members secretly envied Granddad and wished they could do what he did now and then, but everyone agreed it was a trial to have to deal with him during these episodes. But deal with him they did. Their goal was simply to make sure he didn't hurt himself or anyone else when he was crazy, and to keep him out of jail and out of bankruptcy. This was not easy. He lost all his money one night in a poker game the family didn't know about. Another time he tried to buy the local hotel—and he would have, if the owner hadn't known about Granddad and demanded he go home and think about it.

It wasn't so long ago that manic behavior of the kind Tyrone's granddad showed was understood simply in terms of eccentricity or even evil spirits. But now we know that bipolar disorder is genetically influenced. We have also recently discovered that it can break out in children, even children as young as Tyrone. Once I heard of his family history, Tyrone's tantrums began to make much more sense. All the behavioral interventions his parents had tried made sense, too, but they missed the underlying genetic component. This was a biologically based condition Tyrone had, and it warranted treatment that was also biologically based, at least in part.

I recommended a mood stabilizer for Tyrone. There are several such medications we use for children. I could have picked one of many, but the one I chose for Tyrone is a medication also used to treat seizures, called Tegretol (or carbamazepine, its generic name).

The decision to use medication was not made hastily. Tyrone's family and I discussed it at great length. And medication was by no means the whole treatment. Developing a thorough understanding of Tyrone's condition was just as important as the medication. Behavioral interventions, such as time-outs and rewards for controlling behavior, continued to play a key role. But no treatment would be completely successful unless it took into account the genetic component of Tyrone's condition.

After Tyrone started taking Tegretol, his tantrums abated. They did not cease completely, but they did subside dramatically. Mom and Dad were no longer worn out, and Tyrone no longer felt like an unpredictable volcano.

How much of basic character and personality is "bred in the bone"—genetic? How much of who we are is inescapable, present since birth and destined to stay with us until we die? Probably more than we think, but not as much as we fear.

If there is a depressive vein in your family tree, it is good to know of it. If there is a tendency to drink too much, that is important to know. If there is a tendency to overworry, you should know of that as well. But the mere presence of the gene does not mean you will necessarily develop the problem.

Genetic knowledge will not tell you for sure how your children will turn out, but it will at least enable you to look for the genetic influence on your child in an informed way.

2. The problem—or the explanation—doesn't make sense. As one of my teachers used to say when a student was missing an obvious point, "There's an elephant in the room and no one is talking about it." It is strange how people will nod in sage agreement when they think they are supposed to agree, or fear they will look stupid if they do not pretend to understand.

Parents fall into this trap when they do not trust their instincts but instead go with the flow of opinion regarding their child. A clinician can fall into this trap by accepting someone else's diagnosis without questioning it at all. A teacher can fall into this trap by accepting another person's evaluation uncritically.

Often a parent will say to me, as we are concluding our diagnostic workup, "I have known in my gut all along that we were missing something. I didn't speak up, but I knew there had to be another explanation. It just didn't make sense." The problem is that such silence can go on for years, during which time the child does not get the help that is actually needed.

If what you are told about your child's problem doesn't make sense to you, don't accept it. Don't settle for far-fetched explanations or for homespun wisdom that doesn't sit well with you. Remember, only a few decades ago a boy who had a problem learning how to read was often supposed to feel guilty over unconscious hostile feelings toward his mother. Respectable specialists of diverse backgrounds subscribed to this belief, which we now quickly reject.

There are many scenarios where the explanation you're given for your child's problem may not add up. Let's say your daughter starts doing poorly in school, she has trouble getting out of bed in the morning, and she hangs listlessly around the house. She starts gaining weight, and feels cold even when the temperature is comfortable for everyone else. Until recently she was a peppy, energetic child who did well in school and jumped out of bed in the morning. Why this change?

As you look for explanations, you find nothing. All your daughter can tell you is to go away, everything is fine. Teachers can't understand why she seems different; all they can say for sure is that she is. She has lost her energy and spark. Is something wrong at home? people ask, trying to be tactful. You say you're not aware of anything, but you begin to wonder if you are doing something wrong. Siblings and other relatives have no clues to offer. A conversation on the sly with your daughter's best friend reveals nothing except that the friend is worried, too.

When you ask your own mother what she thinks, she says it's just a phase all girls go through. Your pediatrician tells you not to worry; she'll grow out of it.

However, this homespun wisdom does not make sense to you. You do not remember such a "phase" from your own childhood, and you are really worried by how isolated your daughter is making herself both at school and at home. You take it as alarming evidence that even her best friend is concerned, and concerned enough to share that worry with you. You think that the other adults just don't know how bad things are for your daughter.

The pattern continues, and you can think of no explanation. This is the tip-off that it is time for you to get more help. Get a second medical opinion. (No doctor should ever object to this.) When what you are seeing in your child does not make sense to you, when the explanations you receive don't ring true, then you might think of a hidden biological cause. However, you are not an expert; you can't make the diagnosis yourself. What you can do is insist that the question of what is wrong not be dismissed until you get an explanation that makes sense to you.

The daughter in the story above may have developed a medical condition called hypothyroidism. Listlessness, weight gain, excessive sleep, intolerance of cold, and social withdrawal are all signs of thyroid dysfunction. There are other diagnostic possibilities as well, but the main point here is that when the behavior or mood of your child changes significantly for an extended period of time, it is worthwhile to have him or her checked out medically before you assume that "it's just a phase."

If you and your daughter do not know that such a thing as hypothyroidism exists, and that it can strike without warning or apparent environmental cause, then the condition may go undiagnosed until it becomes really dangerous.

The general principle is simple, but you must stick to your guns and follow it: If what you are seeing in your child does not make sense to you, and if the explanations you are given do not add up, then seek another explanation. Consider hidden temperamental or biological factors that may be shaping your child's behavior.

Of course, there may be other explanations as well, both grave and benign. Your daughter may have experienced some trauma she is afraid to talk about: She may have been sexually abused or have witnessed some terrifying event. She may have developed a substance abuse problem as a means of self-medicating an underlying depression. Or your mother and pediatrician may be right;

she may just be going through a phase. But it is worth pursuing the matter until you feel satisfied. If you sense that something is wrong beyond what your eye can see, trust that sense, and don't ignore it.

3. *You observe a major change in behavior or attitude.* If your child's behavior changes enough for you to notice it, you may be seeing the influence of physical factors. Most parents know in advance about the major changes that occur during puberty. But your child is developing in more subtle ways all the time. Adults' physical development levels off, whereas children are always growing —physically, neurologically, and endocrinologically, as well as mentally and emotionally. Adults continue to grow mentally and emotionally (we hope), but our physical growth tapers off. For children, physical change is constant.

While we usually look for social causes to explain a change in a child's behavior, the true explanation may be developmental. A surge in hormones in an adolescent may produce bad moods or a desire to withdraw. A growth spurt in a toddler may produce a cranky period. A delay in development of certain memory circuits in the brain may create learning problems at school. Unless biological possibilities are considered, parents may automatically assume the cause lies in their parenting or some other interpersonal domain.

In fact, parents do not overlook the biological so quickly in a newborn or a toddler. We routinely think of lack of food or lack of sleep—two fundamental biological factors—to explain the emotional state of a newborn or a toddler. But about the time our children enter first or second grade, we begin to forget—or to remember less quickly—that they are made of tissue as well as temperament.

Unexplained changes in our children may be evidence of physical factors at work. Such factors may be normal, like the onset of menstruation, or they may be a reason to worry. For example, one of the signs of depression in a fifth-grader is a change in sleep habits. The child may start staying awake late into the night, or may start wanting to sleep all day.

4. *The condition is context-independent.* If the behavior is the same regardless of what context the child is in, this is evidence that it may be biologically rooted rather than environmentally induced. For example, if your child cannot pay attention in school but pays attention just fine at home, then his attention is context-dependent; this is evidence that the cause is in the environment at school. However, if your child has trouble paying attention everywhere—at school, at home, and elsewhere—then the difficulty is context-independent. This is evidence that the cause may be biological, and conditions such as attention deficit disorder or other physical causes of inattention (such as hyperthyroidism, lead poisoning, or substance abuse) should be considered.

5. *Your child can give no explanation for what is going on.* Often our kids can't explain why they're doing what they're doing, so this sign is hardly a dead giveaway of a biologically based problem. But it *is* suggestive of one. If a child can't see the blackboard, he may spend a long time squinting and moving closer to the front of the classroom before it occurs to him that he is developing nearsightedness. Someone who's never been nearsighted may not think of nearsightedness to explain blurry vision, even if he sees other kids wearing glasses. Instead, he rubs his eyes and squints. When Mom or Dad asks why he's doing poorly in school all of a sudden, and coming home with a headache, he answers honestly, "I don't know." And if Mom or Dad, or his teacher or his pediatrician or his older sister—somebody—doesn't ask, "Can you see clearly?" he may never volunteer the crucial information that everything seems blurred. And sometimes even asking isn't enough, because the child has no point of comparison to establish what is normal. How do you know what sharp vision is, if all you've experienced is blurry? In these cases, the parent must take the child for an eye exam, or other professional evaluation.

In general, if your child can give no explanation for what is going on, and if what is going on is a problem, and if it goes on for a long time (that is, for longer than you, the parent, feel comfortable with), then include biological causes on your list of suspects. These are the most common hidden medical causes of emotional problems:

1. Vision problems
2. Hearing problems
3. Learning disabilities
4. Attention deficit disorder
5. Sleep problems
6. Substance abuse
7. Depression
8. Undiagnosed allergies
9. Lack of exercise
10. Undetected mistreatment or neglect

Any of the conditions above can make your child cranky, irritable, anxious, underachieving, or just not himself—and he may be unable to tell you why.

6. Your child is taking some prescribed or over-the-counter medication. This is an obvious but easy-to-forget possibility. Even aspirin can make you irritable. Common over-the-counter cold and allergy remedies can induce lethargy or grumpiness. Antibiotics can make a child feel out of sorts. Any medication can cause changes in mood.

7. Your child's eating habits or sleep patterns have changed. We do not know exactly how diet and sleep affect mood and behavior, but we do know that they influence and reflect both. Not only do diet and sleep influence mood and behavior, but emotional problems may be first manifested in a change in how a child eats and/or sleeps. Increased *or* decreased appetite may signify depression or some other emotional problem; so may trouble getting to sleep at night or a tendency to wake up too early in the morning or to want to sleep too late.

There are many myths in the food-and-behavior domain. For a long time we all believed that sugar made kids act up. Although that belief is still widely held, recent evidence indicates the connection has been exaggerated. Michael Jellinek of Harvard and Massachusetts General Hospital has written a book entitled *What Should I Feed My Kids?* which analyzes some of the faulty restrictions on diet that have been promulgated.

However, all clinicians would agree that food does influence behavior in some way. On the most basic, obvious level, if you don't eat, you don't live. And if you eat too much, you may become obese. Chronic obesity usually leads to emotional problems. Excess caffeine intake (from cola or coffee, for example) can underlie an anxious or hyperactive personality.

Can more subtle effects be produced? Probably. Many mothers can tell you what foods they believe produce the best behavior in their children. Certainly many parents express some of their nurturing, loving feelings through the food they give their children. They can also smother, bribe, or otherwise emotionally mistreat their children through food.

Without going into detail, it is enough to say that food may contribute, positively or negatively, to the emotional makeup of your child, and diet may be a hidden cause of emotional problems.

Similarly, sleep may provide the tip-off that your child is upset or worried over something he or she's not talking about. If your child can't get to sleep at night or is waking up before the sun rises or wanting to stay in bed late, consider that an emotional problem may be causing this change in sleep pattern.

Just as problems may be reflected in sleep patterns, sleep patterns may cause problems. We all know that children who do not get enough sleep tend to be irritable or moody. It is also not a good idea for your child to vary his or her sleep schedule widely. The common adolescent practice of sleeping very late on nonschool days, enjoyable as it may be for both the sleeper and the parent who gets a few free hours, is not a great idea. Large shifts in sleep patterns decrease the quality of sleep in general. The long sleep becomes less refreshing than depressing.

8. The season has changed. More and more we are recognizing that changes in climate can affect moods. In adults, a condition called seasonal affective disorder, or SAD, causes depression in the months without sunshine. Countries that get little sunshine have a higher incidence of depression than regions closer to the equator. Although this subject has not been well studied in children, it is logical to assume that climate—especially sunshine—may affect children's moods to a significant degree.

9. Your child has many physical complaints. Children may express depression through complaints about their bodies. Particularly in adolescence, a child's self-image may be distorted. A slender girl might think she is fat. A handsome boy might think he looks like a geek. Either of these body-centered complaints may relate to an underlying depression.

10. Your child gets sick or is injured more often than he/she used to. Sometimes a child's body expresses emotional discomfort. The child gets sick—physically—rather than saying she feels sad. Or the child gets into accidents or is injured rather than saying he doesn't really care what happens to him anymore.

These illnesses or injuries are not imagined. They are real. However, they may be rooted in emotional distress. We now know that emotional turmoil can impair the immune system, an impairment that can in turn lead to a greater susceptibility to infection. We also know that someone whose attention is preoccupied by his emotional distress can become careless, and thus predisposed to physical injury.

Chapter 3

....

Twenty-five Practical Tips for Managing Emotion and Learning

The chapters that follow will discuss various emotional and learning problems outlined in the introduction. At the end of certain chapters there will be specific suggestions on how to manage the problems discussed in those chapters. Here, however, I would like to emphasize some general, practical suggestions on the management of emotions and learning in children and families—techniques of brain management, so to speak. These suggestions apply to all children at all ages and are not specifically geared toward any one temperament, learning style, or emotional state.

1. Increase the amount of connectedness in your child's life. By "connectedness" I mean a feeling in the bones of being a part of something larger than oneself. The "something larger" may be one's family, extended family, school, neighborhood, or church; a set of shared beliefs, a club, a political party, a town, a state, a nation, an athletic team (that one plays for or roots for); one's ethnic or racial group; nature and the environment; one's best friends or workplace; or any other person, group of people, ideal, or institution one feels a part of, involved in reciprocally, connected to. Such connectedness sustains us.

Connectedness is the key to mental health in children and adults alike. Unfortunately, over the past fifty years, people's sources of connectedness have eroded. The extended family, nuclear family, neighborhood, church, and most other strong connections have weakened. People feel more on their own now than ever before. This is ironic, because we are technologically more connected than we've ever been. But humanly we are increasingly isolated and set apart.

This is not good for children. Their development of confidence, optimism, and security depends upon their establishing a solid sense of connectedness early on. Try to build that sense into the lives of your children as much as possible.

There are specific, concrete steps you can take to develop and increase connectedness in your family's life. Have conversations with your children about this and that, instead of speaking to them just to give them a direction or correct their behavior. Tell them stories and anecdotes from your own past. They'll be fascinated; also, this is a good way to develop roots and keep alive a sense of connectedness to the past through the oral history of the family. Develop and honor family traditions and rituals. Arrange gatherings and parties. Make sure your children get to know as many members of their extended family as possible, even if they live far away. Get to know your neighbors, too. Reach out, even if you are busy or shy or both. Develop connectedness to ideas and morality by talking to your children about the big issues—the meaning of life; what happens after death; the nature of right and wrong; God—and give your child a sense of being involved with you with these questions, even if you do not have all the answers. Connectedness includes connections not only to people, but to ideals, and to institutions and organizations, to information and ideas, and to nature and whatever is transcendent.

If you can focus on connectedness in all its many forms, and develop and increase it in yourself and your family, you can be certain that you and your family will become stronger, happier, and better able to withstand adversity.

2. Eat dinner together as a family. If you cannot do this every night, do it as often as you can. Try to make it a priority. Family dinners, even if they are full of confusion and little spats, glue families together. They provide an informal forum for general discussion, as well as a stage where everyone can perform.

3. Know the rules of your house and make sure everyone else in the family knows them, too. Rules are actually very stabilizing, at least when they are fair and are enforced consistently. They cut down on unnecessary struggles. The truth is that all families have rules, whether they consciously know them or not. It is worth the effort to spell out what your rules are so that (a) you'll know what they are; (b) everyone else will know what they are; (c) they won't change every day; and (d) you can enforce them more easily. It is much easier to enforce a rule that has been stated in advance than to enforce one you have made up on the spot. Sit down over your family dinner and spell out your rules. Keep them simple and few. You don't have to have a rule to cover every detail, just the basics. Debate, negotiate, haggle, do whatever you have to do, but establish your rules. Then write them down; otherwise you and everyone else will forget them. They can always be changed.

For example, a family that was having trouble at dinnertime had a little meeting while Dad was doing the dishes one night and set up the following rules, which the seven-year-old daughter composed, wrote down, and posted on the refrigerator, after discussion with her five-year-old brother and Mom and Dad:

1. No complaining about the food.
2. No begging for dessert. If you ask more than twice for dessert, you can't have it.
3. Sit down during dinner.

Dinners went much more smoothly after the rules were established.

4. Have a dictionary in full view in some important room in the house, like the living room or kitchen. Dictionaries should not be hidden.

Use your dictionary often, and make sure your children see you use it and learn to use it themselves.

5. *Sleep well.* Many families sleep poorly. Lack of sleep is becoming a part of modern life. This is inevitable when little babies are around, but once your children are able to sleep through the night try to set up a consistent bedtime for everyone. Your brain likes to get into a set rhythm if it can.

6. *Get lots of exercise.* Exercise is one of the best tonics we have for the brain—in children and in adults. Of course, it's good for the rest of your body, too, but it is marvelous for your brain. It helps it focus, makes it less sluggish, and gives it the food and nutrients it needs. Exercise works wonders for a child who is grumpy, distracted, or rambunctious. Be active with your children. Play tag. Get into sports of all kinds—picking ones that you like, of course. Chase your kids around outside. This is fun and good for everyone.

7. *Get rid of the words "smart" and "stupid."* Tell your kids those are inaccurate terms. "Smart" and "stupid" don't really mean anything—and yet children use them all the time, mostly in ways that make them feel envious, inferior, or awestruck. This book uses more accurate terms: "learning styles," "multiple intelligences," "temperaments," and "variations in attention." Tell your children early on that everyone's brain has strengths and vulnerabilities, that no one is totally smart or totally stupid any more than the United States is totally hilly or totally flat. Some people play music well, others field ground balls effortlessly, others can take cars apart easily, others can memorize anything, and others can learn a foreign language seemingly at a glance. There is no such thing as simply smart or simply stupid; we all have relative strengths and vulnerabilities.

8. *Value learning.* Talk about the importance of learning. Tell your child why learning matters. Give him or her a reason to learn, other than to please you or the teacher. Ask your child over dinner, "What did you learn today?"

9. *Applaud questions.* Emphasize that *the only stupid question is the one you don't ask.*

10. *Unlink fear and learning.* The most common learning disability is also the most preventable: fear. Many of us parents grew up in an educational system that used fear, shame, and humiliation as pedagogical tools.

For too long it has been standard procedure for teachers to "motivate" children by scaring them or humiliating them, calling on them when they know they aren't paying attention, holding up poorly done papers for others to laugh at, posting bad grades for others to chortle over, or literally calling students insulting names. Most of us grown-ups had teachers like that somewhere along the line. That method of teaching, although time-tested, should not be time-honored. Its day should be over.

While fear may promote learning in the short term, in the long term it turns children off to the whole process of education. Learning should be a long-term, not a short-term, undertaking. Instead of instilling fear, teachers should use other tools, such as clarity of expression, patience, finding the apt analogy or vivid demonstration, humor, praise, and structure. These techniques create an atmosphere of learning in which there is pleasure in the work; there may be pain, but it is only the necessary pain that often accompanies learning anything new, not unnecessary pain inflicted by a teacher.

11. *Read aloud to your child.* Reading aloud helps develop the imagination, because it allows the listener to form his own picture in his mind. It also helps develop a sense of the music and timing of language. Jim Trelease's *Read Aloud Handbook* is an excellent resource.

12. *Praise your child's efforts to learn, and give lots of reassurance.* Remember, learning is hard. You should shower the learner with praise and reassurance. This is not "empty praise." Some parents and teachers feel that they should praise a child only when he has done something marvelous to "deserve" it. While understand-

able, this point of view is counterproductive. It is like adding oil to your car's engine only when it "deserves" it. A child needs praise all the time, just as an engine needs oil all the time. Learning generates heat and friction in the brain; praise and reassurance lubricate and smoothe the process. They makes the gears of the brain mesh more easily. Never withhold praise and reassurance. Your child will know when he or she has done something marvelous; you do not need to hold back your praise for only those special moments. In fact, frequent praise and reassurance will make those special moments come more often.

13. Have music in your house. Anecdotal studies have suggested that workers do better work when Mozart is playing, and children learn more. Many children study better when listening to music of the right kind.

14. Eliminate sarcasm. If you're angry, say you're angry. If you're disappointed, say you're disappointed. If you think what someone else said was foolish, say you disagree. But try never to make sarcastic remarks to children. Also try not to make them to your spouse, as listening to you is one way children learn how to be sarcastic themselves. Persistent use of sarcasm instills fear in children and curtails their willingness to be open.

15. Make sure your child knows that it is safe to fail. No one learns without failing first. The only way you can develop a new skill is by passing through a period of doing the task poorly, then gradually improving. If your child is afraid to fail because she fears ridicule or disapproval, she will learn much less than the child who is bold and brave enough to learn new skills.

16. If your child is "fighting with his brain," pounding his head, and saying, "I'm dumb!" as he does his homework, give him reassurance and then stay with him for a while. Help him bear the tension of learning. Tell him that the pain and frustration he feels are okay, a normal part of the learning process. Ask him whether he needs some help, or whether there is another approach to the problem that he might try.

17. Know your child's brain. This tip is the neurological equivalent of "Know thyself." As this book stresses throughout, getting the best out of your brain begins in knowing your brain well. Ask yourself: What are the strengths of my child's brain? What are its vulnerabilities? Under what circumstances does it learn best? When does it learn poorly? It is a mistake to assume that everyone's brain is the same or functions best under the same conditions that work well for someone else. Help yourself and your child get to how know his or her brain operates best.

18. *Assess the "goodness of fit" between you and your child.* If you are naturally quiet and you have a voluble child, try not to blame the child for getting on your nerves; be aware of the issue of fit, or relative lack of fit. If you are naturally uninhibited and you have an inhibited child, try not to force the child to change temperament, which is like changing handedness; instead try to adjust to the difference of fit. Since you are the parent, it is appropriate for you to try to adjust to your child rather than force your child to adjust to you.

19. *Help your child name feelings.* One of the best ways for someone to avoid being overpowered by a feeling is to be able to name the feeling. Giving a feeling a name puts it at arm's length, rather than right up in your face where it is most threatening. When your child is in the grip of an unpleasant feeling, help her not only to name the feeling but to tell someone else about it. The statement, "Mommy, I'm feeling sad," can mark the beginning of feeling better.

20. *Also when an unpleasant feeling comes upon your child, help her to get in the habit of knowing it will pass.* No feeling lasts forever. Tell her it will pass, even if she gets annoyed at you for saying so. This is one way to instill the basic tool of self-reassurance, a very important skill to acquire.

21. *Diet matters.* Exactly how does it matter? We don't really know. However, we do know you should not ignore the issue. The food your brain uses comes from what you eat. We used to think sugar was a big problem, but most evidence now refutes that. Be an empiricist. See what diet works best for your children. Talk it

over with your pediatrician or a nutritionist. Above all, watch what your child eats and try to see how individual foods affect him. The best advice is still probably the tried-and-true advice: Eat a balanced diet, eat three meals a day, and stay away from candy, junk food with lots of additives, and between-meal snacks.

22. *Use structure.* Make sure there are rules, schedules, and consistency in your child's life. If you do not have a schedule, sit down with your family and make one. If you can't stick to it perfectly, fine. But at least you have a template that each day should more or less follow. This is reassuring to kids.

23. *Pray or meditate.* And teach your child to do the same. If you are religious, try to pray every day. If you are not religious, learn meditation or self-hypnosis or some other technique that allows your brain to go into a controlled trance at least once a day for at least a few minutes. This is not the same as sleep. It is extremely good for your brain. Meditation, prayer, quiet time, and even pleasant daydreaming all have a relaxing effect upon the brain. They drain it of its goal-directed, present-centered frenzy, a state in which too many of us, and our children, live too much of the time. Children who can pray, meditate, or quietly reflect can replenish their mental energy by doing these activities. You can learn to meditate by buying a book on the topic. There are many in paperback—look for a title that includes self-hypnosis and meditation, but avoid a book that pushes a certain religion or single point of view. Herbert Benson's book *The Relaxation Response* is excellent. It is old, but not out-of-date, and it is a classic in the field.

24. *No illicit drugs.* Obvious, but worth mentioning. It is highly unlikely (if you count caffeine, almost impossible) that your child will go through life without trying some drug or another. However, you should teach your child what each drug does. It is up to you, as a parent, what standards and rules you want to set, but try to make this decision early in your child's life so you can start talking about drugs of all kinds in a consistent way from early childhood on.

25. Ask your child what works best for him or her. Ask your child what techniques or habits help with studying, playing, and getting along in everyday life. If you ask, your children will tell you. However, most of the time we prescribe what we think is best for our children without asking them first. This is a great mistake. Always ask your child first what works: "How can you get this project done best?" "What is the best time for us to talk?" "How can I help you talk to your sister so you won't fight with her?" Often children have specific suggestions that could really help, if only we would ask.

Chapter 4

··

Confused: Variations in Learning

If I can't learn the way you teach,
can you teach the way I learn?
—*A student*

The headline on the front page of the Hartford, Connecticut, *Courant* on August 29, 1995, read as follows: "Yale Law student is young, gifted and dyslexic."

The story described Benjamin Bolger, who in 1995, at nineteen years old, became one of the youngest students ever to enroll in Yale Law School. He has dyslexia, and reads at about a seventh-grade level. However, he also finished at the top of his graduating class at the University of Michigan.

How did he do it? He and his mother understood his brain. They understood that although Benjamin read poorly, he could easily understand *what was read to him*. He used books on tape, but also his mother read to him from six to ten hours a day. She will accompany Benjamin—her only child—to New Haven to help him in law school.

Benjamin Bolger not only had a very devoted mother but also used the accommodations that are now standard for students who have learning disabilities—for instance, taking tests on an untimed basis. In this way he was not unfairly penalized for being a slow reader.

His unusual mind required some unusual help to shine. But shine it surely did. One of his professors at Michigan was quoted as saying, "My first reaction was, 'Give me a break.' I figured this guy was obviously not going to be a very good student." But the professor said Benjamin's papers were brilliant. "He was just out of this world. His writing was kind of out of control yet filled with brilliant images, creative insights. When he told me he was 17 years old, I couldn't believe it. If there is such a thing as an audiographic memory, he has it. He absorbs everything that is said to him."

How do you know if your own child has a learning disability? You can begin by observing him or her at home. Then be in close touch with school, as teachers are experts on normal development in children. Tell your child's teacher what you observe at home, and with the teacher's help you should get a good idea of whether your child needs additional testing or help or is within the range of "normal."

Be on the lookout not just for specific problems but for the most common learning disability of all. The most common learning disability *by far* is not dyslexia, although dyslexia is common. It is not attention deficit disorder, although ADD is not rare. It is not a mathematics disability or a foreign-language disability or a nonverbal learning disability, although these conditions appear in every large group of children.

By far the most common learning disability we know of is fear. At one time or another it affects 100 percent of the population. Every one of us has felt afraid at some time or another in learning a new subject or a new task.

Fortunately, while it is the most common of all learning disabilities, fear is also the most treatable. A reassuring teacher, a well-written instruction manual (if you can find one!), or a friendly classroom can all help overcome fear.

In the absence of fear, most people can learn most things. *Most children can learn more than they are learning now.* The great failure of education today is a failure of the heart as much as of the head.

In our rush back to basics and to fundamentals and to rigor, we must remember one of the oldest principles of teaching: "Instruct by pleasing," the Latin poet Horace wrote. The ancients knew this; we moderns should keep it in mind. Learning begins in emotion, in a positive attitude. Parents and teachers need to pump children up about learning. "You can do it!" "Go for it!" "Atta girl!" "Atta boy!" We need to turn children on. One of learning specialist Priscilla Vail's books is entitled *Emotion: The On/Off Switch for Learning,* and that title tells the truth.

Anyone can learn, and at any age. Some of the most talented members of society have a learning disability or some unidenti-fied idiosyncrasy in the way they learn. In fact, I dare say that all of us could identify some area of learning in which we considered ourselves different, if not weak. It is important to help children identify these areas and not feel bad about them. Shame over one's intellectual capabilities can be crippling. It is unnecessary. It can be avoided.

John Irving, today one of our foremost novelists, graduated from high school thinking he was stupid. Imagine how many potential John Irvings are buried under the weight of negativity heaped on them during their school years. (Even the positive feedback we hand our "A" students is misleading. The glorious straight-"A" high school valedictorians sometimes leave their best years right there in high school and end up working for the "D" student who plugged his way through school, then founded a new company after college.) The whole caste system in school based on the smart/stupid dichotomy is misleading—in both direc-tions.

We cannot expect our schools to make our children's educa-tion painless; learning often hurts. We can, however, expect schools to eliminate unnecessary pain.

Eliminating unnecessary pain is the single best "treatment" for any learning problem, and we all have problems learning now and then. Make the classroom, or whatever place you happen to be in when you learn, safe. Make it okay to struggle, okay to fail, okay not to get it right. If you do this, you do most of what needs to be done. If you do not do this, no treatment plan and no "individualized educational plan," no matter how brilliantly conceived, will work. A scared child learns poorly. More significantly, a scared child can't wait to stop learning. A scared child wants out. So don't scare children.

❊

In addition to various kinds of intelligence and styles of learning, there are specific learning problems, such as dyslexia, that parents should know of.

How many children have a diagnosable, namable learning disorder? One in ten children would be a conservative estimate. This is figuring that 5 percent of the population has dyslexia, 4 percent has attention deficit disorder, and 1 percent have other disorders; all these are conservative figures. Figures for learning disorders are extremely difficult to determine because the criteria used to define learning problems vary according to who is conducting the survey. As has been stated, all children (and all adults) have difficulties in learning at one time or another. And all children have a "cognitive style," a profile of strengths and vulnerabilities. Exactly who receives a diagnosis and who doesn't becomes slightly arbitrary.

Excluding mental retardation, the more common learning disorders include, in descending order of prevalence, dyslexia, or difficulty with reading and/or writing; attention deficit disorder; and a mathematics disorder with or without the syndrome of nonverbal learning disabilities.

Dyslexia is defined by Bruce Pennington, a leading expert on learning disorders, as an unexpected difficulty in learning how to read and spell one's native language. The definition therefore excludes problems in learning a foreign language. "Unexpected," says Pennington, "means that there is no obvious reason for the difficulty, such as inadequate schooling, peripheral sensory handicap [for example, poor vision or hearing], acquired brain damage, or low overall IQ." Dyslexia is common. Millions of Americans have it. Depending upon how it is defined and who does the measuring, the prevalence of dyslexia may vary from 5 percent to as much as 30 percent of the population.

Some of the exciting current brain research is in the field of dyslexia. Major projects were started at the Beth Israel Hospital in Boston by Dr. Norman Geschwind and continued by Dr. Albert Galaburda, looking at the biological basis of dyslexia. The research from Beth Israel has shown that the dyslexic brain has certain minute anatomical differences from the nondyslexic brain.

Others in centers across the country have looked at various aspects of dyslexia. Priscilla Vail has written widely and lucidly on the topic of working with dyslexic children in the classroom. Paula Tallal has done work on the brain's processing problems in dyslexia. Judith Rumsey has devised a rhyming test for detecting dyslexia. Sylvia O. Richardson has written penetrating descriptions of the phenomenology of dyslexia. I mention these researchers to stress that there was a time, not very long ago, when dyslexia was looked at askance, as if it were an invention or an excuse rather than a natural fact. The work of these people, and of many others, has dispelled such skepticism.

There was also a time, not so very long ago, when a child's difficulty in reading was thought to derive from underlying emotional conflict, specifically unconscious guilt over aggressive feelings toward his or her mother. We now know that in the vast majority of cases difficulty in reading creates, rather than derives from, emotional conflict, and that Mother is usually the one most instrumental in getting the problem dealt with properly. And we recognize the genetic rather than environmental basis of most cases of dyslexia.

To figure out if your child's reading problem is due to dyslexia, talk with your child's teacher. Children do not all learn to read at the same time. If your first-grader is behind his or her peers in reading, that does not necessarily indicate the presence of a reading disability. Teachers have a good feel for the normal range of progress in learning to read. If your child is significantly behind, your child's teacher will know it. Then you might consult with the school psychologist or learning specialist to get more formal testing.

One problem is that many schools have abandoned the teaching of phonics. They use, instead, what is called the whole language approach, by which the student learns to read by osmosis, by immersing himself in words. This is fine for some children, but others need a more structured method, one that includes a way to figure out what a word sounds like. Phonics provides such a method: You "sound out" the word. But if you don't know phonics, you can't sound the word out. Children with reading problems often become completely lost and confused if they do not learn phonics. Then they start to believe they are stupid, or they take a dislike to reading—both of which are, of course, undesirable outcomes. If your child has a reading problem, even if dyslexia has not been formally diagnosed, consider teaching him phonics, or hooking him up with an Orton-Gillingham tutor (the Orton-Gillingham method emphasizes a multisensory approach to reading, using phonics) or some other tutor who specializes in teaching phonics.

If the cause of your child's reading problem is dyslexia, a good place to turn for help is the Orton Dyslexia Society (see Chapter 11 for the address and phone number). This is a wonderful organization, full of knowledgeable, experienced men and women, dedicated to advancing the cause of literacy everywhere. This society trains people all over the country in the Orton-Gillingham method mentioned above, and provides tutors for children and adults.

Attention deficit disorder, or ADD, is another problem that can impede learning. ADD, too, is common, affecting anywhere from 2 percent to 10 percent of the population. I will discuss ADD in the following chapter.

The other learning disorders are less common. Some have

been recognized only recently, such as the syndrome of nonverbal learning disabilities, or NLD, described by Byron Rourke, Jane Greene, and many others. Rourke believes that NLD is caused by damage to the "white matter" of the brain, the part of the brain that lies beneath the thinking cortex, which is called the gray matter. The term "nonverbal" refers to the fact that the main problems in NLD are in functions governed by the nondominant, nonverbally oriented hemisphere of the brain. (In most people, this is the right hemisphere.) Children with NLD can speak fluently, but have impaired nonverbal skills, such as interpreting body language or facial expression and picking up on the mood of a group or an individual. Hence, their social skills are poor.

The child with a nonverbal learning disability can make use of what he hears, but has trouble taking in information he gathers by seeing or touching, and with complex motor tasks and in dealing with new material of any sort. He has trouble understanding anything that can't be "spelled out." In other words, he has trouble getting the gist of an idea, or the spirit of a situation.

Because he can be so verbal, able to talk up a storm, this child can puzzle you with his inability to "get" what is going on around him. At first glance he seems socially and intellectually facile. However, as you stay with him you begin to see that the unheard, nonverbal part of life passes him by. Words are so preeminent in our lives that we sometimes forget how much we rely on what words cannot tell us, information we gather by means other than words. We forget how much we rely on nonverbal cues in understanding each other socially, and also in understanding new concepts. Often, as you are learning about something new, there comes a moment when you suddenly get it, when the idea pops out at you, when you say to yourself, "Oh, now I understand how a pump works," or whatever the concept might be. Children who have NLD lack the cognitive apparatus to make the idea pop out, to get it. They do not intuit; everything must be spelled out.

The child with a nonverbal learning disability also develops problems in reading comprehension; although he can decode the words, he has trouble making use of them, trouble being guided by them. He can define the words he hears or reads, but he cannot necessarily do what the words are telling him to do or reach the conclusion they are leading him to reach. This making use of words is the nonverbal part of comprehension, the part we do intuitively, without words. We first decode a word—that is, read it or hear it—but then we have to put it into a context with the other words that surround it in order to get the bigger picture —that is, understand the meaning of the sentence, paragraph, or book. The child with a nonverbal learning disability has great trouble doing this.

Day-to-day difficulties also include problems with mathematics, science, general problem-solving, and social relatedness. The child has trouble "seeing" the social cues that are so crucial to getting along with others and sensing the attitudes of other people. NLD is rare, affecting perhaps one-half of one percent of the population, but it is important to know about should your child have some of the symptoms. Because most people don't know about NLD, the diagnosis is usually missed. These kids are simply thought of as "maladjusted" or "weird" or "stupid." Their difficulty reading social cues leads them to experience frequent rejection from peers. By adolescence they are usually lonely and low-spirited. While early diagnosis cannot prevent the primary neurological problems, the secondary psychological problems can be anticipated and more effectively dealt with.

Rourke summarizes the assets and deficits in NLD as follows:

Assets
1. Handwriting (early on a problem, but the child catches up)
2. Word decoding (the child can tell you what the word is, though he can't necessarily comprehend what he reads)
3. Spelling
4. Verbatim memory

Deficits
1. Handwriting (a problem early on, but it improves)
2. Reading comprehension (gets worse over time)
3. Mechanical arithmetic and mathematics
4. Science (major problems in reasoning)
5. Adaptation to novel situations (the child tends to rely on rote methods)
6. Social competence (the child tends to withdraw as he gets older)
7. Emotional instability

What do these add up to? What does a child with NLD look like? By fifth grade he is probably socially set apart, is a good memorizer, but has trouble in school with math, science, and reasoning and comprehension, and may be a little depressed. The point of diagnosis and treatment is to try to help him make the best of what he can do, and not suffer unnecessarily for what he can't.

Medication may help with some of the symptoms of NLD, as may other approaches such as social coaching and tutoring. Parents need, first of all, to learn as much as they can about the condition so that they can have realistic, informed expectations for their children.

Children with NLD need much more coaching than the average child. They do not get what others get so naturally, and parents and teachers must understand that this is not because they have an attitude problem but because the nonverbal processing centers in their brains are not working properly. It can be exasperating to talk to someone who doesn't get what seems to be so obvious to everyone else. But these children need our patience. They are trying. However, they are limited by what amounts to a kind of blindness. They can see literally, but they cannot see metaphorically. They cannot see what everyone else sees easily: anger on a teacher's face, the logical next step in a series (such as 2, 4, 6, 8, ?), or what to do when a friend starts to cry. With coaching, direction, reassurance, and structure these children can be helped, but helping them requires knowledge of their disability—and, of course, patience.

Finally, we should mention a condition called central auditory processing disorder, or CAPD. This condition, which is diagnosed primarily by speech/language pathologists, includes a great deal of crossover with the symptoms of attention deficit disorder or ADD; ADD will be discussed in the next chapter. The core problem in CAPD, as the name implies, is using what you hear. The child with CAPD does not make use of what he hears as fluently as other children. The American Speech-Language-Hearing Association stated in 1992, "Central auditory processing disorders are deficits in the information processing of audible signals not attributed to impaired peripheral hearing sensitivity or intellectual impairment."

If you cannot use what you hear, then you will get into many other difficulties. You will have trouble paying attention, because you will be lost. You will have trouble getting organized, completing work on time, showing up where you should, participating in classroom discussions or conversations with friends, and maintaining a positive outlook. After a while, you may easily become depressed or feel frustrated due to lack of success both academically and socially.

If the primary problem is in processing language, then the diagnosis of CAPD is made. If the primary problem is in paying attention consistently, then the diagnosis of ADD is made. The two conditions can often coexist. How can they be distinguished? Only by a careful evaluation by a professional, and even then it is not easy. A speech/language pathologist will tend to diagnose CAPD while in the same child a child psychiatrist will tend to diagnose ADD.

True CAPD can be helped with a variety of exercises aimed at improving the language processing skills of the child. These exercises must be set up and supervised by a professional, usually a speech/language pathologist. Unlike ADD, we do not treat

CAPD with medication, unless ADD coexists, in which case medication may help.

In diagnosing any of these conditions, it is most important that you seek a thorough evaluation by a professional. Because of the proliferation of knowledge in the field of learning, self-proclaimed "experts" have proliferated as well. Be careful. Don't use the Yellow Pages as your first referral source. Find someone who knows the person to whom you are being referred. Ask your pediatrician or your child's school, or call the medical school nearest you and ask for the department of child psychiatry or pediatric neurology to get a referral. The evaluation will cost you a significant amount of money; don't waste it. A wrong evaluation will cost you not only money but also years of wrong treatment. These are lost years.

All children, not just the children who have diagnosable learning disabilities, experience some frustration when they learn. To find out what really helps your child, experiment. Follow the steps already suggested, then take an empirical approach. See what works best. Maybe studying in the morning works better for your child. Maybe listening to tapes of classes. Maybe summarizing books immediately after they've been read. I got through medical school largely by using index cards upon which I wrote down the key information about a specific topic. I had stacks of index cards, but they made the information manageable for me. Encourage your child to find whatever works best. It doesn't matter how your child learns, as long as the method is safe and legal. Learning styles can be unique. I once consulted with parents whose child read best if she held the book *upside down*. We do not have a name for this "method," no diagnosis or label, but this child, who was an excellent reader, learned in a way that for almost everyone else would be impossible.

In helping your child get along well in school, you need to be able to deal with the school effectively. It is crucial that you develop a good relationship with the teachers and administrators. To that end, the following tips are offered here:

TEN TIPS ON DEALING WITH YOUR CHILD'S SCHOOL

1. Make friends with the teacher and with the school. This is by far the most important tip. When parents and teachers or parents and school administrators get into struggles, the person who suffers is the child. Do all that you can to build a positive relationship with the teacher and the school—help the teacher with photocopying; show up for every meeting; participate in supporting the school. Struggles almost always lead to hurt feelings and trouble for the child. Bite your tongue. Realize teachers have it tough in many ways you probably don't even know about. Make friends, not enemies, at school.

2. Get to know your child's teacher. This is a corollary of number 1. It helps to know the teacher as a person before you have to deal with a crisis or conflict. It is much easier to hear bad news about your child from someone you've had coffee with and laughed with than from someone you only know as a name.

3. Keep the school informed about what problems you see your child having and ask the teacher to do the same for you. Take five minutes every week just to chat with the teacher. This way you will not hear for the first time in March about a problem that started in October.

4. Look at the fit between your child and the school. Ask if the school is aware of different learning styles, and try to make sure you get a teacher who is. Try to work with the teacher to make sure your child is being taught in the way that best enables her to learn within the limits of what a school can reasonably provide. If the school cannot accommodate you, you might want to change schools.

5. Once you have decided that your child is, in fact, in the right school, let the school do its work without your hovering over too much. It is good to be in communication with the school, but don't pester the teacher. Let the school teach; you be the parent.

6. *Don't do your child's homework for him.* If he has more than he can do, tell the teacher. If he does not understand the work, the teacher should know about that as well. It is fine to answer a few questions for your child, but if you find yourself spending hours every night working on homework with your child, this is something the teacher should know about. You should not be doing your child's homework.

7. *Hold on to teachers' comments and compare them from year to year.* They make an excellent, quick review of problems and progress.

8. *Remember, not all children learn all things at the same time.* Some children read sooner than others. Some do math earlier. Some talk early, some late. Don't ask your school to hurry your child. Children are hurried enough as it is.

9. *Also remember, your school is only as good as you help it to be.* Try to make your criticisms concrete, and try to offer solutions if you can.

10. *Don't expect teachers to know everything.* It is impossible these days to keep up with all that is being learned about learning. If you know some subject better than the teacher, don't be shocked or disappointed. Share what you know.

Chapter 5

····························

Confused: Variations in Attention

"Maggie, why do you seem to be lost in the clouds all the time? I can never tell if you hear me or not," the teacher says, looking concerned.

"I can hear you," Maggie answers.

"But are you *listening* to me?" the teacher asks.

"I'm trying to," Maggie answers, "but sometimes my mind goes away."

What is wrong with Maggie? Is she lazy? Is she tired? Does she need more motivation? Is she just bored? Or might she be hard of hearing?

What does it mean to pay attention, and why do so many children have such a hard time doing it?

It means a lot. And it matters a lot—particularly in school. One's brain is not always equally tuned to all topics. Far from it: Attention is fickle, settling down on one subject only as long as that subject keeps its interest.

There are many reasons children have a hard time paying attention, particularly in school. We are asking children to do an unusually difficult task in most classrooms. It is not natural for a child to sit still and listen for extended periods. We have to remember this before we start making unrealistic demands on them.

In my work, I give many lectures to audiences of schoolteachers around the country, teachers of all ages who teach all grades. I am always amused at how unruly and rambunctious these audiences invariably are! Let out of their classrooms, and out of their roles as authority figures, teachers become as bubbly and noisy as any fifth-grade class. They are impossible to bring to order, they persistently ignore directions, they interrupt, they pass notes, they daydream, they leave the room without permission, they blurt out answers to questions without raising their hands, they whisper among themselves, they forget what they have been told to do, they use colorful language, they sometimes knit or tap their pencils or make strange noises—in short, they are impossible in precisely the same ways kids in classrooms are impossible. I love it! I enjoy reminding them of what they are doing, not to ask them to stop, because I relish their enthusiasm, but by way of asking them to perhaps purse their lips less severely when their students do the same.

Beyond the fact that paying attention in groups is difficult for all of us, many other factors lead to distraction in the classroom. Sometimes the material is too taxing, so the child tunes out. Sometimes the child finds another activity—like talking to a friend or gazing out the window—that is more engrossing than what is being written on the blackboard. Sometimes the child is preoccupied with some other concern, such as what his girlfriend is thinking, or what lunch will be.

Instead of "Why *doesn't* a child pay attention in school?" the pressing question is "Why *does* a child pay attention?" Since there are so many reasons not to pay attention, how do we persuade *any* children to listen as well as hear?

We use many methods. One is authority: We command children to listen. Another is achievement: We give them prizes for listening. A third is fear: We tell them we will do bad things to them if they do not listen. A fourth is peer pressure: Some schools create an atmosphere, a school culture, that dictates that every student sit still and listen. Perhaps the best method of all is for the teacher or parent to compete with everything else that is vying for the child's attention—and win! We've all had teachers who could do this; weren't they amazing?

But in addition to these external influences, internal biological factors regulate attention as well. Some minds, it turns out, wander more easily than others. Over the past hundred years a great deal of research has been done into the phenomenon of attention. One of the fruits of this research is that we have learned that not everyone attends in the same way. Some people are amazingly hard to distract; these are the people who are good with details. I sometimes think of them as having attention *surplus* disorder. Then there are the majority of people who attend pretty well most of the time, but can get distracted easily when they're tired, bored, or preoccupied. And finally there are the 5 percent or so of us who show great inconsistencies in attention, at times hyperfocusing on a task and at other times ricocheting in a zig-zag of distraction; this group has what we call attention deficit disorder.

When I was a child, if you didn't pay attention you were sent to the principal's office. Now we diagnose attention deficit disorder. But if ADD is such a big deal, why didn't we know about it when we were children? Are we involved in some sort of ADD epidemic, or is the epidemic just an epidemic of excuse-making?

It is understandable that the majority of people, who have worked hard to take responsibility for their actions, should grow impatient at what might appear to be just another excuse offered up by a lazy and irresponsible minority. But the symptoms of ADD have been with us since the dawn of consciousness. There have always been children who couldn't sit still and focus on their work, just as there have always been children who paid attention particularly well. There have always been children who disrupted classrooms and car rides and dinnertime conversations.

What *is* new, and certainly a godsend for millions of children and adults, is the diagnostic term ADD. Instead of the old diagnosis—a moral diagnosis such as "bad" or "wayward"—we now know enough to apply a more useful diagnosis, the medical diagnosis of ADD. And with a medical diagnosis comes medical treatment, instead of "moral" treatment—some form of reprimand, insult, or physical punishment. This shift from moral condemnation to medical treatment is what is new, not the symptoms. And that shift is great good news for us all.

The classic symptoms of ADD include easy distractibility, impulsivity, and physical restlessness or hyperactivity. We have solid neurological evidence that something is going on in these children's brains to make them behave the way they do. Now that we have medical treatments that drastically curtail their negative symptoms, these children and their adult counterparts can get an even chance at life.

Having ADD myself, and having written two books on the topic, I am closely involved with the subject. This involvement has taught me at least two lessons. First, ADD is a seductive diagnosis. We have to be very careful not to overdiagnose ADD. *Everyone* has trouble paying attention at one time or another. That does not mean everyone has ADD. The diagnosis only makes sense when the symptoms are severe and when they are causing some problem in the individual's life. Only a professional can make the diagnosis, and even then it is a tricky one to make. Many other conditions can mimic ADD; not the least of those conditions is modern life.

In children and adults, modern life induces a syndrome I call pseudo-ADD. This is not true ADD, but looks just like it. There are two main reasons why our world is "ADD-ogenic." First is the electronic communications network that envelops all of us. The fax machine; the telephone with its cousins, the cell phone and the answering machine; the television and VCR; movies; the radio; the personal computer, with its modem and access to the Internet, America Online, Prodigy, and CompuServe; the remote control; satellite communications; FedEx; and on and on—all these technical wonders have so connected us that we are constantly reachable. This means we are constantly expected to reach back. Consequently, a round-trip message—you to me, and back to you—that used to take a week now takes a minute or less. We have so speeded up our lives, and our children's lives, that we feel constantly distracted and restless, two of the cardinal symptoms of ADD.

Children love this feeling. It is almost addictive. The faster they go, the faster they want to go. The more stimulation they have in their lives, the more they want. If parents are not careful, they play into this frenzy and create an ADD-like atmosphere in their own homes.

The second factor that contributes to creating pseudo-ADD in modern life is the reverse of the first. As hyperconnected as we are electronically, we are disconnected socially. We used to live in neighborhoods where we could drop in on each other all the time. Many eyes watched our children. We looked out for each other. Now, many children do not even know all the members of their extended family, let alone see them on a regular basis. Neighborhoods have broken down. People do not keep up with their friends or take the time to connect. The church is not the force it once was. People do not feel that they are part of something larger than themselves. Loyalties to businesses and institutions have eroded. We often feel disconnected from national government and local policy-makers. All this disconnectedness creates distraction, insecurity, and displacement, all typical feelings in ADD.

We therefore see two powerful factors, electronic connectedness on the one hand and social disconnectedness on the other, combining to create a modern landscape that induces the symptoms of ADD. While only 5 percent of the population has true ADD, I'd guess about 50 percent has pseudo-ADD.

Additionally, a number of medical and psychiatric conditions can mimic ADD—conditions such as hyperthyroidism, hypothyroidism, drug abuse, depression, manic-depressive illness, and post-traumatic stress disorder, to name some of the more common ones. There is no definitive diagnostic test for ADD; like a diagnosis of depression, a diagnosis of ADD depends on the intensity and duration of the core symptoms. Therefore, proper diagnosis requires a careful professional evaluation.

The second great lesson I have learned from working with children and adults who have true ADD is the reciprocal of the first: While we do not want to overdiagnose ADD, we must strive never to miss the diagnosis either. Missing this diagnosis can leave a child in a dark world of daily reprimands and physical punishments. Children and adults with undiagnosed ADD endure years of unnecessary pain. As much as we worry about overdiagnosing ADD, we should worry even more about missing the diagnosis when it is there.

One of the great rewards of my professional life has been seeing the progress patients have made after being diagnosed with ADD. They tell me being diagnosed and treated was like a miracle for them. At last they could understand themselves. At last their brains made sense to them. At last there was a noncondemning name for what was going on. And at last there was treatment, instead of punishment. It is exciting to watch a person, when given the key of new knowledge about himself, change from feeling stupid and misunderstood to feeling confident and being successful.

How do you make the diagnosis of ADD? What signs should you look for in your child (or even in yourself) as tip-offs to ADD?

Look first of all for the hallmark symptoms of easy distractibility, impulsivity, and restlessness. If these symptoms appear in your child to a much greater degree than they do in other children of the same age, they may indicate ADD.

The terms "distractibility," "impulsivity," and "restlessness" are rather vague; what, specifically, should you look for? The following signs are typical:

1. Your child has trouble getting organized in the morning. Just getting dressed can take forever.

2. Your child is impossible at the dinner table or at restaurants. He or she cannot stay seated, instigates spats with siblings, and generally disrupts everyone else's meal.

3. Your child can't seem to remember more than one instruction at a time. If you ask him to go into the next room and get you a pair of scissors, he'll go into the next room, but then forget what he went there to get.

4. Your child interrupts constantly.

5. Your child often agrees to do something, then doesn't do it. He says, much to the annoyance and disbelief of others, that he forgot.

6. Procrastination is a major problem.

7. Your child exhibits many positive qualities, such as high energy, enthusiasm, warmth, a "special something" or twinkle in his or her eyes, creativity, intuition, and persistence or pluck.

8. Your child impulsively makes up tall tales or improbable explanations for failures.

9. Your child is often late for appointments or forgets them altogether.

10. Teachers complain that your child doesn't pay attention in class. You complain that your child doesn't pay attention at home.

11. Getting organized is an ordeal.

12. Your child loves adventure, risk, and all forms of high stimulation.

13. At times, your child pays attention very well, even hyperfocuses, particularly when engaged in a task that interests him.

14. Your child can't sit still.

15. Your child speaks out of turn, often blurting out remarks that are deemed inappropriate by teachers or parents.

16. Your child is the class clown.

17. Your child demands a lot of attention.

18. Your child is moody.
19. Your child is impatient; he or she just can't wait for anything.
20. Your child has very little sense of time. There are only two times: "now" and "not now."

If you find these symptoms much more intensely in your child than in other children, think of ADD as a possibility. If you find only a few, you and your child need to work on them, but it's unlikely that the problem is ADD. But if you find more than fifteen, then you should get a professional to evaluate your child.

Who can diagnose ADD? Child psychiatrists are specifically trained to do so, but many others can also make the diagnosis—neurologists, pediatricians, psychologists, social workers, nurse practitioners, or other trained professionals. Somewhere in the process an M.D. (pediatrician, neurologist, or child psychiatrist) should be involved to rule out medical conditions such as hyperthyroidism or lead ingestion that can look like ADD.

What does the evaluation entail? The diagnosis of ADD depends first and foremost on the child's history. The history is the oldest and most telling "test" in medicine. To take the history, the doctor sits down with the child and asks the question doctors have been asking for centuries: "Where does it hurt?"

The child may say it hurts in school, or it hurts to think or to pay attention, or it hurts to get yelled at. Then the doctor asks why it hurts in school, or how it hurts to think, or why the child gets yelled at. The story begins to unroll.

Then the doctor asks the same question of Mom and Dad: "Where does it hurt?" It hurts, they might say, to watch our son try, and then fail, and then try again. It hurts to have to yell at him so much. It hurts to go on vacation with him. It hurts to watch him miss so much. The doctor asks for more detail, and the picture begins to enlarge.

Next the doctor asks the same question of the schoolteacher:

"Where does it hurt?" The teacher says it hurts to see a child with so much talent achieve so little. Or she might say she sees him stare out the window all the time instead of look at the blackboard; or it hurts to see him be distracted easily by his friends, or to watch him dawdle over simple work. A teacher's comments add key information to the history because the teacher is in the unique position of observing the child all day in a group with other children of the same age. Also, the teacher is usually more objective than parents.

After gathering the history, the doctor can usually make a diagnosis. However, sometimes additional testing is needed. These may be medical tests, such as thyroid function tests, but most often they are psychological tests. These are paper-and-pencil tests, sometimes taken on a computer screen as well, given by a psychologist. Their results describe the child's thinking in a variety of ways. Tests assess memory, attention, distractibility, language comprehension, vocabulary, fund of knowledge, pattern recognition, spatial relations, computational skills, and abstract reasoning. Psychological tests can also assess emotional well-being, picking up on hidden signs of depression, hostility, confused thinking, fear, or other emotional problems.

As a group, these tests are quite sophisticated and can illuminate hidden domains of a child's mind. But the fact is, we do not have a foolproof test for ADD. Psychological tests, which many people erroneously think of as being "the test" for ADD, can mislead you in the following way: Three of the best treatments we have for ADD include structure, motivation, and novelty. How is psychological testing done? It is done one-on-one, just the psychologist talking to the child. Nothing could be more structured than a one-on-one situation. The process is full of novelty: puzzles, games, sometimes flashing lights on computer screens. And the child is motivated because he is being tested; the cameras are on, so to speak. Hence, the process of psychological testing has built into it three very good treatments for the condition it is trying to diagnose. This leads to a number of what are called false negative results.

This can be deeply harmful for a child who clearly has all the symptoms of ADD but is refused treatment because the psychological tests were negative. When the history—what you see with your own eyes—tells you the child has ADD, that should take precedence over what a few hours of psychological testing seem to reveal. In other words, if the history and the testing are at odds, believe the history.

This is not to say that psychological testing is irrelevant. It can help elucidate associated learning disabilities such as dyslexia or a math disability, or it can uncover emotional problems. It can be highly informative, as long as you know it is not infallible.

Once the diagnosis is made, what is the treatment? The treatment of ADD divides into five components. The first is the diagnosis, which in itself is therapeutic. To learn that you are not, say, retarded, but instead have a treatable neurological condition gives great relief.

The next component is education. The more you learn about ADD the better equipped you are to deal with it in your child, in yourself, and in the rest of your family. There are many books and tapes available on the subject. Speaking to someone who has a child with ADD can help a great deal as well. Education is key to managing the condition.

The third component is structure. By "structure" I mean lists, reminders, schedules, assignment books—all the boring things folks with ADD tend to avoid. But they are essential. Although learning new habits of structure takes work, the payoff is great. Once you train yourself always to check your pocket for your wallet before you leave a room, or always to put your keys in the same place at home; once your child learns always to write down his assignments in the same place, large amounts of frustrating search time are saved. You can use that time for better things. The individual with ADD needs to structure his or her life to compensate for the lack of internal structure.

For children, the following kinds of structure are particularly helpful:

1. Make sure the rules are clear.
2. Make sure the rewards and penalties are clear.
3. Try to keep to a schedule at home; when are meals, what is study time, and so on.
4. Post lists to help with repetitive tasks. For example, put a list on the door of the bathroom stating in big block letters what your child is expected to do before leaving the bathroom: pick up towel, flush toilet and put seat down, wipe toothpaste off sink, turn off all faucets, and so on.
5. Give warnings before transitions. Say, "We are leaving for Grandma's," well before you intend to leave. Repeat the warning several times as departure time approaches.
6. Protect study time.
7. Make sure time is set aside for reading aloud or silently.
8. Intervene quickly if your child starts to "lose it." These kids need to be destimulated, for example by sitting out, before they really explode.
9. Enforce rules, but stay out of arguments. ADD kids love to argue because arguing is so stimulating. It is more fun to argue about why you do not want to do your homework than it is to sit down and do your homework. These arguments are counterproductive.
10. State goals and ideals often. The kids lose sight of the big picture. If the long-range goal is to make the soccer team, remind him of that often, so he'll know where he's heading. If the long-range goal is to go to college, remind him of that so he'll have some rationale for school. If as a family, you believe in God, state that, so he'll remember it.

There are also a number of structuring devices for the classroom that can help a child who has ADD. If these techniques are applied, they will help all the children, not just the ones with ADD. If a classroom is made ADD-friendly, that is good for everyone.

1. Make frequent eye contact. When the teacher makes eye contact with a student, it is almost impossible not to pay attention.

2. Speak the child's name often. Say, "As Joey told us yesterday," or make some other inclusive remark (not "Earth to Joey" or similar derisive remarks of the kind that used to be common in school). It is hard not to pay attention when you hear your own name spoken.

3. Use touch. Of course, schools have various rules about touch, but it should be allowed for any teacher to put his or her hand on the shoulder of a student. This gesture is centering and reassuring.

4. Have the kids with ADD sit near the teacher, but not all together in a group.

5. Break down large tasks into small tasks. Instead of saying, "Write a book report," break the task down into its component parts.

6. Try to introduce new material in terms of old material that has already been mastered. For example, when you say, "Today we start fractions," the ADD child (as well as some others) may feel suddenly overwhelmed, afraid he or she can't learn such a vast topic. But if you quickly add, "Don't worry, fractions are just another kind of division, and we've already learned division very well," that will help recast the new material in terms of old material that has already been mastered.

7. Give frequent feedback. Children with ADD need to know often where they stand. "That's it, keep at it, you're getting it, good job": These are the words the child needs to hear. Don't give feedback once a week or once in a while. Give it often.

8. Just as at home, the rules of the classroom need to be clear, simple, and consistently applied.

9. At the end of the day, check with the children who have

ADD to make sure they have not left behind anything they need.

10. Praise, praise, praise. Children with ADD need lots of encouragement to overcome the regular beat of negativity they so often feel about themselves.

The fourth component of treatment is coaching and/or psychotherapy. Sometimes traditional psychotherapy is needed, but more often a coach can help the child with ADD. A coach is a person (usually not a professional) who checks in with the child on a daily basis. In a ten- or fifteen-minute session the coach and the child go through the following steps, outlined by the acronym HOPE.

In HOPE coaching, the coach begins simply by saying hello. That is the "H." It is important to emphasize the need to focus at the start. The next step is to ask, "What are your three main objectives for today?" Objectives are the "O." The question asks the student to set priorities for the day by naming the top three goals; many individuals with ADD can name a hundred goals, but stumble over naming just three. By reducing the number of goals to three, you increase the likelihood that they all will be achieved. Next the coach asks, "What are your plans to achieve those objectives?" The plans, of course, are "P." The question calls on the student to put a set of plans into words. Stating one's plans out loud also increases the likelihood that they will be accomplished. Finally, the coach ends the session by providing encouragement; this is "E." Most children (and adults!) with ADD contend with a huge burden of negativity; they can't get started because they feel they will fail. An injection of positivity, in the form of daily encouragement from the coach, can help counter this negativity. All four steps together—HOPE—send the student off with a clearly defined game plan for the day, and some encouragement to get him started.

Finally, as I see it the fifth component of the treatment of ADD is medication. We have a number of different medications to help children and adults who have ADD. One or another will help about 80 percent of the people who have ADD; that means 20 percent will derive no benefit. Since the medications are quite safe, it is worth a trial of medication if you have ADD, unless you are opposed to this for some reason. When the medications work, what they all do is increase mental focus. What is mental focus? It is the ability to read an entire page without drifting off. It is the ability to listen to a conversation without just watching lips move. It is the ability to have a great idea when you are taking a shower and remember what that idea was once you step out of the shower, instead of just remembering that you had a great idea. We all struggle with mental focus, but in ADD the struggle is severe. Medication can improve mental focus, much as eyeglasses improve visual focus.

What are the medications used to treat attention deficit disorder? We use a variety of medications—stimulants, antidepressants, and others.

Of the stimulants, the most common are Ritalin (methylphenidate), Dexedrine (dextroamphetamine), and Cylert (pemoline). Stimulants were first used in children in this country to treat the symptoms of ADD in 1937. Since that time a tremendous amount of research has documented their usefulness as well as their safety. They receive negative publicity from time to time, but the medical facts are clear: When used under a doctor's supervision, the stimulants are extremely safe and effective in treating ADD.

Many people ask how it can be that a stimulant, of all things, can help a child who is hyperactive or appears to be overly stimulated already. The answer is that the stimulants act to stimulate inhibition. One way to look at ADD and hyperactivity is as a general lack of inhibition in the operation of the brain. The brain has trouble inhibiting what is coming in, which leads to distractibility, and it has trouble inhibiting what is going out, which leads to impulsivity and hyperactivity. The brain has two kinds of nerve cells, ones that stimulate action, others that inhibit it. In ADD, the inhibitory cells are less active. Therefore, by giving a medication which *stimulates* the *inhibitors,* the brain's circuitry comes back into balance.

If the stimulants do not work to improve mental focus, other medications have been found to be helpful; among these are certain of the tricyclic antidepressants, as well as the antihypertensive medication clonidine. We cannot tell in advance which medication will be effective, so there is often a period of trial and error until the right one is found. Of course, sometimes no medication helps, and we rely on the nonpharmaceutical approaches to treatment that have already been mentioned. These can work very well by themselves.

Only about 3 percent to 5 percent of children have true ADD. What about the other kids, who have trouble paying attention but don't fit the actual diagnosis? Is there any such thing as a lazy child anymore?

Of course there is. All children are lazy now and then—and all adults are, too. We all have our lazy days, and we have our industrious days, and that is how life is.

But if you find yourself calling your child lazy day after day, you might want to think twice. What does "lazy" really mean? Children are not innately lazy. If a child is lazy all the time or most of the time, or if a child is daydreamy much of the time, or if a child just doesn't "get with the program" at school or at home, it is worth looking past the descriptive labels—"lazy," "uncooperative," and the like—to what they *might* signify neurologically.

Many treatable conditions can masquerade as laziness or daydreaminess or irritability. A list of some of the more common would include depression, hypothyroidism, sleep disorders, a reaction to hidden trauma, or simply unhappiness. It is useful to think of laziness as a symptom or a signal of some deeper problem, rather than simply a defect in the child.

This is not to say that children don't have defects or that every child who won't work is in some sort of trouble. However, before you rest easy that your child is simply another Tom Sawyer, you should check out the other possibilities.

If the diagnosis can be made during childhood, a lot of pain can be averted. I could cite literally hundreds of examples of adults who have come to see me to say, "If only...": If only someone had looked past my veneer. If only someone had asked me what was wrong. If only someone had given me a second look. If only someone had known there was such a thing as ADD.

The time to think about it is now.

Chapter 6

....

Mad: When Children Act Up

The art of being wise is the art of knowing what to overlook.
—*William James*

"I couldn't believe what was happening," Leslie said to me. "I was becoming afraid of my own son. Every day I would wake up and wonder what he was going to do next. Every time the phone rang, I flinched, wondering what bad news would be on the other end. Sometimes I even felt like I hated him—my own son, the child I know I love so much. But I felt hatred for him some days. Isn't that unforgivable? How can you hate your own son, especially when he's only in the fifth grade? But I did. He would just make life so miserable for us all. I couldn't work, I couldn't spend time with the other kids, I couldn't comfortably leave the house, for fear he would do something while I was gone, and since I couldn't afford any help I was basically a prisoner in my own home. I brought him to doctors and they all said, Well, try this or that and come back in a month and we'll see how he is. They didn't even hear me! I really don't think they listened. How could they have heard me and not done more than they did? Or if they did hear me, they couldn't have believed me. They probably just thought I was a hysterical female who had lost her husband and didn't know how to handle life. But Dr. Hallowell, I tried. I tried everything I could think of. I read books on Tough Love, I asked, advice from relatives and friends, I tried everything anyone suggested I was so desperate. I hit him, I grounded him, I pleaded with him, I bribed him, I begged him, I ignored him, I screamed at him, I threatened him with kicking him out or giving him to the police, and he just laughed in my face. He knew I couldn't kick him out. But some days I sure did want to! Maybe someone else could have handled him, but I don't know how. If any of those doctors had really known what was going on, they wouldn't have dismissed me so easily. It was making me crazy. No one knew what we were going through."

"What else could the doctors have done?" I asked.

"They could have listened to me. They could have believed me. Instead, they just sent me away."

Leslie's problem with her son Alex isn't all that rare these days. With the increase in single-parent families, many boys are growing up without dads. Boys use fathers to learn how to modulate aggression. When fathers are absent, boys' aggression often careens out of control. Leslie needed outside help. The situation was really too much for her to handle on her own. I was able to help her first of all by listening to her and believing her. Not being heard and believed can drive anyone crazy. Then we had to think of a way of establishing some authority in Alex's life that he would respect.

But how do you do this with an out-of-control eleven-year-old?

You bring in reinforcements.

I was the first. Alex met with me, and we tried to figure out why he was being such a difficult kid. He didn't know why, of course, but at least after we met he knew that I knew what was going on. Then we tried to make a diagnosis. There are various conditions that can make a child overly aggressive: attention deficit disorder, Tourette syndrome, lead intoxication, seizure disorders, and substance abuse—(we do see this in eleven-year-olds) all can result in disruptive behavior. However, Alex had none of these. His behavior seemed to stem mainly from his family situation.

The next step was to set up a contract among Alex, his mom, and his younger brothers as to what the rules of the house should be. Alex's father, Bennett, who lived an hour away, also had to agree to abide by this contract when Alex went to visit him. Bennett's involvement in this process was key. Thankfully, he was more than willing to cooperate. He came to the family meeting we had in my office to negotiate this important contract. Bennett's presence was extremely helpful; if he had refused to cooperate, as sometimes happens, the solution to the problem would have been much more difficult. If you are a mother, you need to make every effort to involve your child's father in solving a problem like Alex's even if you do not get along with him yourself. If you, as the main parent, cannot bring Dad in by your own invitation, then try to find a persuasive therapist who can. Most reluctant fathers will end up participating if they know a referee, in the person of a therapist they have established a positive feeling for from an initial telephone conversation, will be there to prevent big squabbles or struggles.

Once the contract had been negotiated and Bennett's involvement was made clear, the major work was done. Alex's "impossible" behavior had mostly been an effort to get some rules set up and dad involved—exactly what he got.

What if his disruptive behavior had continued despite these interventions? This happens. There are three suggestions I make in these situations: *Persist persist, and persist.* Add more reinforcements. Involve an uncle or a teacher or a coach. Sign up with a Big Brother. Join the Boys' Club, the YMCA, or any local club or organization your son wants to join that you feel is safe, appropriate, and, of course, affordable. Positive groups (not gangs, of course) help contain and redirect aggressive behavior.

Also, keep coming back to the contract you made with your son and the rest of the family. Sometimes this process simply boils down to a battle of wills, a battle you must win. The only way to win is to make sure you don't get worn down. So *never worry alone.* Share your concerns with friends, physicians, clergy, other parents, colleagues—anyone you trust who has time to listen. Make contact. Your child must understand that you have a bigger circle of support than he can fend off. Sooner or later, he will do what he has been waiting and wanting to do: shape up.

Leslie and Alex provide just one example of what is probably the most common problem parents face: What do I do about my child's misbehavior?

First, you need to get a sense of what is normal. In other words, you need to know when to worry and what to overlook. That was the question Marge and Steve, parents of Sonia, asked me: Is our daughter a problem child or is she like other kids her age? Sonia was a six-year-old who was becoming increasingly feisty with each year of her life. She had always been strong-willed, a quality her parents valued and wanted to preserve, "but not at the expense of my sanity," as her mother put it. Sonia was stubborn. She would dawdle endlessly while getting dressed in the morning, often making herself late for school and her mother late for work. She would object at the last moment to what she was wearing, making fussy complaints such as "This blouse is too scratchy" or "These tights don't match my skirt" or, just as she was on the way out the door, "I think I want to wear the pink dress instead." Marge, a patient woman, was reaching the end of her rope. "I've had it with this stuff. She has just got to start obeying me. I can't put up with her whining and complaining."

I suggested setting up a contract according to which Sonia would be responsible for certain tasks, such as getting dressed on time, in exchange for certain rewards. Sonia and her mom could decide what the terms of the contract would be. That worked for a while, but then the novelty started to wear off, and Sonia's old habits emerged. Marge started setting limits, like putting Sonia in her room when she talked back or not allowing her to have friends over if she had not completed her chores.

Sonia, who had previously accepted her mother's authority, now began to test it more aggressively. When Marge sent her to her room, she went, but started to throw things around when she got there. She didn't break anything, but she made a lot of noise. One night, when Steve sent her to her room, she decided to sing at the top of her voice. Her parents tried to ignore the racket, but after almost an hour of singing Steve went in and told her if she didn't knock it off, she could not watch TV for a week. Sonia screamed at him that he was not her "boss" and she could do whatever she wanted to. Steve then became very angry and yelled back that no, she couldn't. And how would she feel about getting spanked? Sonia told him to go ahead, she didn't care. At that moment, Marge intervened, having heard the commotion from downstairs. She pulled Steve out of the room before he spanked Sonia, and she told Sonia she would have to stay in her room after school tomorrow.

"Dr. Hallowell," Marge asked me, "is this normal? We agreed long ago that we wouldn't spank or hit our children, but if I hadn't been there at that time Steve would have spanked Sonia, and I can't say I would have blamed him."

"This is normal," I said, "but that doesn't mean it is easy. As for spanking, I advise against it. But how to control Sonia? You won't be able to do so totally. Remember, some acting up is okay. You're not trying to run the tightest ship in the Navy, and some six-year-olds are just very feisty. Basically, what you need to do is set up some parameters—what is okay and what isn't—then establish some consequences for when the rules get broken, then stick to them. If you don't believe in spanking, as you say you don't, then don't bring it out as an option when you're really mad. Keep some other option up your sleeve for those moments."

Many kids are like Sonia—feisty, rambunctious, a real headache sometimes, but not such a problem that they need professional help. (Though the parents may need some counseling.)

Anger and aggression are built into every child (and adult), so the question often comes up, "How aggressive is normal?" Since all children have aggressive feelings, but over a wide range of intensity, parents often must assess on their own, without much guidance, where their child fits on the spectrum. How strict should you be? What sort of limits should you set? When should you get worried? When should you seek help?

You should worry, and think of getting help, when any of the following describe your situation:

1. Your child stands out from his or her peers as being markedly more aggressive or out of control.
2. You hear repeatedly, from reliable others, that your child is extremely aggressive or disruptive, even if you rarely see such behavior yourself:
3. Your child often behaves in a way that is dangerous to himself or to others.
4. Other children do not feel safe around your child.
5. You fear your child.
6. You often dislike your child because of his unruly behavior.
7. Your child is consistently disobedient.
8. Your child seems to lack empathy or conscience.
9. You feel as if you might lose control of your temper in your attempts to control or discipline your child.
10. You are at a loss as to what to do with your child.

If any of the situations described applies to you, this is not usually normal, neither part of a predictable phase nor on an appropriate developmental continuum. Particularly these days, when expected levels of anger and aggression seem to be continually revised upward, it is difficult for a parent to tell if his or her child is abnormal or just a child of the nineties. However, it is important to identify as early as possible any significant problems your child is developing with anger and aggression, because the sooner you intervene the better your chances become of taking care of the problem effectively.

If you want to know if your third-grade son, for example, is normal in how he handles aggression, what do you do to find out? You may think he is a handful, but how can you tell if this is just the way most boys his age usually are? In extreme cases, this is not a tough call. A child who can never play with others without fighting, a child who is frequently destructive to property, a child who flies into rages or tantrums all the time is not within the normal range. This child needs help.

However, the great majority of children do not present the question so simply. For most parents who have feisty children, the problem is more subtle: How feisty is too feisty? Where does Tom Sawyer leave off and a criminal in training begin? Where does self-assertion leave off and an abrasive personality start to emerge?

The best way for a parent to begin to answer the question of what is normal is to compare her child to other children. However, sometimes this is not easy. Neighborhoods are not as tight as they used to be. The grapevine is not as efficient as it once was. Parents do not receive the constant flow of information they used to get about their children's behavior. Furthermore, many parents do not have a ready pool of same-age children with whom to compare their own child. The next best thing—maybe even the best thing, period—is to ask the schoolteacher. Experienced teachers are experts on normal child development. Teachers get that hourly flow of information. They work with children all day. Talking with the teacher is an excellent way to find out if your child is within the normal range. Another good person to ask is your pediatrician; however, he or she will not have the benefit of continuous observation of your child, which the teacher has.

Over the spectrum of anger and aggression, we can roughly divide children into three groups. The first group, perhaps 10 percent to 15 percent of children, have one of what child psychiatrists call the disruptive behavior disorders. These include conduct disorder and oppositional defiant disorder; we can include attention deficit disorder here as well, because it often leads to disruptive behavior. In addition, some adolescents develop what is called borderline personality disorder, which can lead to highly erratic, impulsively aggressive, and/or self-destructive behavior.

The parents of children with any of these conditions must constantly worry over how to manage their children's aggressive and disruptive behavior.

The second group of children—by far the largest group, taking in perhaps 70 percent to 80 percent of children, present problems with anger and aggression from time to time, but not with the intensity or frequency of children who have a diagnosable disorder. The children in this group may get angry, squabble, and fight like most children, but they do not stand out as being difficult or as differing from their peers. Their parents worry from time to time about anger and aggression in their children, but do not lie awake every night worrying, as do the parents of the children in the first group.

The third group, taking in perhaps another 10 percent to 15 percent of children, lies on the other end of the spectrum from the first group. They almost never get angry. They are polite and obedient to a fault. Their parents almost never need worry about controlling the children's anger and aggression. Indeed, the worry parents feel for these children is that they are *too* well-behaved, perhaps too inhibited. Parents wish these children *would* act up from time to time. Their problem with anger lies not in controlling it but in releasing it. They need to learn how to get mad.

Most parents will recognize immediately where their child fits. You know if you have a difficult child, and you know if you have a docile child, and you know if your child is somewhere in between.

Group I	Group II	Group III
Diagnosable disruptive disorder (10%–15% of children)	Management of anger at times a problem, but not a major concern (70%–80% of children)	Rarely, if ever, gets angry, almost never physically aggressive (10%–15% of children)

At what age do the children who fit into Group I begin to stand out from their peers? Most children go through a defiant or "no"-saying period around age two. This negativistic behavior usually subsides by the time the child reaches three or four. Child psychiatrists use the diagnostic term "oppositional defiant disorder" (unfortunately abbreviated, ODD) to describe the more extremely difficult children among whom negativity doesn't fade. Perhaps 5 percent to 10 percent of all children would fit that diagnosis. Of the children who have ODD, most resolve their problems before they become adolescents. About a third of them, however, go on to develop the next stage of behavioral disorder, called simply conduct disorder (CD).

Conduct disorder develops gradually. Children who begin as negativistic or oppositional-defiant usually improve. If no intervention occurs, or if the child doesn't "shape up" on his own, as sometimes happens, the symptoms will worsen. These increasingly severe symptoms can be divided into stages. In Stage 1 the child is unusually aggressive to people and/or animals. In Stage 2, the child also begins to destroy or damage others' property or belongings. In Stage 3 the child becomes extremely deceitful and/or steals things. And in Stage 4 the child violates important rules or laws and/or abuses drugs. Not many children reach Stage 4 of conduct disorder. Usually the progression is halted before this stage of lawbreaking behavior. Those who do reach Stage 4 need intensive professional help, usually a combination of psychosocial interventions such as parental counseling and education, child retraining and social coaching, individual and group psychotherapy, family therapy, and usually medication. Most children who have Stage 4 conduct disorder also suffer from some other condition. This is called a comorbid diagnosis. Common comorbid diagnoses with conduct disorder include attention deficit disorder (ADD), learning disabilities, and mood disorders such as depression. In addition, children with conduct disorder often have major family problems, medical problems, economic problems, or all of the above.

These extremely troubled children can break the spirit of a parent or a teacher or even a professional who tries or is forced to take care of the problem alone. To help these children properly requires a team effort. No one, not the best parent, doctor, or teacher in the world, can do it alone. Most effective approaches to treating such children use a full team of professionals working together with parents, at first with the child hospitalized and later on an outpatient basis. The team includes a psychiatrist, a family physician or pediatrician, a psychologist, a social worker, an occupational therapist, a representative from the school, and others as needed. Such treatment is expensive; it is essential that insurance and government funding be made available, because not only are these children's lives a human tragedy, but also children with conduct disorder cost society millions of dollars if they grow up without receiving treatment. Childhood is the time to intervene; by adulthood it may be too late to make a real difference.

The main reason for bringing up such a severe disorder in this book is to point out the developmental continuum, from the relatively mild "terrible twos" through conduct disorder. Aggressive behavior can be a problem at any age, and it can be due to many factors. Obviously, the sooner you can intervene the better for everyone—parent, child, family, school, and society at large.

The other severe condition mentioned is borderline personality disorder, or BPD. As I said earlier, we do not usually diagnose children or adolescents with personality disorders, because their personalities are still being formed. However, in extreme cases, where the symptoms have been constantly present over at least a year, the diagnosis of BPD may be made. Even if it is not made, the presence of the symptoms may give a warning as to what might lie ahead, in early adulthood.

BPD is extremely vexing for parents and other caretakers. The symptoms are intense; indeed, emotional intensity is the hallmark of BPD. Other symptoms include frantic efforts to avoid abandonment (either real or imagined); an unstable sense of personal identity; a tendency to idealize someone, then utterly devalue the same person in the next minute; impulsive behavior, particularly with respect to sex, money, drugs, eating, or driving; recurrent suicidal gestures such as wrist-cutting or intentional overdosing; mood instability; prevailing feelings of emptiness; frequent rage attacks; and a tendency to become paranoid when under stress.

Obviously, such a collection of symptoms can create major problems for everyone involved. Parents of a child who has BPD, or the early signs of BPD, often blame themselves for having created such a tortured, and torturing, human being. If the parent, not knowing that a condition such as BPD exists, tries to manage the entire situation at home without any help, the prognosis is bleak. Daily life becomes agony for everyone in the house. Every waking moment is tense, as each family member anxiously watches for the next explosion. When the teenager with BPD erupts, as she or he does regularly, no one is spared. These individuals have a knack for striking where others are most vulnerable emotionally. They can inflict great pain, both upon their loved ones and upon themselves. It is imperative that parents seek help, that the diagnosis be made, and that a clinician skilled in treating the borderline patient become actively involved.

What determines where your child will lie on the continuum from "never angry" to having conduct disorder or borderline personality disorder? Is his fate all due to parental influence? No doubt some misbehavior is due to lack of discipline at home, or to inconsistency on the part of a parent. But upbringing does not tell the whole story. Not every child with severe conduct disorder has "bad" parents; in fact, most do not. Studies have demonstrated a definite genetic influence in both conduct disorder and borderline personality disorder.

When a child acts up, we usually blame the parents (for being divorced or too lenient, permissive, or uninvolved) or society (TV, video, bad schools, gangs). Sometimes we blame the child, but we invoke only the most primitive of explanations: We say the child is "bad."

But in so doing we overlook many factors. Language development, for example, can play a key role in how a child handles anger and aggression. If you can't put your feelings into words, you are more likely to become violent. Genetics affects violence: Some children are simply born with tighter wiring than others, and are more likely to explode easily. Some children are less inhibited than others, and that lack of inhibition can have a genetic basis. Some children are genetically more likely than others to become lawbreakers. *This does not give them an excuse* to misbehave, break rules or laws, or in any way violate the rights of other people. However, it does give us an additional, powerful means of understanding them so that we may help them, and their parents, *take responsibility more effectively.* It is the major theme of this book that blame does not point the way to correct behavior; knowledge does.

The first question to ask about aggressive behavior is "Why?" "Why does my Debbie behave so compliantly, while my Matthew just will not obey?" a mother asks. "What has gone wrong, so that my son wants to join a gang?" a dad wonders. "Where do these tantrums come from?" another parent asks.

Usually, the answer can be found in one or more of the following five categories. Once you have an idea of the cause of aggressive behavior you can begin to work out a solution in a rational way. The main causes of overaggressive behavior, and some remedies directed toward each cause, are summarized in the table opposite.

I. BIOLOGY

We know that genetics contributes to aggressive behavior. How much genes contribute is the more pointed question. One excellent study looked at adopted children and then researched the records of their biological as well as their adoptive parents. The study found that only 3 percent of adopted children became criminals if neither their adoptive nor their biological parents were criminals. If the adoptive parents but not the biolog-

Aggressive or Violent Behavior in Children:
A Summary of Causes and Remedies

Cause of Aggressive Behavior	Possible Remedies
1. Biological and genetic factors	Diet, sleep, exercise, medications
2. Inability to use language well and to put feelings into words	Develop language skills. Read aloud to your child. Limit TV and video. Play word games. Role-play conflict situations.
3. Insufficient structure (e.g., schedules, rules, expectations) and supervision	Develop more effective, consistent structures in the child's life. Make sure he has a sensible plan for each day.
4. Parental influence	Modify parents' behavior; develop an authoritative presence in the child's life.
5. Peer group	Pay attention to your child's peer group. Have friends over. Get to know your child's friends' parents. Develop a peer-parent network. Plan together how to regulate your children's lives.

ical parents were criminals, the figure rose to 7 percent. If the biological parents but not the adoptive parents were criminals, the figure increased to 12 percent. This might seem to demonstrate that environment alone gives you a 7 percent chance of becoming a criminal, and genes alone give you a 12 percent chance. However, all of us are influenced by both; what is their combined influence? In this study, the children whose adoptive parents *and* biological parents were criminals stood a 40 percent chance of becoming criminals themselves. Genes plus environment proved much more powerful than either by itself.

Most parents are not concerned about outright criminal behavior in their children, although some have to be. But criminals can teach us about the biology of aggression, even aggression in the normal range. Why, if not for biological reasons, is criminal behavior so predominantly male? In 1994, there were about 1 million adults in a state or federal prison in this country. Of the million, 950,979 were men; that is about 95 percent!* More than any other single statistic, that one proves a biological basis for violent, lawbreaking behavior. Men are more violent than women.

Why? More than social conditioning is at work. More than social stress or deprivation must also be at work. It has to take more than social factors to produce a statistic of 95 percent. After all, women are subject to the same—if not even more damaging —social stressors and deprivations as men are. What is there about the physiology of men that leads them into violence?

Begin with hormones, particularly testosterone. The hormones that bathe the male brain differ from the hormones that bathe women's brains. This is one of the predominant physiological differences between men and women, and it is a profound one. But why do most men *not* commit violent crimes? All men secrete testosterone, but only a relatively few become violent. Are there physiological differences that identify the ones who become violent?

It looks as if there are. John Ratey, my colleague and co-author on two books, has pioneered some of the work in this area, particularly in his studies of pharmacological interventions with violent patients. Research is coming in from many other quarters as well. We may not be far from being able to predict early in life who is at highest risk for becoming a criminal. We're not there yet, but the data bank is growing fast. What we will do with that information once we have it poses tough ethical questions. But for now

* The source of this information is the Bureau of Justice Statistics.

we can simply learn from what we're finding, and realize as we try to regulate our children's aggression that not all brains are alike.

For example, some children show significantly less behavioral inhibition than others. They are born thrill-seekers and risk-takers. There is likely a biological basis for this. Some children are much more avid in pursuit of a possible reward than they are fearful in avoiding a possible punishment. In scientific terms, this means their brains' activating systems are more powerful than their brains' braking, or deactivating, systems. In real-life terms, this translates into the little boy who will scale the fence that has jagged glass cemented on top because he wants to swim in the pool on the other side. Or the older boy who will leap from rooftop to rooftop, with no regard for a possible fall. Or the young adult who will make losing bet after losing bet at a casino, urged on by the hope of winning the jackpot, not a bit discouraged by his repeated losses.

We say these kids are daring, but what does "daring" mean physiologically? Why do some children readily take risks, while others do not? Some of the reasons relate to what is allowed in the child's home and school. But physiology also plays a role. In addition to a relatively tamped-down inhibitory system, children who readily take risks may be underaroused physiologically. This means *they need to seek excitement in their external environment* in order to come alive, so to speak. They need to find some high stimulus in order to wake up, get activated, engage. They feel slowed down in an average environment. They need to pump up the voltage in order to light up.

This child is like an extreme version of the adult who needs to splash cold water on his face in order to wake up in the morning. For underaroused kids, their resting state is closer to a sleep state than to wakefulness. They feel the need to splash a lot of cold water on their faces—or to use some action-packed, sometimes dangerous or violent equivalent of cold water—in order to engage the world alertly. They're bored until the heavy action begins.

Can we measure or test for this trait in a child? We probably will be able to, in the not too distant future. There are some physiological measurements that may indicate baseline underarousal in these children; they include a low heart rate, increased slow waves on the electroencephalogram (EEG), and low skin conductance. Most people are familiar with the fact that heart rate rises with physiological arousal. Increases in EEG activity and in the skin's ability to conduct electricity also indicate physiological arousal. But these values have not been normalized or introduced into the standard workup in your pediatrician's office. They are, rather, tools for research at this time.

For practical purposes, children who are underaroused may not be unusual in any way except that they seek highly stimulating situations more avidly than other children do. For these kids, it is important that they learn, or be taught, to find stimulation in socially acceptable ways (such as heavy exercise, organized sports, onstage performance, or a demanding activity such as a paper route) rather than seeking it in disruptive or dangerous ways, such as misbehaving or engaging in reckless stunts. In the extreme, the thrill-seeking child may pose a serious risk to his own life or the lives of those around him. Children who are more moderately underaroused are the ones who always act up or find a way to disrupt the party.

Children may be biologically predisposed to aggressive behavior not only because of underarousal but because of anomalies in the frontal lobes and other parts of their brains. The frontal lobes play a key role in impulse control, social understanding, the ability to sustain attention, and the calculation of risks and benefits. If the frontal lobes are at all dysfunctional, or even just different, the child may be naturally more of a risk-taker and less likely to pause before acting, less able to reflect. He or she will therefore behave more impulsively. In addition, damage to other parts of the brain—particularly the temporal lobes and a small almond-shaped region called the amygdala—may lead to overaggressive behavior. Adrian Raine, an expert on aggression, emphasizes that no one theory explains all aggressive behavior, but that we do know that variations in the brain contribute to it.

These factors, combined with the ability, or lack of ability, to use language and to put feelings into words, which will be mentioned next, combine to set up the major biological contributors to aggressive behavior in childhood. To summarize, the biological factors predisposing to aggressive behavior in children are these:

1. Being male
2. Difficulty using language
3. Difficulty inhibiting behavior
4. Physiological underarousal
5. Variation or dysfunction within the brain, particularly the frontal and temporal lobes.

How can a parent test for the presence of these factors? Mostly just by observation. You can assess Factors 1, 2, 3, and 4 by comparing your child with other children or by talking to your child's teacher.

The assessment of Factor 5 requires the assistance of a professional. In cases where disruptive, uncontrollable anger in a child persists, it is worthwhile to get certain medical and/or psychological tests done. Neuropsychological testing, which is paper-and-pencil testing administered by a psychologist, can reveal a great deal of helpful information about the functioning of the brain, including the frontal and temporal lobes. Sometimes a brainwave test, or EEG, will reveal a problem in some other part of the brain. In addition, the EEG is helpful in defining seizure disorders, some of which may result in violent behavior. Seizure disorders are an important biological cause of unusually aggressive behavior in children.

Sometimes these seizure centers are hard to locate by EEG or any other means of testing. Indeed, some violent behavior originates in seizure activity that lies too deep in the brain to be detected by the EEG. Sometimes seizure activity in the amygdala, an important center for anger control, does not show up on EEG tracings, so the child would not be diagnosed with a seizure disorder. However, she might improve dramatically when treated with an antiseizure medication. But the medication would not normally be prescribed unless the seizure disorder were diagnosed on the EEG.

These hidden seizures may be much more common than we have believed. Since they cannot always be diagnosed by the EEG, they go undetected and untreated. Children with ongoing anger and rage problems may benefit from an empirical trial on an antiseizure medication. The potential side effects are few, if the medication is properly monitored. Since children with uncontrollable rage rarely lead normal lives until that rage is controlled, the potential gain is enormous.

The more common biologically based syndromes associated with excess aggression in children are listed below.

1. Conduct disorder or oppositional defiant disorder
2. Attention deficit disorder
3. Tourette syndrome
4. Seizure disorders of different types
5. Borderline personality disorder
6. Bipolar (manic-depressive) illness
7. Genetically based hair-trigger temper; frontal lobe dysfunction
8. Fetal alcohol syndrome or fetal alcohol effect (due to alcohol ingestion by mother during pregnancy)
9. Lead poisoning
10. Use of drugs such as alcohol, cocaine, or PCP
11. Space-occupying lesion in the brain, such as a tumor, cyst, or subdural hematoma

These conditions point up the wide range of genetically or otherwise biologically based conditions that can lead to violent or excessively angry behavior in children. All these conditions require attention by a medical professional for diagnosis and treatment. You should not try to diagnose any of these on your own. However, you may want to discuss them with your pediatrician or other professional to see if they might be relevant to your own child's situation.

The good news is that with an accurate diagnosis, effective treatment becomes available. Sometimes, but certainly not always, this takes the form of medication. There are a number of medications that can help with overly aggressive behavior. But they can be given only when an accurate diagnosis has been determined.

For example, if the cause of the aggressive behavior is a seizure disorder, an antiseizure medication such as Tegretol (generic name carbamazepine) or Dilantin (phenytoin sodium) may provide definitive treatment and put an end to years of turmoil. Or if the cause is attention deficit disorder, we have many medications that can help, the most common ones being the stimulant Ritalin (methylphenidate) or an antidepressant such as Tofranil (imipramine). If the cause is behavioral disinhibition or a genetic "hair trigger" a class of medications called the beta-blockers, like Inderal (propranolol), can help diminish violent behavior and increase the ability to reflect before acting. In the rare cases when the aggressive behavior is due to massively deranged thinking, antipsychotic medication, such as Haldol (haloperidol), can help. Sometimes excessive aggression is part of Tourette syndrome, a genetically transmitted condition whose hallmarks are involuntary twitches, or motor tics, as well as involuntary utterances, or vocal tics. If the child is impulsively aggressive because of Tourette syndrome, Haldol (haloperidol), an antipsychotic medication that is a dopamine blocker, or Catapres (clonidine hydrochloride) an anti–high blood pressure medication that is in the class of drugs called alpha-2 agonists, have been found extremely helpful. None of these medications is a cure, but all can offer dramatic help for some children, when used in the proper circumstances under professional supervision.

Summary of Childhood Conditions That May Include Aggressive Behavior for Which Medication Is Often Helpful

Condition	Medication
Seizure disorders	Anticonvulsants, such as Tegretol and Dilantin
Attention deficit disorder	Stimulants, such as Ritalin; antidepressants, such as Tofranil
Tourette syndrome	Alpha-2 agonist, Catapres or dopamine blocker, Haldol
Impulsive anger, rage	Beta-blockers, such as Inderal
Psychosis	Antipsychotic medication, such as Haldol
Bipolar disorder (manic-depressive illness)	Mood stabilizers, such as lithium or Depakote
Extreme anxiety	Antianxiety agents, such as BuSpar
Conduct disorder, oppositional defiant disorder, and borderline personality disorder	Various medications from different classes, including Catapres, Inderal, BuSpar, Prozac, Tegretol, Haldol, and lithium, depending upon details of child's history

II. LANGUAGE

Two keys to success in managing anger are the ability to reflect and the ability to use words. Those two capacities often separate the children who can manage anger from those who can't. (And those who can't are to be distinguished from those who choose not to. Children who *choose* to become violent pose much more difficult problems; fortunately these children are rare.)

But every child has to deal with angry feelings. Every child (and every parent) must decide what to do when he or she gets mad. How does this decision get made? Is it really a decision, or is it more of a reflex? What is the difference?

The difference between a decision and a reflex is that a reflex goes only through the spinal cord or the base of the brain, while a decision is made at the top, in the cortex of the brain. Management of anger is more successful if the decision about what to do with an angry feeling is made in the "parlor" (the cortex) of the brain, rather than in the "switching station" (the spinal cord) or just above it, in the primitive "basement" (the brainstem). Spinal and brainstem "decisions" are not conscious decisions; they are reflexive acts.

We need these reflexes. They allow us to react more quickly than decisions made in the cortex allow, and when instantaneous action is needed, reflexes save our skins. However, an instantaneous reaction can get us into trouble, particularly when we are dealing with anger. If we cannot reflect, at least for a millisecond, before we act, we may act in ways we regret.

Some people lack the intermediate reflective step between impulse and action. They can get into a lot of trouble because of their impulsive behavior. A prime example is seen in attention deficit disorder. One of the three core symptoms of ADD is impulsivity (the other two are distractibility and restlessness). People with ADD at times lack the inhibitory controls—the brain's brakes—that intercept an impulse before it becomes an action. I say "at times" because the brain's activity is not a steady state. The symptoms of ADD wax and wane. Impulsivity may be a problem one hour and not a problem the next, depending upon how engaged in a particular task the child or adult happens to be.

Inhibition, which sometimes connotes emotional narrowness, is in fact a necessary component of healthy mental life. We need to be able to inhibit in order to control our behavior. We need to be able to inhibit in order to pay attention. Indeed, the act of paying attention to one event means that the individual is trying to inhibit all other incoming or outgoing stimuli. Problems with too little inhibition or too much impulsivity, or both, may in fact derive from problems in the frontal lobes, which I discussed earlier.

However, language also plays a pivotal role in one's ability to reflect or inhibit. One good way to enrich the brain's inhibitory system and the concomitant ability to reflect before taking action is to develop one's ability to use language. In contrast to what happens when we think in waves of feeling or bursts of impulse, when we think in *words* we must reflect. In fact, "to reflect" usually means to use words internally to describe one's situation before acting upon it. If we can think by speaking to ourselves before acting, then we can reflect. But if our ability to use language is underdeveloped, then our ability to reflect and inhibit impulsive actions will also be impaired.

These two tools—the ability to reflect before acting and the ability to use language—are linked. When one tool is missing the other often is. If one grows stronger, the other usually does, too. People who are deficient in both—people who are innately impulsive and also deficient in language skills—are at great risk of getting into serious problems on account of their anger. When anger swells up in the impulsive, language-impaired individual, he is at its mercy. If he cannot reflect upon what he wants to do and cannot use words to shape and express his feelings, it is highly likely that he will act upon the feeling with little or no conscious control. When we act upon anger without thinking first, violence often ensues.

If you look at children and teenagers who habitually have trouble controlling their tempers, you will find time and again a language disability of some sort, or an impulse control problem such as attention deficit disorder, or both. Indeed, the prison population and the population of ex-convicts includes a disproportionately high number who can't read or can't write or have great trouble articulating what they think or feel. And an innovative program developed in the juvenile court system in Redmond, Washington, reduced recidivism among juvenile offenders from 67 percent to 27 percent, by implementing a program that included teaching the effective use of everyday language.

III. INSUFFICIENT STRUCTURE

Many children who behave too aggressively or cannot control their anger suffer from a lack of structure in their lives. What is structure? Structure comprises all the external devices that keep us on track each day. An alarm clock is a good example of an instrument of structure. It gets us out of bed on time. The rules of the road provide structure. A daily schedule offers structure. Traffic lights are part of structure. Supervision adds to structure by trying to make sure people abide by it.

Many children lead lives in which they simply do not know what the rules are. The rules change from class to class or home to home or town to town or day to day. These children find no consistency, so they begin to make up their own rules. They get no supervision, so they break rules whenever they want to.

Without structure, consistency, and supervision, children become angry, confused, and anarchic. They do what they want. Might, instead of any internalized code of morality, begins to make right. Charisma takes the place of proper authority. What's cool rules the day.

From the moment their child is born, parents must start deciding what their rules are going to be. Then they have to enforce them. This is rarely easy, but it is essential. Aside from the presence of high technology in the forms of TV, video, CDs, cell phones, and the like, the lack of structure and supervision in the lives of today's children is probably the most obvious difference between this generation and generations of the recent past.

You may feel that you are swimming upstream in setting up rules at home. You may feel the culture conspires against you. Or you may feel you do not have time. But make time. Sit down with your spouse, or if you are alone, sit down with someone you trust, and answer this question: "What are the rules of this house?"

The answer does not have to be a long one. There was just one rule in my daughter's kindergarten classroom, and that one rule was only one word long. The one word was posted in big red block letters where no one could miss it: R E S P E C T. Whenever anything went awry in the class, the teacher pointed to the word and asked, "Was that a respectful way to treat your classmate?" Or "Was that a respectful way to treat the environment?" Or "Was that a respectful way to treat that book?" Virtually every problem in any child's behavior could be brought back to that one rule, the single word "respect."

When you keep the rules that simple, children begin to internalize them quickly. It wasn't long after Lucy started kindergarten that if I honked at a driver in traffic she would ask me, much to my embarrassment, "Daddy, was that a respectful way to treat the man in that other car?" This is what we mean by moral education: the taking in of certain precepts so that they become felt beliefs that can be applied in everyday life. It all begins with structure, with defining the rules and expectations.

If your child seems to lack respect for rules or authority, or if he seems to lack a moral sense, it may be because he doesn't know what the rules are, or because he has never seen how someone with a moral sense acts.

At the end of this chapter, in the section on tips on anger management, I recommend the frequent use of negotiation and contracts. This is a good way to set up structure at home. Have a family negotiation session to work out what the household rules are, and what the contract is governing their enforcement. Then post the contract, complete with the signatures of all family members, on the refrigerator or in another highly visible place where it can be referred to daily. *Use it.* Don't just make it and then forget it. Use your rules and your agreements to run your daily lives.

In the presence of rules, organization, consistency, and supervision, the chances that anger will go out of control greatly decline. And when anger does flare up, the structures will be in place to deal with it. There will be an already agreed-upon consequence for swearing, or hitting your brother, or slamming your bookbag against the screen door so that it breaks.

IV. PARENTAL INFLUENCE

Not so long ago, this would have been the only factor discussed here. The discussion would have taken on a tone of subtle blame. "It is up to the parents," the writer would state, "to make their child behave." The issue of children's behavior boiled down to a contest of will: you against them.

This book, I hope, makes it clear that the issue is more complicated than a contest of wills. However, parents do matter. They probably matter more than any other single factor, particularly before children hit school. When it comes to controlling anger and aggression, parents make a big difference.

How? That is a question all kinds of experts have been trying to answer for centuries. A few principles seem clear, however, not only in managing anger and aggression, but in helping children deal with life in general.

First of all, in order to be an effective parent you must be present in the lives of your children. You do not have to be present twenty-four hours a day, but you must be present enough to be involved. How many hours does this mean? There is no precise number, but you can feel it in your bones when you dip below the minimum-visibility line. Your children treat you differently. They don't rush up to you. They may even behave more "respectfully," as they would around a stranger. It is very difficult to have a formative influence upon your children, except economically, if your are absent almost all the time.

Second, have a plan. This emerges from the discussion of structure. Try to agree with your spouse, or within yourself, on a plan

of action in advance. What am I going to do if Julie starts screaming at her brother? What am I going to do if Joey refuses to get
dressed in the morning or takes so much time I'm late for work
waiting for him? What am I going to do if Reba calls me a bitch?
What am I going to do if I find out Caleb has been smoking pot?
What am I going to do if Nathan tells me he is too busy to do
chores around the house? What am I going to do if . . . ? The list
is a mile long. You cannot anticipate every contingency, but it is a
good idea to have a general plan for dealing with angry, aggressive, defiant, or disruptive behavior. If you do not have a plan you
are much more likely to be erratic, handling problems one way
one day and quite another the next. Such inconsistency is confusing and ultimately damaging to children.

Third, establish an authoritative presence. Children need to
know that you are in charge. Children want to know that you are
in charge. At some level, children need to believe that you rule
the world—even though you don't. In generations past, parents
established this presence by fear, usually by means of physical
punishment. Dad would take off his belt, or Mom would grab a
wooden spoon—threats of beatings to come. But this is not such
a good idea. Fear may work in the short run, but in the long run
it is not good for parent or child.

There are other ways of establishing an authoritative presence.
Being there, noticing, being consistent—these are key. Learning
how to say no and mean it is also important. If your child knows
that a few tears or a little pleading will break you down, you
will never establish an authoritative presence. Behaving properly
yourself is also, of course, very important.

Raising your voice can help establish your authority, but do it
only rarely. Lowering your voice can be highly effective, even
more so than yelling: "Uh-oh, watch out. Whenever Mom starts
talking so soft you can't hear her, she really means business."

Above all, stand for something, and stick by it. Whatever "it"
is, is up to you.

V. PEER INFLUENCE

When children reach adolescence, the peer group becomes the prime mover. As a parent, you exert your greatest influence when your children are young. As they reach high school, they start to separate and become more independent, if not secretive. They look to peers for approval and acceptance.

As a parent you need to plan for this. Consider, in choosing a school, a neighborhood, and a career, what kind of peer group you will be introducing your child into. It is far easier to control your child's choice of peer groups by not introducing him or her to a certain group in the first place than by forbidding contact with people he or she has already met.

Sometimes, you must at least try to put your foot down. Sometimes your child will basically test you by associating with someone he or she knows will make you hit the roof. Sometimes you should ignore this, so as not to rise to the bait unnecessarily. But sometimes you must hit the roof, both to prevent damage to your child and to demonstrate that you still notice and care. Your child will tell you to back off and mind your own business, but he or she doesn't really mean this. She says, "Go to hell, Mom," but she means "Thanks, Mom." Don't worry, someday she'll tell you so.

But much better than exclusion is inclusion. Try to get to know your child's peers as much as possible. And *get to know their parents.* Form a peer-parent network. If the kids exclude you from what's going on in their lives, at least you can create an effective parental grapevine. In these days of declining neighborhoods and communities, it can be extremely helpful to be friends with the parents of your children's friends.

TEN TIPS FOR DEVELOPING SKILLS TO MANAGE ANGER IN CHILDREN (AND THEIR PARENTS)

All the following tips help in mastering any strong feeling, but since anger is usually the most destructive of strong feelings, I have included them here. All these tips can be used at home, require no professional assistance, and cost nothing. And they work.

1. Get plenty of exercise. Exercise may well be the best tool we have for helping children (and adults) work off anger and aggression. Overall, physical exercise is one of the best tonics you can take for your brain. It helps all brains—children's, adults', old people's, animals', even babies' brains. It helps in many different ways. It increases the levels of blood the brain receives. With more blood comes more oxygen and many other good nutrients. Exercise produces increased levels of a class of chemicals known as catecholamines (epinephrine is one) that help in focusing the mind. It produces endorphins, substances that bind to special receptors in the brain to create feelings of well-being. Exercise also produces "neurotrophins," a whole series of nutrients for the brain that the body puts together to supply the nerve cells with the precise substances they need to grow and stay healthy. How does exercise do this? We don't know exactly, but we do know it happens because we can measure these substances in the blood before and after exercise.

Exercise also helps in managing anger by providing an acceptable outlet for aggressive feelings. Exercise is controlled aggression. As you pump your legs in running, or jump off the ground to catch a thrown ball, or reach for the basket to tap in a shot, or swing your racket at a tennis ball, you are directing aggression. It feels good. It *is* good. It drains off helter-skelter aggressive feelings that build up during the time a child spends in a classroom or engages in other sedentary pursuits.

Exercise also relieves anxiety. It is a better anti-anxiety agent than any medication, and it has no side effects (unless you exercise too much).

Aside from these beneficial effects on the brain, exercise is good for us in a host of other ways as well. Most people know of the good effect exercise has on the cardiovascular system. Exercise is also good for your bones, your skin, your lungs, and virtually every other organ in your body. It is only bad for you if you do it too much, too fast, or irregularly.

A regular routine of exercise should be a part of the lives of us all. Every child should exercise every day. Every parent should exercise at least three times per week.

2. Use words. Read aloud. Play word games at dinner and while driving in the car. Role-play the resolution of conflicts by talking them out. Next to physical exercise, using language to express feelings may be the best antidote we have to destructive or violent behavior. If you can't put what you feel into words, or if you can't argue or debate coherently or ask for what you want articulately, you feel frustrated. Frustration leads to physical acting up, sometimes to violence. This point may sound obvious, but many children are growing up these days unable to find words for what they want to say. They don't read, they don't write, they don't even talk coherently as much as they should. They watch and they listen: to TV, radio, video, CDs, and the like. But these are all passive activities. Watching and listening do not "work" the imagination the way reading, writing, and talking do. Language, like all neurological tools, is not a permanent fixture; if you do not use it, you lose it.

Encourage your child to use words as much as possible. When he is frustrated, say, "Use your words, Sammy." Or when she is angry, say, "Annie, tell me how you feel, in words." This is often easier for girls to do than for boys, but it is essential for both. If your child can say, "I'm so mad I feel like hitting you!" that is much better that actually hitting you. Applaud the use of words rather than punishing the sentiment expressed. Aside from "dirty," blasphemous, or disrespectful words, the definition of which is up to the individual family, there are no bad *words* a child can say. The use of words in itself constitutes a victory, a victory of the child's cerebral cortex over sensate experience.

Words help a child take the fangs out of anger. Once you channel angry feelings into words, you have won, at least for the moment. You are in command. This is not to say that words cannot hurt. Words can do great damage, as we all know. But the first step for a child in mastering anger is to learn to use words, rather than physical acts, to express that anger. Then he or she can try to learn to use the words wisely, an effort that will continue for the rest of his or her life.

One of the best ways to encourage the use of language is to make a habit of reading aloud to your child. Although this is a form of listening, it is listening to *words*, and it requires the imagination to rouse itself and form mental pictures and scenes as the reading progresses.

I will never forget my great-aunt Nell reading the *Oz* books to me (there's a series of at least ten or fifteen of them, as I recall). I remember that when her house was being built we sat on two-by-fours and had picnics accompanied by readings of *The Wonderful Wizard of Oz*. Great-aunt Nell had very little money to buy me presents, but the gift she gave me of reading aloud was worth more than any present she could have bought. I can only begin to imagine what those picnic readings planted in my brain, how many words have grown from those roots.

Besides reading aloud to your children, play word games with them when they are young. Spelling games are great for facilitating language development. There are many, many word games families can play together on long drives, at dinner, in waiting rooms, on airplanes, or while standing in line anywhere. Your local librarian can help you find several books full of good games. Those written by Priscilla Vail are particularly good.

3. Limit TV and Video. This is a hot debate among experts in child development. What does TV do to the developing brain? What does witnessing violence on TV or in movies do to a child's mind? What do video games do to a child's imagination?

We're not sure of the answers to these questions. But I think it is safe to say that TV and video don't do much good for children's brains, and in excess may do a lot that is harmful.

From the standpoint of language development, which I have already mentioned, TV and video take away the chance for the child to supply his or her own mental pictures. In this way they retard the development of the crucial connection between words and mental images, and they retard the development of the imagination. From the standpoint of controlling aggression, there is the obvious fact that TV is filled with images of violence. The debate over whether watching violence is bad for children has become unfortunately politicized.

All children make up violent images at times—in daydreams, nighttime dreams, games, stories, and fantasies. Fairy tales are full of violent images, rife with people being eaten, maimed, and killed. Wolves and bears and dangerous giants abound. This is the part of the folklore of childhood. Violent imagery, per se, is not bad for children; what matters is the context. As a child psychiatrist doing play therapy, I often encourage children to play out their violent feelings in some made-up game or supervised fantasy. Playing out a fantasy often helps them feel better. However, this involves imaginative work on the part of the child, who is much like a novelist telling a story. The child gets off his chest something that has been bothering him, and he orders it and masters it as he does so. Also, the play is supervised by an adult, in this case me, who is ready to answer questions, provide reassurance, and stop the game if matters get out of hand.

So supervised imaginative play including violence is a far cry from a child sitting alone or with other children, passively watching violent scenes on TV, scenes that are thrown at the child whether he is ready for them or not, whether he can handle them or not, whether he knows what they mean or not. I am of the opinion, not from a political standpoint but from a psychological one, that watching violence—on TV or in real life—is bad for children.

The most practical way to limit a child's watching violence is to keep peace at home and to regulate what your child watches on TV and video and at the movies. You don't have to be fanatical about this, and you don't have to become a Quaker or a complete pacifist, but I think you do your child, and yourself, a great favor by severely restricting how much violence you allow him to watch.

He (or she, although the appetite for violence seems to be higher among boys) will fantasize plenty of violent scenes on his own. This is normal. You can model for him what to do with these feelings in real life by showing him how you behave. Fathers are particularly helpful to boys in this way: They can show their sons constructive things to do with aggressive feelings. If you let him learn from TV or from violent movies, you risk his learning that physical violence is appropriate, exciting, and even noble. Perhaps worst of all, you let him feel over time that violence is routine, even banal, so that he is no longer shocked and outraged, as he should be, when he sees it in the real world around him.

4. *Train your child to think of anger as an important signal.* Like fear, anger is a signal. Your body secretes certain chemicals that activate your nervous system when you get angry. It is up to the cortex of the brain to modulate this signal rather than letting the lower brain take over and go berserk. Child-rearing is, in large measure, training your child's brain how to do this. It is important for children to get to know their anger as a signal to be interpreted, not simply as a sensation to be acted upon.

Let's say, for example, your six-year-old explodes when you tell him he cannot have another cookie. "I want one right now!" he screams.

Instead of just telling him to hush up, which you might quite justifiably do, you might also try telling him to listen to his anger more closely. His anger is telling him he has hit a brick wall, the wall of Mommy's no. How has he dealt with this wall in the past? Does screaming help? Usually not. So he might try negotiation. Whenever he feels the sudden burst of anger that "No" triggers, he might, over time, try to train a new reflex: the reflex of negotiation.

5. *Encourage negotiation and the making of contracts.* This is what "working it out" is all about. Hear both points of view. Negotiate, negotiate, negotiate. Make a deal. Sign a contract. The more you can do this with your children, the better. When a dispute comes up, don't impulsively bark out a response; instead, negotiate.

Teaching your child to learn to negotiate, make deals, initiate agreements, and stick to contracts provides him or her with a lifelong skill. Successful adults are usually the ones who have mastered these skills.

It is never too early to start. Make deals with your three-year-old. Put together a contract with your six-year-old in the form of a chart or other daily monitoring device. Negotiate with your twelve-year-old regarding the rules of everyday life. If your family gets in the habit of reflexively negotiating, rather than fighting, demanding, or arguing, you will not only build a happier family but also give everyone skills that are of great value in the world outside home.

Most of us parents react instead of "proact." We react to anger instead of planning in advance how to deal with what will come up.

If you have a contract (or an agreement, if the word "contract" sounds too business-like) that bedtime is nine P.M., then when nine P.M. comes you can confidently say, "It is time for bed." If you are met with screams, all you have to say is, "Our agreement is that you go to bed at nine." Now, saying that will not turn off the screams like a radio on/off switch, but it will put you in a much better position for enforcement than if you had no such agreement, in which case your child could respond, "But yesterday I went to bed at ten, and the day before that at ten thirty, and the day before that I stayed up till ten, too."

With agreements there should also come contingency plans. If you do not have contingency plans, the consequences of broken agreements become blank and vague. Make the consequences standard, not variable. If you do not have a standard consequence for a given infraction, anger will often make you overreact. Have you ever said to your children, "If you do not go to bed *right now,* I will never buy you another Christmas present!" Much better if there had been a standard consequence: "You don't get a star on your star chart," or "You can't listen to the radio as you fall asleep"—whatever.

Since consequences come up so often in anger management, let me give some suggestions about them. First of all, *never hit*. I explain the whys of that injunction fully in Point 8. But you do need to provide some effective consequences. In general, rewards work better than consequences, but the possibility of a consequence must exist.

For little children I recommend time-outs. Make them brief—a minute or two—and ask the toddler to explain them. Use this as a chance to work on putting feelings into words: "Why did you get a time-out?"

"Because I hit Abe."

"Why did you hit Abe?"

"Because he took my truck."

"That must have made you very angry."

"Yes."

"When you get angry, do you have to hit?"

"Yes."

"Can you think of any other way to solve the problem?"

"No."

"How about asking Abe to give you back your truck?"

"Okay."

"Let's rehearse it that way." Then you can take your child through a little scene where you take the truck and he asks for it back, in words, and tries to negotiate its return, also in words. Teach the meaning of the word "negotiate" young. As I keep stressing, I think negotiation is one of the two or three most valuable tools for parents and children to use, both at home and everywhere else.

For older children I recommend productive physical labor as a consequence: Mowing the lawn. Washing the car. Picking up around the neighborhood or around the school grounds. I think detention periods are counterproductive. Better to have the child doing something useful than just sitting in a room dreaming up ways of getting into more trouble. Also, physical labor helps work off some of the aggression and excess energy that may have landed the child in trouble in the first place.

Grounding is okay for major offenses, but try to add to it some physical labor, with the promise that if the chore gets done promptly or particularly well, the period of grounding can be reduced. Build a positive activity—physical labor—and a positive incentive into the grounding.

Try not to use food as a reward or a consequence. Your child's nutritional needs should not be linked to discipline. That can lead to strange feelings about food, and even to eating disorders.

6. Get a proper diagnosis. When angry, disruptive behavior persists beyond the bounds of what is reasonable for your child's age, talk to a professional about it. You might start with your pediatrician, who might in turn refer you to a psychiatrist or a psychologist. As I mentioned above, there are a significant number of causes of disruptive behavior that only a trained professional can diagnose.

7. Keep a journal. If your child has had angry outbursts repeatedly, try to keep your own journal of the episodes as they occur. It does not have to be lengthy or terribly involved; just include the basic facts. After a month or so, you will be able to learn a great deal about what is going on by reading the journal entries. A written record can correct many mistakes that our memories make. It can also provide a perspective from which certain patterns may quickly be detected.

8. Never hit a child. This is the safest policy for child and parent alike. A generation ago—even today, in many places—it was routine for children to be hit at home and at school. The Bible encourages physical punishment ("Spare the rod and spoil the child"), and cultural lore from around the world seems to sanction various forms of striking a child's body in order to improve his behavior, attitude, effort, or some other failing.

However, it is the parent or the teacher who has failed when the only method he or she can think of to promote correct behavior is to inflict pain upon a child's body and humiliation upon that child's spirit. It is time for this practice to stop. Civilization should have advanced far enough by now for us to give up hitting children. Spanking, paddling, whipping, caning—whatever form they take, these practices are wrong. They should be obsolete.

How can I say this when corporal punishment has been in use for centuries? I believe the collective sensibility of humankind progresses over time. Practices that were routine in one era come to exceed the bounds of proper action in another. The stocks, the ducking stool, the dunce cap—these are punishments most of us now consider primitive and cruel, but they were once routine. Tradition is not an absolute validator. Slavery, too, has a long history.

Hitting isn't the answer to discipline problems. It is only a matter of time before the various forms of hitting children go the way of the ducking stool. I doubt any civilization, or any parent, would express pride in hitting a child. What a culture, or a parent, might well take pride in is developing an effective form of discipline that excludes physical punishment.

I have never met a parent who spoke with pride about beating his or her children. On the other hand, I have met many parents who do indeed speak with pride about *not* hitting their children. "I have never laid a hand on him," many a mom or a dad has told me gladly. In particular, parents who were hit themselves speak movingly of their resolve not to do to their children what was done to them.

This is not to say that we do not *feel* like hitting our children at times. Almost every parent has felt the urge to give his or her child a swat. This feeling is normal. But it should be a feeling we resist, like the feeling of wanting to hit our spouse, or our boss, or the car that just cut us off in traffic. There are *always* better ways to solve the problem than hitting.

Can I give you three good reasons not to hit your child? Sure.

A. *It is wrong.* This is the best reason. But if you do not feel the truth of it in your gut, move on to Reasons 2 and 3.

B. It may do serious damage. When you give yourself the option of physically punishing your child, you open yourself to the *possibility* that you will physically abuse your child. I am not saying that all physical punishment constitutes physical abuse. Certainly not. However, I am saying that *physical abuse becomes impossible if you do not allow yourself the option of ever hitting your child.* It only takes one episode of losing control of yourself as you hit your child to do a lifetime's worth of damage. Suppose it's a hot summer evening, after a bad day at work; you come home and find yourself constantly pestered by your five-year-old, who finally breaks his dinner plate by dropping it on the floor seemingly on purpose. You might find your blood rise to the point where you lose yourself, and you do something you have only read about: You hit that child, and then begin to beat that child, and you take out the whole day's frustration upon the body of that child. And as you continue to beat that child you change into a different person altogether, a person who is pleased at how easy it is to beat this child; how glad you are to let it all out, not only the day's frustrations but the week's and the year's and the lifetime's. You are no longer hitting your child. You are hitting some object. You are hitting back at all that was done to you; you are inflicting pain upon it, and you are in charge. Later you see "it" was your child. But later is too late. It only takes one such episode to do irreparable damage. I have interviewed many adults who remember the *one time* that Mom or Dad "really lost it" and beat them up; they remember that one time as the moment they lost trust in that parent forever.

Hitting just is not worth it. In the name of discipline or of all the good intentions you may have, it is not worth taking the chance of abusing your child. *Keep the option of hitting permanently closed.*

C. Hitting doesn't work. This is the irony of ironies. All the studies that have been done of physical punishment reach the same conclusion: It does not work. It does make children scared; it does humiliate them and cause them physical pain; but it does not stop them from acting up. If anything, it causes them to act up more. This is because when a parent or teacher relies on physical punishment, he or she tends to neglect working on the development of the internal controls a child needs. In essence, physical punishment is the easy option for a parent or teacher. The more responsible option, the option requiring greater patience and imagination, is also *the option that works best: Never hit.*

9. Take charge. Establish an authoritative presence in the life of your child. While I advocate never hitting, I also know that the adult in charge must make sure the children know that that adult is, indeed, in charge. All of us can remember the pathetic plight of the substitute schoolteacher when we were in school. Being there just one day, with no chance to get to know us or to establish authority, he or she didn't stand a chance against the average classroom of seditious and rebellious any-graders. It was a field day for us and a bad day for Mr. or Ms. X. Unless, of course, Mr. or Ms. X happened to be one of those leadership geniuses who know how to take charge immediately.

"There's something in his tone of voice," people often say about a teacher or parent who takes charge easily. It is not how loud you talk, it is how you say what you say. Do you say it as if you mean it? Do you say it with respect for those you are addressing? Those are key: sincerity and respect. But there is a third ingredient, I think, that all "take-chargers" have, and that ingredient is confidence. You have to believe you are the person for the job. You do not have to think you are perfect in all respects, but you do have to believe that you are the right person to be doing what you're doing. Confidence, sincerity, and respect. These are the ingredients of taking charge.

When I was in school we had a music specialist who looked about ninety years old and couldn't have been much over four feet, ten inches tall. We were all bigger than she, by far. We were faster on our feet, by far. We knew much more of the pop lingo of the day, and we knew many more of the jokes that were in. But no teacher ran a smoother class than Miss McAvoy, or Miss Mac, as we all called her. She would totter into our classroom for our music period, or we would swarm into her room, depending on the day's plan. In either case, the minute the bell rang all mouths were shut and all eyes were focused on Miss Mac. We did what she told us to do, and we did it when she told us to. In many schools, music period is the most disruptive of all, because it involves singing, noise-making, and many self-conscious moments. But in the hands of Miss Mac music was easily the most orderly of all classes.

Other teachers often visited our music classes—not only from our school, but from elsewhere as well. Miss Mac was a legendary teacher, from whom many wanted to learn.

How did she do it? I'm sure that when she was asked she'd say she didn't know. She liked children, and she liked music, and she expected us to cooperate, and we did. Somehow those ingredients all seemed to reinforce each other. She made music fun, more fun than cutting up would be. We didn't want to waste our time with her by misbehaving. We also didn't want to hurt her feelings. We really loved Miss Mac. The cynic might say she was just using her age and slight build to her advantage, making us all think of our most kindly grandparent or even great grandparent. But so what? All teachers must use whatever they have, whoever they are. The trick is to use what you have well, and Miss Mac did that.

She used love to take charge. Not simpy, smarmy, sticky love, but strong, real love. She never spoke her love, but she showed it all the time: her love of music, love of school, love of children, love of life. She had a calm about her that calmed us all, and she had an energy about her that kept us all in step, attending, hanging on her next word or direction.

Not every parent or teacher can be Miss Mac. Very few of us can. I know I can't, but I can learn from her, as all of us can learn from the teachers, parents, or even drill instructors we have known who did their jobs well, who took charge with skill.

10. Bring in reinforcements. Never worry alone. Reinforcements may come from anywhere. An uncle or an aunt, a godparent, a coach, a teacher, a neighbor's parent, an older sibling, a friend. When you need fresh troops to deal with a child's excess aggression, get them. Remember, you live in a community. You do not have to worry alone. Even these days, no one has to be totally alone. Local Boys' Clubs or other athletic facilities, the Big Brother and Big Sister organizations, your school, neighborhood churches or synagogues or other religious institutions—all can be places to make contact, if not for your child then for yourself. This is one of my prime rules for parents: Never worry alone.

Chapter 7

·····································

Sad: When Children Are Unhappy

I was born with a vile melancholy, and it has made me mad all my life—at least not sober.

—Samuel Johnson

One wintry Sunday morning I got a frantic call from Mrs. Ellerbee, the wife of the man who manages the building where I have my office.

"What's the problem?" I asked.

"It's my sister, Shannon," she said. "Well, actually it's her son, Luke. He got arrested this morning walking down the railway tracks playing chicken with the trains. Can you believe that? Shannon is hysterical. She's going down to the police station now to get him out, but she was really crazy on the phone. She was blaming herself for everything. How could she have let this happen? she said. Why didn't she know what was going on with Luke? Was he ever going to be all right? I tried to console her but I didn't know what to say. I'm not a professional. I think she needs help. You were the only person I could think of."

"Sure," I said. "I'm glad you called. How old is Luke?" I asked.

"Sixteen. He just got his license. He's in the tenth grade."

"How has he been lately?" I asked.

"I'm not sure, Dr. Hallowell. He and his mom and dad argue now and then, but it's a pretty happy family, I think."

"Well, why don't you give me your sister's phone number, and I'll give her a call."

"Would you? Oh, thank you. I don't know what's going to happen to them. If anyone can help them, I'm sure you can."

"It's my pleasure," I said. Actually, it was not exactly a pleasure to give over a Sunday morning to crisis intervention, but Norm Ellerbee had bailed me out of many tense moments. I can still remember him finding a plumber at midnight on New Year's Eve for a burst pipe. I thought that was a miracle.

When I called Mrs. Ellerbee's sister, I got an answering machine. As I listened to the cheerful message, it seemed an ironic counterpoint to what the person who'd recorded the message was doing now, bailing her son out of jail. As I began to leave my message, someone picked up. "Dr. Hallowell?" a man's hoarse voice inquired.

"Yes," I said. "Mary Ellerbee asked me to call."

"Yes, thank you. Mary is my sister-in-law. This is Dave Haskins. Did Mary tell you what's happened?" Dave gave me the headlines again, and then I suggested that we get together in person, since that would probably feel better than the telephone.

"That would be great," Dave said. "When Shannon and Luke get back from the police station. God, I can't believe this."

"I know," I said. "It feels like the end of the world right now, but it's not. Lots more kids than you'd ever believe end up at the police station some time or other. Call me when they get back, and I'll give you directions to my office. Listen, I know you're upset, but crises like these have a funny way of turning out to be good news in the long run."

"Good news?" Dave said, incredulously.

"I know that sounds absurd right now, but a crisis calls attention to something that needs attention paid to it," I said.

"Well, it's a hell of a way to get attention," Dave said with a grunt.

I arrived at my office building before the Haskinses, and unlocked the front door, and cranked up the heat a bit, as the New

England winter had settled in overnight. Then I walked up to my third-floor office. While I waited, I drank the coffee I'd bought along the way and munched on a Danish.

Three quick knocks on my door announced the Haskinses. As I opened the door, three figures filed past me—somewhat sheepishly, it seemed—and stood in the middle of my floor, awaiting instructions. "Sit anywhere you'd like," I said, extending my arm around the room, which included a couch, three easy chairs, and a straight chair, with some folding chairs stacked against a wall. Shannon Haskins and Luke sat on the couch, while Dave took the easy chair next to them.

"Thanks for seeing us on such short notice," Shannon said.

"No problem," I said. I looked at all three of them for initial signs of distress. They each looked stunned. "This hasn't been your average Sunday morning," I said.

"No," Dave said. "Not average."

"How did things go at the police station?" I asked.

"We posted bail," Shannon said. "Luke has to appear in court tomorrow morning. Know any good lawyers?"

"In fact, I do. I'll give you a name and phone number if you like, when we're done."

"We could use a lawyer, that's for sure," Dave said.

"Fine," I said. "So who can tell me what happened?"

It was Dave who replied. "We got a call this morning from the police saying Luke had been brought in after being found walking on the railroad tracks. When they stopped him, he swore at them and told them he was just playing chicken with the trains."

"That's not all that happened, Dad," Luke put in. "Why don't you ever get it straight?"

"Okay, tell me—what did I leave out? That you'd been drinking? Okay, I left that out. The police said Luke had been drinking."

"Dad, that's not it at all. They had no right to come up on me like they did. I was just walking along minding my own business and they drive up and put on their big flashing lights and get out of their car and push me down on the ground. They had no right to do that. Or don't you care, Dad? Are you just worried about how the neighbors are going to react?"

Dave turned red. "Don't push your luck with me this morning. I have really had it with you."

"Ooooooh, Dad, I'm scared. What are you gonna do? Ground me? Maybe hit me? Did you ever think maybe I've had it with you?"

"Luke, Dave, please," Shannon interrupted. "Let's try and tell Dr. Hallowell what's been going on."

"We *are* telling him, Mom. This is exactly what's been going on. It's not your fault. Don't get upset." Luke noticed tears dripping down his mother's cheeks, and he handed her a tissue from a box on the table in front of the couch.

"So it's my fault, is that the idea, Luke?" his father asked, digging his thumbs into the arms of his chair.

"Dad, you are so weird."

"Why am I weird? Because I'm upset you got drunk and got yourself arrested?"

"Yes, Dad, that's just what I meant. You are so dumb!"

"Look, if we weren't sitting in this office taking up this doctor's time I would end this conversation right now. You're right: I *would* like to hit you. But I won't. As far as I'm concerned there's no point in talking with you as long as you're going to be like this."

"Everyone is tense, and understandably so," I interrupted, holding up my hands, palms out, like stop signs. "This is not an easy way to start the day. Luke, can you tell me why you were walking along the train tracks?"

"If *he'll* let me." Luke said, nodding at his father.

"Go ahead. I won't interrupt," his father said.

"I was out walking because Jeannie had just blown me off. She was back with Carlos, and I was ripped. I love her."

"How can you love someone at your age?" Dave interrupted.

"Dave!" I said, beating Luke to the punch by about a milli-second.

"I know. I'll be quiet," Dave said, rubbing his hands together.

"What Dad does not understand is that I'm not a little boy anymore. Dad, I love Jeannie. You must have loved Mom like this once. Well, I love Jeannie."

"But I treated your father better than she treats you," Shannon said.

Peace began to emerge in the room bit by bit as Luke told his story. His father sat back in his chair and crossed his legs at the ankles, instead of at the knees as they had been before. Mom stopped crying. And Luke became less sarcastic and defensive as he talked about love.

His story was as he'd said. His girlfriend had given him a hard time and he'd set off down the railroad tracks, beer in hand, to contemplate everything from suicide to love to loneliness to the taste of the beer. When the police found him they did treat him roughly, as police are sometimes wont to do, but now he had to face legitimate charges.

"I doubt the law will come down very hard on you," I said to Luke. "I'm no lawyer, but I have had experience with this sort of situation."

"You've been arrested?" Luke asked me, with a touch of admiration.

"No, that's not what I meant, although I was once brought into a police station because I didn't have my license or registration and I got wise with the cop who stopped me. One piece of advice, Luke. Never get wise with cops. It's like taunting the IRS. You just don't do it. They hold all the cards."

"But that's not fair," Luke said.

"I know," I said. "But you gotta get smart about these things. You can't take on the Concord Police Department all by yourself at age sixteen."

"You sound like my mom and dad."

"I'm sorry," I said. "I know you don't need another parent telling you what to do. It's just some friendly advice."

"I thought shrinks didn't give advice," Luke protested, as

though he'd caught me making a mistake. "Jeannie's shrink will never tell her what to do even if she begs her to. What's the deal with you guys, you only give advice when the patient doesn't want it?"

"I guess it seems that way," I said with a smile. "Anyway, what I meant was that on the basis of my experience with quite a few other patients of mine who were in your position, I doubt you'll have a lot of trouble in court. You don't have a record, you're going to be polite and cooperative with the judge—" I paused. "Right?" I asked, looking into Luke's sweet blue eyes. Luke nodded. "So that means, assuming you didn't really piss off whoever arrested you, that things should go okay."

The tension in the room decreased some more. Dad even smiled. Luke smiled, too, I think because I had said the phrase "piss off." Now I thought I could ask for more detailed history without everybody yelling at each other.

Luke was the oldest of three children. Neither he nor any other member of the family had ever been to a psychiatrist before— "Not because we couldn't use one," his mom said, "but because we didn't have the time or money."

Actually, the story of the family was pretty smooth, as family stories go. But as we dug into Luke's story a little more deeply, the smooth family picture roughened a bit. The fact was that Luke had been pretty unhappy for a long time, and had been telling only his girlfriend, Jeannie, about what was really on his mind.

"But if you've been unhappy, why didn't you come to us?" his mom asked, almost pleading. Luke just looked at the floor. That was his answer. I looked at Dave Haskins, expecting to see him angry or impatient. Instead he looked sad and concerned.

"What's been bothering you?" I asked Luke.

"Nothing in particular, I guess," he said, still looking down. "I don't know."

"Have you been thinking about suicide?" I asked, wanting to get everyone's worst fear out on the table.

"Sure," he said. "But I'd never do it. I'm too chicken."

"Oh, Luke," his mom cried out, "how can you say you've been thinking about suicide? Oh, this is awful. This is really awful. What has been going on? What have we done to you?"

"Mom, please," Luke said, "it's not you or Dad. It's no one. It's me. It's life."

"But suicide? How could you even think of such a thing?" Shannon's tears came out quietly, as tears do, but her face was red with pain.

"Mom, don't worry, I'd never do that. He asked, so I answered. But don't worry, okay? I hate it when you cry."

"Luke," his dad broke in, "I'm sorry I got mad at you this morning. I'm beginning to think that this was a damned good thing that happened last night. Now we know what's going on. We're going to help you, and you can count on that. It's just that this is a shock."

The more we talked the more the family came together. The more Luke talked, the more clear it became that he had been depressed for about six months, ever since last summer. It wasn't obvious why he was depressed. He had girlfriend problems, school problems, and family issues, but nothing out of the ordinary, nothing that virtually any sixteen-year-old wouldn't be dealing with. So why was life feeling so onerous to Luke?

We do not understand depression entirely. All we know for sure is that from time to time some children and adults become unusually sad for an extended period of time. It was crucial for Luke's mother and father to get past guilt and blame in order to understand him. Neither guilt nor blame is good treatment for depression. Honest talk helps. Understanding helps. Listening helps. This is what Luke's family started to do that Sunday morning in my office.

As his father so bravely said, it was a good thing that Luke got picked up by the police. Sometimes it takes an extreme event to unearth the true distress in a child.

It was perfectly understandable and appropriate that Dave and

Shannon Haskins first reacted with anger, shock, guilt, and tears. A bomb had exploded underneath them, and they needed to react. Each of them had to speak his piece.

But what should happen next is key. What do we do with our children's feelings, and with our own feelings regarding our children? How can we move in a constructive direction?

Shannon and Dave Haskins continued in family therapy with me for a while, and I referred Luke to an individual therapist. Therapy is certainly not needed for all families, but in this case there was a crisis, and the family wanted the refereed forum that family therapy provided. Also Luke expressed a wish to speak to someone privately about his own concerns. He started in therapy, and was also started on an antidepressant medication.

The outcome was excellent. In six weeks, Luke, Shannon, and Dave all said they were in a much better place than they had been before Luke got arrested. His case was in fact suspended, then dismissed. There was no punishment other than the pain and humiliation of the arrest. It impresses me how often these apparent disasters turn out to resolve very positively.

It wasn't so long ago that depression was thought to be a disease of the will, a sign of weakness, or even a sin. Now we know that it is an illness, a condition that can attack any one of us and for which we have a number of effective treatments. Depression is just one example of many conditions we now recognize in children but that only a generation or two ago were hidden or dismissed as moral failings.

There are some children who, like Samuel Johnson, seem to have been born with "a vile melancholy," a feeling of sadness that is out of proportion to their life circumstances. These children are constitutionally sad.

Other children, like Luke, develop depressive feelings out of the blue or in response to some mild stressor. Normally a short burst of sadness passes quickly, like a cold current when you are swimming in warm waters. But in some children the feelings do not easily go away. A child may be happy during early life; then, at a certain age, he or she may turn sad for no apparent reason. The child cannot explain this change of mood, and neither can those around her. But she is not herself. She is down in the dumps and hard to console. The low period may last weeks, months, even years. This is childhood depression, and it is much more common than we used to think.

We now know what any observant grandmother could have told us all along: Some children are chronically, inordinately sad. They are depressed.

What are the signs that suggest your child may be depressed? Obviously, if your child tells you he is sad, this is a sign. Not all sadness equals clinical depression, but if sadness persists intensely depression is the likely cause. If your child withdraws from friends or fun activities, this may signify depression. Or if your child becomes extremely sensitive and testy and starts to fall off academically, these symptoms may indicate depression. Also, depressed children frequently complain of physical ailments, such as stomachaches or headaches or unexplained aches and pains in various parts of their bodies. Sometimes they become highly agitated and skittish, and they have great difficulty separating from Mom or Dad. Children younger than age 10 who are depressed sometimes state that they hear voices that aren't there, a symptom called auditory hallucinations.

As children get older, they more frequently show some of the typical signs of depression in adults: feelings of helplessness and hopelessness, an inability to experience pleasure or joy, and a physical slowing down, or what is called psychomotor retardation. Adolescents, more than younger children, may sleep excessively or use illicit drugs or alcohol as part of a depressive episode. Both younger, prepubertal children and adolescents also commonly experience poor concentration, lack of sleep, and feelings of being sad or down in the dumps as part of their depression.

In addition, all depressed children are at risk for other problems, particularly disruptive behaviors (such as conduct disorder and oppositional defiant disorder), anxiety disorders, or attention deficit disorder. These so-called comorbid conditions can mask the sad symptoms by drawing attention to the disruptive, anxious, or distracted symptoms instead. If your child is acting up a great deal, it is important to look underneath the misbehavior and ask, "Are you unhappy about something?"

What is the current medical definition of depression in a child? It is basically the same as that of depression in an adult. According to the *Diagnostic and Statistical Manual of Mental Disorders,* fourth edition, the standard psychiatric handbook, these are the criteria for a major depressive episode:

> Five (or more) of the following symptoms have been present during the same two-week period and represent a change from previous functioning; at least one of the symptoms is either depressed mood or loss of interest or pleasure.
>
> (1) depressed mood most of the day, nearly every day, as indicated by either subjective report (e.g. feels sad or empty) or observation made by others (e.g., appears tearful). In children and adolescents, can be irritable mood.
>
> (2) markedly diminished interest or pleasure in all, or almost all, activities most of the day, nearly every day (as indicated by either subjective account or observation made by others)
>
> (3) significant weight loss when not dieting or weight gain (e.g., a change of more than 5% of body weight in a month), or decrease or increase in appetite nearly every day. In children, consider failure to make expected weight gains.
>
> (4) insomnia or hypersomnia [excessive sleeping] nearly every day
>
> (5) psychomotor agitation or retardation nearly every day (observable by others, not merely subjective feelings of restlessness or being slowed down)
>
> (6) fatigue or loss of energy nearly every day
>
> (7) feelings of worthlessness or excessive or inappropriate

guilt (which may be delusional) nearly every day (not merely self-reproach or guilt about being sick)

(8) diminished ability to think or concentrate, or indecisiveness, nearly every day (either by subjective account or as observed by others)

(9) recurrent thoughts of death (not just fear of dying), recurrent suicidal ideation without a specific plan, or a suicide attempt or a specific plan for committing suicide

As difficult to confront as it may be, it is important that we parents be aware of the possibility of childhood depression. We child psychiatrists used to think that children could not get depressed. We mistakenly believed that they lacked the psychological apparatus for depression. In Freudian terms, it was thought that depression resulted from the superego, or conscience, attacking the ego for its various transgressions. Since the superego was thought to be incompletely formed in children, it followed logically that children "could not" get depressed. This is an intriguing example of how a theory can distort what we see before our very eyes. The theory said children could not be depressed, so no matter how depressed a child appeared to be, we called the phenomenon by another name.

Our natural tendency is to deny depression in our children because we do not want to see it. It is antithetical to what we think of as the nature of childhood. A child may be sad, angry, or disappointed, sure. But depressed? Isn't that just for grown-ups?

Unfortunately, it is not. Probably about 5 percent of children and adolescents suffer from depression at any given time. And of children who suffer a depressive episode, two-thirds of them will experience depression in adulthood as well. In other words, depression tends to recur.

There are some children who never quite know what happiness is, or what the rest of us call happiness. Most of us have known adults who report that they have been unhappy for as long as they can remember. This condition, constitutional melancholy, is separate from episodic depression, though both occur in children. Somewhere in between the two is a condition we call dysthymia (literally, "bad mood"). The diagnosis applies to a formerly happy child who becomes sad and serious for a year or more. He is not as sad as the depressed child, and he does not have the associated symptoms of excess sleep or sleep loss, loss of weight or appetite, or hallucinations. However, the dysthymic child is in pain and needs help, too.

These conditions need not relate to the child's actual life circumstances. A child whose material needs are met, who has excellent parents and lives in an affectionate community, may still feel that life is bleak. On the other hand, there are children who, no matter how bad their external circumstances may be, still manage to keep a cheerful air about them. The factors that protect them derive, at least in part, from their genetic package.

That same package may lead to depression. Sometimes a parent who has been depressed much of his or her life will look at me sadly and ask, "Is this why my daughter is sad? Have I passed myself on to her?" I see such parents feeling they have made yet another mistake. But while the answer to the genetic question may be, yes, that does not tell the whole story. Depression is much more complicated than a set of genes. Not all children whose parents are depressed will become depressed themselves. And, sadly, some children whose parents are not depressed do become depressed. But even if you are genetically predisposed to depression, you and your child can manage this condition successfully throughout life.

The biological perspective can also help. The depression is not the parent's *fault*. It is no one's fault that depression is wired into one's genetic package. It is simply the luck of the draw. If you leave blame aside, and if you realize the gene does not seal your fate—you yourself still have a great deal of control—then you can manage very well.

We have to remember that all brains are vulnerable. No brain is without pain. This is a different way of looking at the age-old wisdom that life is difficult. Brains are difficult. Each brain manages some part of life effortlessly, but struggles with some other part.

If your child is depressed or struggles with a subclinical mood problem—if he is constitutionally "serious," for example—the reason for this condition may be in the way his brain is wired, rather than the way you have raised him or how life has treated him.

Mistreatment of a child can, of course lead to depression. In one study of depression in preschoolers, all the children diagnosed with depression had been victims of abuse or neglect. Not only mistreatment, but all manner of painful life experiences can lead to depression. Rejection, failure, a tragedy in the community, and any of the many vicissitudes of life can trigger an episode of major depression in a child. The key for a parent is to know what the signs are and to watch for them.

Untreated, a single episode of depression lasts quite a while, on average about nine months. In the life of a child, that is a long, long time. You can lose friends and fall far behind academically in nine months. Beyond those consequences, the most dire consequence of depression in children and adults is, of course, suicide.

Suicide is not common among children, but unfortunately it is on the rise. Prepubertal children may think of suicide, but they very rarely complete the act. Adolescents, however, do commit suicide; it is one of the leading causes of death in this age group. The most common method of suicide, accounting for two thirds of completed suicides by adolescents, is shooting oneself with a gun, usually a gun found at home. Overdosing is the most common method among suicide attempts that do not lead to the child's death. Statistically, adolescent girls are more likely than boys to attempt suicide, while adolescent boys are more likely than girls to complete the act—that is, to die if they attempt it. Any child who is depressed should be considered a suicide risk. Most will not attempt suicide, but at least the risk factors should be reduced as much as possible: Get guns out of the home; be careful of any prescription medication, especially the tricyclic antidepressants, which are lethal in overdose; and make sure the child is not abandoned, neglected, or abused.

Mercifully, suicide is not a common outcome of depression in children. However, depression can leave marks that last a long time. A child who has experienced an episode of major depression at, say, age nine is much more likely than other children to get depressed again later in adolescence or adulthood. He is also about twenty times more likely to develop an additional psychiatric diagnosis such as bipolar disorder, substance abuse, or other condition.

Apart from any diagnosable illnesses they may have, children who have been depressed are more likely than other children to be insecure throughout life. They will probably need more reassurance and approval than the average adolescent or adult, and they will continue to be at risk for recurrence of depression. This is not as grim as it might sound. If you know you have this vulnerability, or your child does, you can plan accordingly: Give plenty of reassurance. Give support. Teach your child to feel comfortable reaching out. And remember that some of the most talented, productive members of society since the dawn of time have struggled with depression throughout their lives.

How does a family contend with a child who, though not depressed, is "serious" or constitutionally unhappy?

I could offer many examples, but the one I choose to give is that of Charlie and his parents, Liz and Jacob Michaels. When they came to see me, Liz and Jacob were caught up in blaming themselves. They had been to see several therapists in Charlie's eleven years of life, and they had been given a great deal of advice, much of it contradictory. They had been told to spend more time with Charlie, and they had been told to back off. They had been told to have another child to help take the pressure off Charlie, and they had been told that he was bothered by having two younger siblings already. They had been told to alter his diet, and they had been told that his diet was irrelevant. They had been told he needed psychoanalysis, and they had been told psychoanalysis didn't help. They had been told to get into family therapy, and they had been told that family therapy would only upset Charlie. They had been told that Charlie should get testing for a hidden learning disability, and they had been told that Charlie was intellectually gifted. "Honest to God, Doc," Jacob Michaels told me in his first meeting with me, "it's pretty confusing trying to sort it all out."

I sat and listened while Jacob and Liz sketched out the whole saga. Charlie himself was not present at this first appointment. This is my usual practice in a situation whose background I don't know; it allows the parents to be completely open and also spares the child a recitation of not necessarily enjoyable data.

"Charlie's problem is that he has never been a happy kid," Liz said. "Jacob and I like to think of ourselves as happy—I mean, we *are* happy, as happy as you can be in 1995. Life has been good to us. Jacob makes a good living, and I could, too, if I chose to go back to work. But for now I want to be at home with the kids. Charlie, being our first, has always had a special place. But from the moment he was born he had a different temperament than the others."

"And the others?" I asked.

"Melissa and Rose are just much more lively and outgoing, that's all. Charlie is always so serious."

"Serious enough for you to go see several psychiatrists," I said.

"Maybe it's just the Jewish thing to do," Jacob said with a laugh. "All firstborn children must see a shrink. But I like to believe there's more to it than that. We have wanted for him what we wanted for the others—you know, the usual: happiness, success, health. He has success and health, but I don't think he has happiness. I don't know what we've done wrong."

"What makes you so sure you've done something wrong?" I asked.

"Aren't you sweet," Liz said with a smile. "But it *is* the logical conclusion. You have a healthy baby, you have enough resources to raise him well, and he is unhappy. You must have done something wrong. That is what my mother would have thought, and it is what I think. And in fact we have been led to believe by all the professionals we've seen that Charlie's unhappiness is basically a problem we've created."

"You may have misunderstood what the professionals were saying," I suggested, "because you assumed they were blaming you. Or they may in fact have been blaming you; I don't know. Many of us in this profession come across differently than we mean to. It is difficult for any of us to know how our words will be received."

"Some of them were pretty offensive," Jacob said.

"Just Polansky," Liz added.

"Well, Polansky was enough," Jacob retorted.

"Polansky?" I asked, a little afraid of what I might hear.

"He was a psychologist we went to see. Had this little office in the basement of a hospital. Gray cinder-block walls. No decorations. I suppose that shouldn't matter, but it did. How can you treat people in a bunker? What did he do? All he did was bring Charlie into his office for a while, then bring us in and then bring Charlie in again, then us in once more. The last time he took off his glasses and started polishing them with his necktie while he told us that we were neglecting our duties as parents, that Charlie was socially inept because I worked too hard and that he needed me to play baseball with him. I told Polansky I couldn't play baseball, that I never had been able to play baseball, that I hated baseball. He just kept polishing his glasses and told me I should learn to play baseball. I asked him, did he really think that my playing baseball was the key to my son's finding happiness in this life? Then Polansky put his glasses on and looked at me in this totally condescending way and said, 'Well, if you put it like that, of course not, but I should think you'd be willing to *try* playing baseball, or are you too self-centered?' I'll never forget that line. My head started to spin. I filled up with guilt and rage. I don't know who I was madder at, Polansky or myself. But I went out and played baseball, damn it. Charlie and I played baseball. We both hated it. Finally I asked Charlie if he had told Dr. Polansky that he secretly wished I would play baseball with him. He said geez, no, that Dr. Polansky had told *him* he should play baseball with *me!* I don't need to tell you this experience soured me on the mental health profession. We never went back to Polansky. I mean what was his problem, was his father the commissioner of baseball or something? And to tell me that I am too self-centered, that was—"

"That was unfortunate," Liz said. "But we have seen some people we liked. And the same thing happens. We just feel more and more guilty."

"Does Charlie know you've come to see me?" I asked.

"Yes," they replied. "He said he'd talk to you if you'd like."

I met with Charlie a few times. He was a quiet little guy, cooperative, but of few words. We played gin rummy together, and he won most of the time. He would dutifully pick up the cards and deal again after a victory, or after a rare defeat, with little show of emotion. "Are you unhappy?" I asked him.

"Not really," he said.

"Are you happy?" I asked.

"Not really," he said.

"Can you tell me if there is anything bothering you?" I asked.

"Nothing is bothering me, really," Charlie replied.

"How do your parents treat you?" I asked.

"Good," he answered.

"No problems at home?" I asked.

"Nope," Charlie replied.

"Do you feel any different this year than you did last year?" I inquired.

"I don't think so," Charlie answered, dealing the cards.

I asked for more information. He told me in his succinct way that he loved his parents, that they treated him very well, that they spent lots of time with him, and that basically if I thought anything ill of his parents I should go jump in the lake.

Not much more came out of our sessions. He didn't feel like a very unhappy child, and he didn't feel like a very happy child either. He was a serious boy, and he was a good kid, I thought. I told his parents so.

Over a few weeks I met with Liz and Jacob several times. What emerged was the not uncommon phenomenon of excessive parental guilt. Liz and Jacob had been beating themselves up for Charlie's unhappiness ever since he was born. Some of the beating up had been instigated by mental health professionals, but most was self-inflicted. As Liz said, self-blame was how her mother would have thought and it was how she thought.

In the case of Liz and Jacob—as in the case of most parents who accuse themselves of not doing the job right—the self-assessment missed the mark by a mile. Liz and Jacob were wonderful parents. Even though Jacob hated baseball, he loved lots of other activities. But most of all—and really this is all that counts—most of all, he loved Charlie.

I went over every detail of Jacob and Liz's parenting practices, and I could find nothing to criticize. I gave them a "parent assessment" scale, a set of questions researchers use to identify parents who need help in one way or another. This scale includes five major dimensions of parenting, as follows:

1. Degree of parents' emotional warmth
2. Degree of parents' flexibility
3. Presence of psychiatric disturbance in either parent
4. Parents' knowledge base of principles of child care and physical and emotional development
5. Parents' commitment to family, allowing sufficient time with children, adequate prioritization of child care responsibilities*

* From David Mirazek, M.D., *Journal of the American Academy of Child and Adolescent Psychiatry,* March 1995.

They scored fine on all five points. I told Liz and Jacob that by the most objective assessment I could make, they were excellent parents.

"How is it possible for good parents to have an unhappy child?" Liz asked me.

"Just asking the question gives you away," I said. "You're a self-blamer. Don't you believe in genetics?"

"But Jacob and I are happy," she protested.

"More people contributed to your gene pool than just you and Jacob. You never know whose genes find their way into your offspring."

"So we're prisoners of our genes?" Jacob asked.

"No," I replied. "It's a balance between the two, between the genes and life experience. All I'm saying is that your parenting cannot control and explain everything, any more than the genes can control everything. You can take a child who is genetically upbeat and make him unhappy by treating him miserably. But with Charlie you have the opposite situation. He seems to be genetically downbeat and you have made him as happy as you can by giving him good parenting."

"Well, should we treat his unhappiness with medication?"

"I don't think so," I said. "From all you have told me and all I've seen of him Charlie is not depressed in the clinical sense of the word. He's just constitutionally serious. If he ever goes into a big decline—in other words if his mood takes a big downturn and stays down for a while—that would constitute an episode of depression, which we might want to treat with medication. But temperamental, constitutional seriousness? That is just the way he is, and more power to him. You know *Winnie-the-Pooh*? Maybe Charlie is like Eeyore. Just serious by nature."

On the other hand, the wiring of some children's brains results in depression, sadness that needs to be treated. Not so very long ago, as recently as the 1970s and early 1980s, it was anathema to think of giving antidepressant medication to children. We still do not have convincing proof that medication helps. However, more and more anecdotal evidence supports the notion that medication is effective in treating depression in some children. There is much work to be done to determine which medications work best in children and at what dose.

But before considering which medication, a parent must first come to terms with the idea of using *any*. I will discuss this question in Chapter 10, but simply reiterate here that some medication may help, although it is by no means a definitive treatment. Psychotherapy of various kinds remains the mainstay in the treatment of depression in children.

Since we recoil at the idea of a child's being depressed, we often overlook the signs of depression in children. What we would recognize as depression in an adult friend, we sometimes do not see in a child, even though the signs are right there in front of us.

Sometimes it helps to have a checklist of items to look for to identify depression in children. I have already given the official criteria from the fourth edition of the *Diagnostic and Statistical Manual of Mental Disorders,* known as DSM-IV. The following list is adapted and expanded from the DSM-IV criteria.

TEN SIGNS THAT YOUR CHILD MAY BE DEPRESSED

1. Your child states he or she is sad. This is the most obvious sign of depression. One moment of mild sadness does not constitute depression, but prolonged, intense sadness does. We must be careful not to overlook a child's ongoing complaint of being sad, simply because we can't bear to hear it or we're too busy. Every parent has been guilty of not responding to a child's complaint about something simply because life was too busy and too chaotic at the moment. But if your child repeatedly complains about sadness, this must be attended to. Almost every child who is depressed tells others (not necessarily his parents) that this is how he feels.

2. *Your child seems sad.* This is the more subtle cousin to Number 1, and the one that parents can count on seeing. Sometimes a child will not come right out and say to a parent, "I'm sad" or "I'm depressed." Instead the child shows his or depression through actions, facial expressions, style of communication, body language, and so forth. We can usually tell when our children are out of sorts. However, sometimes it is hard for us to bear the idea that our children are hurting, and so we ignore what we are seeing. This tendency to deny our children's emotional pain may be heightened when we are feeling sad, depressed, or hopeless ourselves, or when we feel at wit's end as to how to help out.

Children, especially adolescent children, can be particularly adept at making their parents feels helpless, as if nothing the parents say could be of any use whatsoever. The child can turn and give her parent such a withering glance that the parent retreats in shame and embarrassment, afraid to intrude on the child's intimate domain ever again. But you must resist this feeling. Your child needs you to risk embarrassment over and over again. Don't take it personally. Don't worry if your child makes you feel like an old fogey, clueless, and almost lifeless in your stupid daze. Just persist. Ask. Inquire. Then lick your wounds somewhere else.

However you feel, it is important that you as a parent ask about the feeling of sadness if you sense it is there in your child. You do not have to know how to solve the problem. Often just giving your child a chance to share it with you goes a long way toward solving it then and there. Trust your instincts and intuitions. If your child says, "Oh, Mom, it's nothing, just leave me alone," this is probably not the best time to leave her or him alone. Back off for a little while, but remember that the request to "leave me alone" does not mean leave me alone forever. Don't stand on ceremony. Ask until you are satisfied you know what is going on.

3. Your child loses interest in activities that used to please him or her, or your child loses interest in regular friends. When a child—or an adult, for that matter—gets depressed, he or she tends to lose interest in the very activities that used to hold interest. It is as if depression acts as a kind of interest-thinner, loosening the glue that holds a child's interest in an activity or pastime.

Just as depression may dissipate one's interest in everyday activities, so it may disengage a child from his or her friends. If the phone stops ringing or if your child stops using the phone, if friends stop coming over as much or if your child starts spending more time alone doing nothing, think of depression as a possible cause.

4. Your child acts or seems unusually irritable. Testy, cranky behavior often masks depression in children (and adults). Instead of telling you that he is sad, your sixteen-year-old may tell you to go jump in the lake, or words to that effect. As obnoxious and off-putting as this moody behavior can be, it is important to consider if sadness may underlie it.

5. Your child pays less attention to dress and personal hygiene. Many children, particularly boys, don't pay much attention to this anyway, but the sign to watch out for is a noticeable change in dress or self-care. If your child starts looking more sloppy than usual, or lets her hair go unattended for uncharacteristically long periods, or seems unaware of his personal appearance, this could be a sign of depression.

6. Your child's memory and attention span shorten. Again, the key is a deviation from your child's usual patterns of memory and attention. Some adolescents become so preoccupied in their depression that they start forgetting their assignments, forgetting to return telephone calls or show up for appointments and obligations. They also demonstrate a marked reduction in attention span, and an inability to carry on an extended conversation without tuning out or to read a page without drifting back into their own personal worries and sense of gloom.

7. *Your child's appetite or sleep pattern changes.* Typically in depression there is weight loss, although there may be weight gain as well. And typically, there is sleep loss, although the individual may try to oversleep as well in an attempt to get away from the problems waking life brings. A variation on this theme is the adolescent who wants to watch hours and hours of mindless TV or go to the movies every day in an effort to escape, as if into sleep.

8. *Your child begins to use some substance such as tobacco or alcohol.* Most adolescents experiment with tobacco, alcohol, or some other substance. However, if your child develops a habit, this may represent an attempt to self-medicate an underlying depression. Dr. Edward Khantzian, president of the American Academy of Addictionologists and a psychoanalyst as well, has written persuasively on the "self-medication hypothesis," the idea that many individuals are drawn to certain drugs of abuse as a desperate means of mollifying or *treating,* so to speak, an unpleasant feeling state, whether it be frustration, low self-esteem, a feeling of being rejected, or depression. Whatever the intolerable feeling state might be, the individual finds a momentary "cure" in the drug. While the cure is short-lived, and the side effects are worse than the original unwanted feeling state, the individual remembers how good the short-lived "cure" felt, and so he returns to it again and again, in a resolute, if misguided, attempt to self-medicate his emotions away.

9. *Your child gets involved in some new, potentially self-destructive behavior.* This is a corollary to sign number 8. Just as a drug may be used by an adolescent to self-medicate, so may an activity be used for the same purpose. A high-risk activity can act as a kind of antidepressant. Driving a car fast can make you forget your troubles for the moment because it focuses your mind elsewhere. Daredevil stunts can give you a rush of adrenaline that purges the depressive feelings, at least for the moment. Gambling or even shopping can be antidepressant activities. Hence, if your child starts to get rather wild, this may paradoxically be a sign of depres-

sion, since the wild behavior may represent an attempt on your child's part to "treat" or self-medicate an underlying, intolerably depressive feeling state.

10. There is a family history of depression or certain other psychiatric conditions. The history doesn't make the present diagnosis, of course; it simply increases the odds, as depression is a condition that can be inherited. The genes for depression seem to be associated with the genes for other conditions. Therefore you should look into a family history not only for depression but also for substance abuse, manic-depressive illness, attention deficit disorder, disorders of impulse control such as gambling, stealing, or fire-setting, as well as for depressive behavior that perhaps was not formally diagnosed.

There are some tips you can use as a parent in managing sad or depressed feelings in children. These tips are applicable to all children, regardless of age or gender.

TEN TIPS ON THE TREATMENT OF SADNESS AND DEPRESSION IN CHILDREN

1. First of all, make sure your child can name the feeling of sadness. Many children, particularly boys, cannot name sadness when they feel it. They literally do not know that what they are feeling is sadness. A friend might be sick and unable to come over to play. Your child will mope, but say nothing. He knows he feels bad, but beyond that he doesn't know what he feels. As a parent you can help him a great deal by saying something simple like, "You seem pretty sad." Whenever you give a feeling a name, it becomes much more manageable.

Teens and adults who commit acts of violence often have a history of a language disability. Because they cannot put their feelings into words, they act on them instead. The ability to use words to express emotion is one of the best protections against our ever resorting to violence.

In the case of sadness, children often feel too embarrassed or confused to know the name for what they feel. They may flail about rejecting consolation rather than acknowledge that what they are trying to cope with is sadness or disappointment. It can help tremendously for a parent, teacher, or other adult to open the steam valve and let the feeling come out in words by giving that feeling its name: sadness. As sadness intensifies it becomes depression. Being able to talk about the sadness first can prevent depression from developing.

Why is this? We don't really know. Why does talking about a sad feeling tend to make most people feel better? We don't know, but the answer to the question lies at the heart of the mind/body duality. It is interesting to speculate that talking about painful feelings activates some neuronal circuit in the brain that communicates with the brain's emotional centers. Words somehow stimulate the limbic system, the center of emotional regulation, and a more pleasant frame of mind ensues. We do know that the brain's language centers connect anatomically via nerve pathways with the limbic system. So it is logical to speculate that language helps regulate emotion.

In this sense, "talk" becomes a kind of medicine or biologically-based treatment itself. It is one of the oldest treatments we have, and probably still the best.

2. *Talk about the feeling a little bit.* This is not to say that you should try to offer psychotherapy. Just discuss whatever it is your child is feeling sad about. As discussed above, talk may produce certain neurotransmitters that ease emotional pain.

3. *Don't feel you must take the feeling of sadness away.* Even if you could, which you can't, you shouldn't. Sadness is part of life, and certainly part of childhood. It is important that your child develop the ability to feel sad. It is important to make friends with sadness.

A chum moves away, a pet dies, the ballgame gets rained out, you don't make the team. Childhood is full of sadness. As parents we sometimes forget how much sadness we experienced in our own childhoods and so we think sadness should not be a part of a normal childhood. Or we take it upon ourselves to protect our children from sadness precisely because we do remember how much of it we experienced as children and we want to spare our own children what we endured. However, it is a mistake to think that you, as a parent, can or should eliminate sadness from childhood. It is unavoidable. Indeed, it is desirable. Just as a child can practice and get good at other skills under his parents' guidance, so can he practice and get good at feeling sadness.

4. *Separate your child's sadness from your own.* As parents we often unwittingly project our own sadness (and other feelings as well) onto our children. If we were unpopular in school, for example, we may seize upon the first rejection our child receives and jump all over it. "Oh, you must feel just awful," we say to our child who in fact was dealing with it very well, at least until we intervened. "I know *just* how you must feel," we go on, pressing our point. "It's terrible when someone else treats you that way. I know. Well, why don't you sit down and tell me how bad you feel?" This is an exaggeration, perhaps, but it is not far from what happens all the time. With the best of intentions, we try to protect our children from what happened to *us,* without first checking to see if what is happening to our child is in fact the same as what we endured, or if it is just pushing a sensitive hot button we still carry.

5. *Give reassurance.* While it is not up to you as a parent to take away the feeling of sadness—indeed, you shouldn't—it is up to you to provide perspective. For some kids, one game getting rained out feels as if all games forever will be rained out. You might say, "Gee, it sure is too bad this game got rained out, but they'll probably be able to play tomorrow or Thursday." Reassurance helps a lot.

6. *Develop connections within the extended family.* Even if geography separates you so that you can't see each other in person, make sure your child is at least in frequent phone contact with extended family. These people used to supply the chicken soup that Mom and Dad can't always. Grandparents and aunts and uncles and cousins can be great antidepressants.

7. *Pay attention to the network of friends your child has.* Not only

are they instrumental in picking your child up when he or she is down, they can provide key information at critical times.

8. Always have a trusted person you can call, other than your spouse. When you and your spouse are at wit's end, or when your spouse isn't available or you just want a different point of view, it is very useful to have a trusted person only a phone call away. This may be a professional, such as a pediatrician or a child psychiatrist or social worker. However, professionals are often hard to get hold of in a hurry, and they usually charge a fee. Better to have a friend—another parent, a former teacher of yours, a neighbor, an "off-duty" professional with whom you're friendly—who is happy to hear from you whenever you call. This person may not have all the answers but he or she is a good listener, knows kids, and likes you.

9. Try to find islands of competence in the child's life. Priscilla Vail's books, *Smart Kids with School Problems* and *Emotion: The On/Off Switch for Learning,* deal beautifully with ways of building self-esteem in children. Robert Brooks, a psychologist at Harvard Medical School who has written widely about self-esteem in children, stresses the importance of finding and nurturing "islands of competence" as building blocks for self-esteem.

These islands become especially valuable when your child is sad or depressed. It is good to go sit on one of those islands with him or her, and see if the world doesn't look better from a vantage point of competence or excellence.

What does "go sit on one of those islands" mean? If baseball is the island of competence, go throw a ball with your child. If reading is the island, have him or her read to you. If model building is it, build a model; and if it's dancing, dance; and if it is nothing at all, go out for an ice cream and think one up. There's always something.

10. If your child is very sad for an extended period of time for reasons you can't understand, it is a good idea to get a professional consultation. This may begin with your pediatrician, who will in turn probably refer you to a psychologist or psychiatrist or social worker. An evaluation will include both parents, if possible, as well as reports from school and from your child's pediatrician. The evaluation may be completed in one session, or it may take a few. In severe cases, if your child is suicidal or posing a danger to others, short-term hospitalization may be recommended, but this is rare. Almost all childhood depression is treated on an outpatient basis, either with psychotherapy alone or with a combination of psychotherapy and medication.

The unusually serious or sad child may benefit greatly from having someone to talk to. This person may be a psychotherapist or a counselor, but he or she may also be an older friend or relative the child relates to well. The whole point is to *make contact*. Close relationships of any kind help protect against depression, and, if depression hits, they help soften the blow.

The lifetime rate of depression during childhood is 18 percent. That means there is a one-in-five chance that your child will be significantly depressed before he or she grows up. Suicide, obviously the worst outcome of depression, is the second leading cause of death in adolescence. Depression is often a silent predator. Children of all ages (and adults, too, especially men) may cover it up and try to hide it, even from themselves. That is why we must watch for it carefully.

Chapter 8

....

Afraid: When Children Are Anxious

Be not afraid of sudden fear.
—Proverbs 3:25

Anita Sparks came to see me to discuss her fear that her first-grader was not outgoing enough. "I was like that," she said, "and I hated it."

"He's unhappy?" I asked.

"I think so. I think he has bad thoughts."

"What do you mean by 'bad thoughts'?" I asked.

"I think he thinks bad things about himself, and then he gets shy and won't let himself join in because he is afraid he will be rejected."

"Has he told you this?" I asked.

"No. He just tells me he feels nervous."

"So why do you think he has these bad thoughts?" I asked.

"Because I used to think them, I guess," she replied.

"And you might be right; he might think the same kinds of thoughts you did," I answered. "But it may be that he was just born with a nervous disposition."

"So you mean when Willie tells me he is too nervous to join in with his friends at recess I should . . . I should what?" she asked.

"You should maybe know that that is simply the way he was born."

"But I don't want him to suffer socially the way I did," she said, becoming upset, reaching into her pocketbook for a tissue. "You have no idea how hard I've tried all along, ever since I gave birth to him, to make sure he would be confident and popular. I never mocked him or put him down. Never. Not the way my mother and father put me down. If he did something wrong or if he annoyed me, I would never say, 'I don't like you.' I would always say, 'I don't like what you did.' And I tried to make sure my husband did the same. I wanted more than anything in the world for Willie to like himself and be popular. I never cared how smart he was. I just wanted him to feel good about himself. You mean I've failed at that? It's all I wanted and I failed at that?"

"No, I'm not saying that at all, Ms. Sparks."

"Please, call me Anita," she interjected. "I'll feel more comfortable."

"Sure," I said, "and you feel free to call me Ned. All I'm saying, Anita, is it isn't all your doing how he feels around other kids. You've done all you can to make him comfortable socially, and what you've done has helped—believe me, it really has helped, but you do not have total control. Willie may have a genetic predisposition to being shy and inhibited, and you cannot undo that with all the love and encouragement in the world."

"You mean he was born that way?"

"Many children are," I said. "We need to help them adapt to the world given the temperament they have, as opposed to trying to change their temperament."

Our discussion resembled those I have with many parents. Parents come to see me wondering if their child is normal. They want to know if their child has a problem they should worry about. They ask me directly: "Is my child okay?" This is one of the most common questions I am asked.

I resumed my interview with Anita Sparks. "Does the idea of

being born with a certain kind of temperament make sense to you?" I asked.

"A little bit, I guess," she replied. "But it sounds too simple."

"It is just one part of who your child is," I responded. "There is a part that is genetic, and there is a part that is environmentally created. Of course, the biggest part is a combination of the two. My job is to help you figure out which is which."

"How do you do that?" Anita asked.

"It's like doing a puzzle. We look at your child together. We try to follow his development and get a sense of what is set in his character and what changes. I can tell you of the research we have that shows what qualities might be inherited. And then we decide together. But more important than deciding what is inborn and what isn't, is for you to realize that not everything about Willie is your fault. You just don't have that much control, Anita."

"Why do I feel as if I do, or at least as if I should?" she asked.

"Because that is the way most moms are," I answered. "Most moms feel totally connected to their children, especially when the children are young. They feel responsible for everything. But this is not realistic. And when I tell you there are factors you can't control, I'm not telling you that you can't control anything. I'm just saying you have limits."

Anita looked down at her hands folded in her lap. "I worry that he is a disappointment to his father," she said softly.

"Why?" I asked.

"His father is very confident," Anita replied. "It is something Zeke values, being social. He is a salesman, and he is super at what he does. He says he never met a deal he couldn't close, and I think he must be right. He loves Willie, I know that, and he plays with him and does all the things a father should, but I can just sense that he feels disappointed that Joey isn't more of a go-getter. You know, a salesman out on the playground. It makes me feel sad for Zeke and for Willie. I want them to have the best father-son bond."

"There's no reason they can't. But instead of trying to make Willie be like his dad, it is probably more realistic to try to help his dad love Willie as he is."

"Is that possible?" Anita asked. "Can you give that kind of total love to a child who is so different from you?"

"You tell me. Would you love Willie if he were very different from you?"

"Yes, I think so," Anita said. "I know so. I didn't have any preconceived ideas of what kind of child I wanted. But Zeke did. He got what he wanted in that he got a son, but I don't think this is exactly the kind of son he wanted."

"So you want me to make him be different?"

Anita paused and thought for a moment. Then she smiled. "Which 'him'?" she asked. "Willie or his dad?"

I smiled, too. "We need to help Willie's father accept Willie to the fullest. You can't dial up your children from some catalogue. You know that, but we need to talk to your husband. Willie's confidence will improve tremendously when he senses his dad loves him as he is."

"Yes, I'd like that. For both of them. It just breaks my heart when I see my husband turn away, or when I see Willie look so lost."

❊

Probably nothing breaks our parental hearts more than seeing a sad or frightened child. We have discussed sadness; now we turn to fear.

Do not be afraid to ask for professional help for your child if he or she has fears that won't go away or that seem unreasonable, out of proportion, and beyond the reach of your reassurance. Once it takes root, fear, more than any other emotion, has a way of hanging around, like alien weeds. A fear that starts in childhood can entangle your entire life. A fear that begins almost as a game, almost as something invented for entertainment, transforms itself before your very eyes into a painful preoccupation. I know many adults who are still bothered by childhood fears, and who wish someone had taken those fears more seriously when they were young.

Sometimes, persistent fear may have a biological basis, as in obsessive-compulsive disorder, or OCD. Originally called the "folie du doute" or "doubting madness" by Pierre Janet a century ago, OCD was described long before it received its current name. It is not uncommon for adults to become obsessed with guilt (a form of fear) and to feel compelled to perform some ritual to try to undo that guilt. Think of Lady Macbeth.

But in children, the problem is less grand. In juvenile OCD the child is plagued by intrusive, unpleasant thoughts that won't go away; these are called obsessions. They do not derive from some great crime the child has committed, but instead seem to come out of nowhere. For example, images and thoughts of both parents dying in a car crash may besiege a child, even though there is no particular risk of such an accident ever occurring. Or the child may fret obsessively over a certain friend, unable to get him or her out of his mind, even though there is no evident problem in the relationship. Besides having mental obsessions, the child often is beset by the need to carry out apparently pointless tasks, feeling that he must complete some specified behavior before he can go on with his day. These behaviors are called compulsions; the most common in children are washing, counting, ordering, checking, and hoarding. In fact, the best book on OCD, by Judith Rapaport, cites one of these ritualistic behaviors in its title: *The Boy Who Couldn't Stop Washing*. Children with OCD may be in the grip of their fears, obsessions, and compulsions in a way that reasonable reassurances can't begin to assuage.

True OCD is biologically based, but environmentally influenced. For example a rigid family may make OCD worse by increasing the child's fears and inhibitions. As childhood psychiatric disorders go, it is fairly common, occurring in about 1 percent of the population. Medical treatment, often including the use of some of the newer medications such as clomipramine (brand name Anafranil) or fluoxetine (brand name Prozac), can usually help.

A psychiatrist, psychologist, social worker, or other trained counselor may help treat other kinds of fearfulness in children, including phobias, anxieties, insecurities, or more subtle states of fear.

For example, most children experience separation anxiety. This is normal; indeed most adults experience it, too. However, for some children the anxiety becomes crippling, virtually tying them to their mothers and tying their mothers to them. In these extreme cases, professional interventions can make a big difference.

Shyness is a common kind of fearfulness in children. Other not uncommon examples of fear states in which professional consultation may be beneficial include refusing to go to school, intense phobias, intense fear of other children, or chronic, severe insecurity. Generalized anxiety, coming out of nowhere, is also a condition for which a parent would be well-advised to seek professional help.

Treatments for all of these conditions begin with a careful assessment. A parent cannot always know what is going on. Another person's opinion, particularly if that person is trained to pick up subtle cues and signs, can direct future treatment. Usually, in children, no lengthy intervention is needed; some knowledge, insight, and redirecting of the parent's efforts help diffuse the child's fear. Sometimes ongoing psychotherapy makes a big difference. A good psychotherapist can work magic with a child and a family. Once in a while medication helps. In any case, if your child is persistently afraid, it is a good idea to get an opinion from someone trained to deal with children's emotional problems.

Most states of fear in children, however, do not require professional assistance. Fear comes in many forms. We have all felt fear as a warning signal. "Watch out!" fear tells us when a snarling dog strays our way. "Be on guard," fear tells us as we go into a business meeting. We also know fear as the gentle anxiety we may feel at a cocktail party or a gathering of friends. Fear goes with us everywhere as our internal warning system. In this capacity it is our ally, and our lives depend on it. If it fails us, as it sometimes does when we drink too much, or if we ignore fear due to peer pressure, we can get into serious trouble or suffer physical harm, even death.

Our children need the right amount of fear. Fortunately, nature builds fear into them. Nature equips us all with a "fight-or-flight" system. This beautifully constructed system in our bodies prepares us to stand our ground and fight or to turn and take flight when we sense danger. At the first sign of danger our adrenal glands secrete adrenaline and our nervous systems set off a series of reactions all of which prepare us to fight or run away. The fight-or-flight reflex sets off changes in all parts of our bodies, from raising the level of glucose (our energy source) in the bloodstream, to increasing the heart rate, to redirecting blood to muscle where it will be most needed, to narrowing the eyes for greater visual acuity, to increasing the rate of breathing to bring in more oxygen. It is such a routine response that we forget how complex and important it is.

The fight-or-flight system is wired into us all from birth. It extends from the tips of our toes to the cores of our brains. Any part of our body can dial 911, so to speak, and set off a panic signal that will be sent to all other parts of our bodies in an instant. Nature has built the system so well that in dire physical emergencies the warning signal can take a shortcut, and go only as far as the spinal cord before a response signal is sent to the distressed region. Control central, the brain, is not informed of what is going on out in the body until after the reparative action has started. For example, if you accidentally touch the hot handle of a pot on your stove, a panic signal will flash to your spinal cord, where it will be processed immediately, without having to wait in line, and the proper response signal will be sent back to your hand. Your hand will pull back before your brain even registers what is going on. This is called a simple reflex arc, and it saves us in all kinds of ways every day. When our brain gets involved, it may add some messages, too—such as an angry expletive, or instructions sent to Memory not to go near that handle again, or other instructions sent to Merchandising to buy a potholder, or ideas sent to Implementation to run cold water over the burn.

The reflex arc, and what the brain learns each time the reflex arc flips into action, are good examples of how our fear system can serve us well.

Sometimes, however, our fear system needs some fine-tuning. Problems in the fear system of children lead to a variety of problems in everyday life. A terrifying experience early in a child's life may inoculate him to live in fear of a recurrence; we see this in phobias and in post-traumatic stress disorder. A child who suffers extreme fear frequently, such as a child who endures abuse, may permanently ratchet up his fear system to red alert and suffer a lifetime of apprehension. Furthermore, fear may develop even without a terrifying experience. But the right amount of fear is protective. Too much or too little can hurt.

Sometimes our reflex arcs trigger too easily. A good example of this is the soldier who comes home from Vietnam and starts rabbit-punching anyone who taps him on the shoulder from behind.

And sometimes the fear generator up at control central works too hard. Some of us are too jumpy for our own good. We fear everything, even before we know whether we need to. Some children become afraid of so many things that they never try anything new, and they miss out on activities they would have enjoyed. Sometimes a child's fear system is set too high even from birth; this child is always a little afraid.

Most fears in children do not rise to the level of a psychiatric diagnosis. However, they still can be extremely painful. If you spend your childhood in fear, you spend your childhood in pain. Fear hurts. It is supposed to hurt. Nature intended fear to hurt so it would function as a good warning signal. The pain of fear gets your attention so you can get out of the way of danger. However, nature did not intend that fear should last long. When fear lasts long, this is harmful.

Sometimes you grow up in fear because you are mistreated. If your parent or a relative or some other person abuses you by hitting you or bullying you or sexually assaulting you or mentally tormenting you, you can develop a sphere of fear that surrounds you everywhere you go. It cripples you. The pain may last a lifetime. Abuse may be the worst of all causes of childhood fears. Judith Herman has written an excellent book on this topic, entitled *Trauma and Recovery*.

After experiencing some trauma, such as a beating or a sexual assault, or witnessing a traumatic event, such as a violent crime or a parent being assaulted, a child (or adult) may develop a reaction that can last a long time. This condition is called post-traumatic stress disorder, or PTSD. In PTSD the child develops three kinds of symptoms. First, she reexperiences the original trauma in some way. She may be unable to put it out of her mind, finding images of the event intruding into her thoughts all the time. She may dream about it in horrifying nightmares. She may actually feel as if the trauma is recurring at some point in her everyday life, even though it is not. This is highly upsetting to child and parent alike, as the cause of the distress is invisible, inside the child's memory. She may panic at the sight of certain objects, cues associated with the trauma, and then feel as if she's experiencing the event all over again.

These symptoms lead to the second group of symptoms, which relate to the avoidance of anything that even vaguely suggests the initial trauma. The child may cease to be interested in activities she once loved, if they in any way remind her of what she endured. She may turn away from certain adults or peers who somehow remind her of the trauma. She may forget big chunks of her past in an effort to avoid having to think ever again about what happened. She may even avoid certain feelings, trying instead to keep a cool air, never wanting to feel very excited, happy, angry, or sad; *any* intensity of emotion calls up the extreme fear she felt at the time of the trauma.

Such avoidance leads to the third group of symptoms associated with post-traumatic stress disorder, the symptoms of increased physical arousal and vigilance. Children with PTSD are wired, on the lookout for any sign of danger, always on red alert. They sleep poorly, have trouble concentrating, startle easily, have a short anger fuse, and never really relax. Tension and anxiety are their constant companions.

This is a terribly painful way to live. People suffering from PTSD need help. First of all, they need safety. Even though the child never *feels* safe, adults need to make sure that the environment is as safe as possible. Second, the child needs a chance to talk about what happened, slowly, at her own pace, with no pressure to "get it all out" at once. Such catharsis can make matters worse. Instead, the child needs a gradual reequilibration, a chance to reset her fear system gradually back down to normal limits. This takes time, patience, and a reassuring therapist, parent, or other concerned person.

In addition to talking her way back to a more normal state, the child may get help from certain medications, such as the serotonin reuptake inhibitors like Prozac or Zoloft. Serotonin is one of many chemicals in the brain called neurotransmitters, so called because they transmit signals from one nerve cell to the next. Most of the medications used to treat emotional or learning problems appear to work by changing the amounts of various neurotransmitters in the brain. The serotonin reuptake inhibitors increase the amount of serotonin available in the brain by blocking its *reuptake* into the nerve cell. Exactly what serotonin does in the brain is another question, one that we cannot answer definitively. But we do know that by increasing its availability in the brain through medications such as Prozac or Zoloft, we are able to improve certain kinds of emotional distress such as depression, rumination, and the kind of anxious worry that often accompanies PTSD. These medications do not undo the trauma, of course, but they can help the child to deal with it.

(Before you seek treatment for PTSD, and certainly before you start accusing people of having committed abuse, think twice. Some people claim to have been abused who have not, and some therapists get carried away with "detecting" in a patient's story "definite evidence of abuse." Just as tragic as the child who is abused is the parent, teacher, or other adult who is falsely accused of such abuse. The damage done by an accusation like that can last a lifetime, too.)

Short of abuse and neglect, children suffer smaller traumas, little incidents that can set a pattern of worry for a long, long time.

I recently saw Addie, a child of eight who was so nervous about everything that she didn't want to go to school. Addie came from a large family; she was the fifth of seven children. Her mother told me she just didn't have time to coax Addie out of her fears every morning since she had six other children to deal with; could I help?

I asked Addie why she didn't want to go to school. She told me she didn't know. Children commonly give this answer when asked why they don't want to do something. Addie and I talked some more. We made friends with each other. Then she told me she was afraid of school. I asked her why. She told me she was afraid of the bomb. I asked her what bomb. She started to cry. "He told me not to say anything or the bomb would go off," she said between sobs.

It turned out some man had approached Addie on the playground and told her there was a bomb in the school and that he would set it off if she ever told anyone about him. That was all. She never saw him again. We told the police about it, but they never found the man.

Unfortunately, there are some strange people in the world who like to frighten children. And children are gullible and easy to scare. Addie gradually became less afraid as we talked. Later that week, we went to school together and spoke to the school principal (whom I had contacted before), who also reassured Addie and, with one of the custodians, gave us a tour of the hidden parts of the school. Pragmatic reassurance helps dissipate fear.

Sometimes, however, fear strikes without provocation. Sometimes a child is born fearful. Some parents or teachers induce fear without meaning to. In other words, no one is abusing the child in any way, and yet, day by day, the child grows more and more fearful. No one is doing anything they should not be doing to the child, and still the child feels nervous and worried in his world. Why should this be?

If it is not due to an abusive or fearsome environment, the child's fearful state may be coming from within. In extreme cases, these children may warrant a psychiatric diagnosis, such as a phobia (which means fear of or dislike of a particular place, thing, or being) or a generalized anxiety disorder. However, most children's fear do not reach that level of intensity. Instead children appear on a continuum, from the fearless, bold child at one end, to the phobic, intensely fearful child at the other.

Some children are biologically primed to be skittish. The early warning system of these children is set too delicately. They get scared too easily. How easily is "too easily"? When fear becomes an unnecessary impediment to the enjoyment of everyday life then we can say the child's fear system is set to go off too easily.

I once treated a high school junior who felt fear in almost all social situations. She was shy, but she forced herself to join in. She never refused an invitation, she joined numerous clubs and organizations, she was accepted in many groups, and she was very well-liked. No one would have described her as shy or retiring. Indeed, her mother told me, "Linda is much more of a social being than I ever was."

That was because Linda deliberately set out to be. Linda saw in her mother's life an example she wanted to avoid. She loved her mother, but saw her as socially crippled by her fear of people. "We're so isolated," Linda told me. "My mother never has people over, and she rarely goes out herself. Dad is the same way, but he has work to keep him busy. And Mom has her books. But I never want to be like that. It just wouldn't be enough for me. She must be so lonely.''

"Does she ever talk to you about it?'' I asked.

"Oh, no, Mom never complains. She wouldn't. It's not like her. She reads instead. I think she lives her life through the books she reads.''

"And you worry you might be like her?'' I asked.

"I fear it,'' she said. It was an odd turn of phrase—"I fear it" —the turn of phrase a person might use when a thought has been spoken internally many times. I could almost hear Linda saying to herself, "I fear it, I fear it, I fear it. . . .''

"But you're not like her at all,'' I protested.

"That's because I work hard not to be,'' Linda said with determination. "For as long as I can remember I have not allowed myself to sit home.''

"It has been an effort?'' I asked.

"Yes,'' Linda replied. "Being friendly and outgoing does not come naturally to me. I'm a lot more afraid of people than anyone would ever guess.''

"Do you know why?'' I asked.

"No, I don't,'' Linda answered. She paused. "I really have no idea. I have not been mistreated or anything like that. My mom and dad love me, and they love each other. They certainly make every effort to help me do the things I want to do, and they offer to have my friends in. I just usually say no because I know they wouldn't enjoy it, my friends or my mom and dad. It's like you've gotta know them, my mom and dad, to appreciate them, and my friends wouldn't understand them. I don't mean they're weird or anything, I just feel like there's this distance I'd rather keep between my friends and my parents. The thing is, I would rather keep that distance between me and my friends, too, and I would, if I didn't try not to. Is this making any sense to you?''

"Yes, Linda, it is. You are very understanding of your parents.''

"Well, good," Linda said, "but why is all this so much work for me?"

"I think you did inherit something from your mom and dad, a temperamental style. It is a style that you understand, and that you feel in yourself, but you want to oppose it in your own life. It is as if you inherited red hair and decided you wanted it blond. You'd have to dye it, and keep an eye on it all the time."

"Yes, that's what I do. I keep an eye on it all the time. But why do I have to? Why is my first feeling always to be afraid?"

"I guess that's just the way you are," I answered. "Did it make school very hard?"

"Much harder than anyone knew. Just walking down the corridors was difficult. All those people. All that eye contact. That's hard for someone like me. Being in class. Having to answer when someone calls on me. Often, just to get the spotlight off me, I'd say, 'I don't know,' when a teacher asked me a question, even though I did know. It made me feel panicky. I felt much safer left in my own thoughts. The cafeteria was miserable, too. Someone always wanted to eat with me. I shouldn't complain, because some girls who were really unpopular would have loved to have people want to eat with them. Isn't life unfair? I, who really preferred to eat alone, always had people wanting to sit with me, but the others didn't. Each day was a struggle, just to be with all those people. People I liked, but I was just afraid of. For no reason. Wow. Pretty weird, huh?"

"No," I said. "There's lots of people who feel like you do."

"But I have always thought it meant we were all dysfunctional, or something. Whatever that word means. 'Screwed up,' that's the phrase I used in my mind. I always thought I was screwed up. Why else did my family stay in when everyone else was out playing?"

"Maybe your mom and dad are just shy," I said.

"But can it be that simple? Aren't they hiding something deeper and darker?"

"You tell me."

"No. I don't think so. They just like to keep to themselves. Actually, I respect my mom and dad more than almost any parents I know. They taught me good things and they taught me to value people, even though they didn't have people in."

"Being shy is a trait some people are just born with," I said. "It can be painful, because life does tend to favor the outgoing types, but it isn't screwed up or bad to be shy."

"I just don't want to be like that," Linda said.

"So you've worked hard not to be. And you've been able to do it, to overcome it, but it's been like changing red hair: You've had to watch it all the time."

"Can you do that? I mean, I know you can change red hair, but can you change your basic nature that you've inherited? Isn't that like changing your genes?"

"You can't change your genes," I said, "but you can change what you do with them. In other words, what you inherit isn't written in stone. You can change almost every human trait to some extent if you want to. We have dye for hair, lenses for eyes, elevator shoes for being short, curlers and straighteners, plastic surgery, and so forth. For inner qualities we have the power of the will. You can decide what you want to be like, and you can override your genetic message, to some extent. Some conditions are much harder to change than others. If you have attention deficit disorder, for example, will alone can help but it can't take away your ADD. If you're prone to depression, will can help, but it can't stave off the black periods completely. If you inherit shyness, as it seems you have, you can force yourself to be more outgoing, but you cannot change the basic feelings of fear that accompany that effort. Over time it becomes second nature, almost reflex, to accept any invitation, but that doesn't mean you won't feel uneasy when you get to the party."

"It doesn't seem fair," Linda said.

It didn't seem fair to Linda, and it didn't seem fair to Jerome

Kagan, the man who pioneered the research on the biological basis of shyness. Reflecting on his research findings that shyness was often innate and not always under the individual's control, Kagan wrote:

It is difficult for an aging, politically liberal social scientist, trained to believe in the extraordinary power of the social environment, to take unreserved satisfaction from the implications of these last fifteen years of research. I confess to an occasional sadness over the recognition that some healthy, attractive infants born to affectionate, economically secure families begin life with a physiology that will make it a bit difficult for them to be as relaxed, spontaneous, and capable of hearty laughter as they would like. Some of these children will have to fight a natural urge to be dour and to worry about tomorrow's tasks. Many will be successful in coping with their dysphoria [troubled mood], but others, like Sylvia Plath, will not. That seems unfair. More troubling is the possibility that, for a very small group of children, neither family love nor personal effort will be able to tame every bout of acute, intense anxiety. I used to hold, with fervor, the nineteenth-century assumption that will was omnipotent; everyone should be able to suppress actions that disrupt the community or hurt others, and everyone should be able—of course, with effort—to gain control over tense, worried moods. . . . I wish that will were stronger.

There is, however, one benevolent consequence of my new perspective. I have become more forgiving of the few friends and family members who see danger too easily, rise to anger too quickly, or sink to despair too often. I no longer blame them privately and have become more accepting and less critical of their moods and idiosyncrasies. Obviously, this has helped my relationships with them, for I no longer demand, with a hint of moral arrogance, that they simply gain control of themselves.

While the facts biology is giving us may not seem fair, they do help us, as Kagan states, to forgive ourselves and others. In Linda's terms, her family isn't necessarily dysfunctional or screwed up; if it's shy, it's simply shy. That trait may make her life less comfortable, but it is not morally negative; it does not constitute a personal failing.

Indeed, many of the great benefactors of mankind have been shy people—scientists, artists, inventors, even actors. Actors, whom one might think of as being naturally gregarious, often are shy and introverted by nature. Henry Fonda described himself as painfully shy. He said he was drawn to acting because he could relax onstage: Someone else had written what he should say. The stage was one place where he didn't have to bear the responsibility of coming up with his own lines.

Psychiatrists have known for a long time that talking about feelings helps. What is remarkable is how difficult it is for many people to do so. Particularly for shy people, it takes courage to come out of hiding. Sometimes a little prodding helps.

Shy people are not mentally ill; far from it. But they are uptight, nervous, skittish—call it what you will. Modern research is telling us that many of these people are the way they are not because anything terrible has happened to them, but because their genes tightened the strings on their nervous systems.

They are inhibited on a physiological basis. They have an acutely sensitive sympathetic nervous system, the part of the nervous system that responds to perceived danger or fear by speeding up the heart, widening the eyes, increasing the rate of breathing, raising the blood pressure, and pumping out adrenaline. Kagan's studies have even shown that some of these people can be identified by monitoring their heart rate while they are still in their mother's womb! Those who have a fetal heart rate averaging over 140 beats per minute several weeks before birth are more likely to become inhibited children, while those who average less than 120 beats per minute are more likely to become the easygoing, relaxed children.

The best one can do is identify this as a temperamental style and not compound the problem by insinuating the existence of other problems or conflicts. If you are shy, it can help you a lot to leave it at that: You are shy.

Fear states, for example, can be especially crippling. Many children suffer with them as Linda did. Many adults never get over a chronic sense of insecurity and fear. They feel it when they enter a store and want to find a salesperson. They feel it when they enter their child's classroom; the other children intimidate them a little bit. They worry about speaking to the teacher—will they be bothering her? They feel fear when they meet people at parties or at business meetings. They even feel fear when they say hello to the man taking their money at the toll booth. There is an old joke about such insecurity: "I'm so insecure, when the football team goes into a huddle I think they are talking about me."

In extreme forms this kind of fear needs treatment by a professional. If shyness is so severe as to be crippling, various kinds of psychotherapy and sometimes medication (for example, Prozac) can help. But in milder forms, it rarely is treated. The problem is that many children—and adults—continue to feel the fear. They may be trained into feeling ashamed of it, so they do not reveal it to anyone, but this only intensifies the feeling inside and deprives them of the natural balm of reassurance.

Fear states in everyday life, so common for us all, can upset a child's development just as much as depression or rage can. A child who is always a little afraid will not try new things. It is essential to be willing to fail or to look stupid in order to learn new skills. We all look stupid the first time we try something new. If we are not confident enough to risk it, then we begin to hold back. We stop developing our repertoire of new skills, or we stop making new friends, or we stop going to new places. We just hang with the same people in the same place and do the same thing. For an adult this is bad enough, but for a child it is unacceptable.

You can identify fearfulness in your child in a number of different ways. If your child has great trouble with separation, with saying good-bye as you send her off to school or staying overnight at a friend's house, this may indicate what we call a separation anxiety disorder. All children feel some separation anxiety, but some kids feel it much more intensely, and at an older age than most.

Some children who are bothered by fear they can't or won't talk about complain of physical ailments instead: "My stomach hurts," or "I have an ache in my foot that hurts really bad," or "I hurt everywhere." Sometimes underlying fear comes out in self-denigrating remarks, like "I'm dumb" or "I'm ugly."

Some practical ways of dealing with fear in children are outlined in the following tips. But extreme and intense fear warrants professional attention. These "at-home" tips are aimed at the child whose problem is not extreme. *Consider professional help if your child's fear persists and interferes with everyday life.*

TEN TIPS ON THE MANAGEMENT OF FEAR AND ANXIETY IN CHILDREN

1. Give plenty of reassurance. This is the great antidote to fear, and giving it is a wonderful act of devotion parents perform for their children. The patient, tactful offering of ongoing reassurance is one of the three or four acts most defining of parental love.

I can still remember my mother sitting on the side of my bed when I was a little boy and telling me in her soft, gentle voice, "The dark is our friend. You don't need to be afraid, because the dark is our friend." Years later whenever I was out in the dark at night alone, and a slight shudder of fear came over me, I would hear my mother's words—"The dark is our friend"—and I would feel all right.

She gave me other reassuring words, and they, too, have stayed with me. "God is everywhere," she would say when I wondered if God would know where I was if I got lost. "Never give up," she told me, especially when she took me to Red Sox games. And above all, she said over and over again, "I'm always here for you, and no matter what happens, I'll always be here, and I'll always love you." And she always did. If anything instilled in me a basic faith in God and the goodness of life, it was my mother's love; and if anything dispelled my fears day in and day out, it was her words of reassurance.

Reassure your children. You plant seeds of adult faith and courage by the tender, simple reassurances you give your children now. The world is a scary place. Your children need to know it can be safe.

2. *Find the cause of the fear and remove it or help your child get used to it.* Obviously, this is the most definitive intervention, if you can do it. If your child is terrified of the spider walking toward him, you might brush the spider aside, or you might persuade your child that it is just a daddy longlegs and can't hurt anyone. Parents are always having to decide which to choose of the two options, to get rid of the cause of the fear or get used to it. Some causes of fear, like death, can't be avoided. The job is to keep the fear in perspective. Some causes you have to get used to, like school, although you can change schools if the fear is caused or worsened by a terrible match between child and school. And some things you can let alone at first but get used to over time, like swimming.

3. *Teach your child to make friends with fear. Think of fear as an important signal.* Tell your six-year-old, "If you feel afraid, that's okay. Ask a grown-up for help. Never be afraid to say you're afraid." Although we do not usually like the feeling of fear—except perhaps on a roller coaster or at a scary movie—it is a valuable ally nevertheless. Teach your child to listen to his fears and never to ignore them altogether. Like pain, fear is one of our body's ways of telling us we may be in danger. Before we choose to overrule that signal, we need to analyze the basis for it. If a child can look at fear in this way, he can begin to deal with it effectively. He can also sidestep the amplification set off by fearing fear. Paradoxically, fearing fear only increases the likelihood

of feeling fear. Like anger and sadness, fear is a friend, an ally, a messenger, a signal.

4. *Make sure your child is never afraid to ask for help.* This is a good talent to develop young. I know many adults who are too scared to ask for reassurance. They can't ask their boss if they're doing a good job; they can't ask their spouse if they are being a good mate; they can't ask their friends if they are being a good friend; and they can't ask anyone to tell them everything is okay when they fear everything isn't.

The giving and getting of reassurance is a skill that can be taught and can be learned, particularly if you start young. Chronic, lifelong insecurity is a terribly painful state. While reassurance can't prevent it totally, it can help assuage it considerably.

5. *Never make fun of the child who is afraid.* We are tempted sometimes to make fun of someone else's fear. We have all done it. "Scaredy-cat, scaredy-cat!" is a chant from the childhoods of us all. To admit to being afraid as a child is to invite taunting from peers. This is because the peer group itself is struggling not to feel afraid, of anything and everything. One frightened member threatens to activate fear in them all, and think of the mess that would make! It is therefore up to grown-ups to help these fearful children. Some parents, particularly dads, feel the urge to scoff at children, particularly sons, who express fear or timidity. An excellent example of a father like this can be found in Pat Conroy's novel *The Great Santini* and millions of other examples can be found in backyards everywhere. We dads tend to expect our sons to be fearless. We feel ashamed of them when they express fear. We feel we need to toughen them up to prepare them for the world out there.

We need to pause before we carry this attitude too far. It is true that a father should model some measure of courage for his sons and daughters, but we should all learn to let children be vulnerable. Teach your child there is no shame in fear—and teach yourself, as well.

6. *Encourage mastery. Build the "can do" reflex.* While it is im-

portant never to mock fear, it is also important to encourage your child to gain mastery over whatever is feared. Achievement matters. You want to build into the child an emotional "I can get good at this" *reflex,* to come into play the instant he or she encounters frustration or difficulty. Where does such confidence come from? It comes from childhood. It starts in our earliest experiences, but it can be stunted there, too. You want positivity to become reflexive; you want the feeling of "can do" to go with your child everywhere and always.

The child needs to feel in his or her bones that life is a state of the possible, not the impossible. As a parent or a teacher you may not be able to eradicate poverty or other external roadblocks, but you can work hard to overcome fear, the great internal roadblock.

You can help a child develop an attitude that's worth a million bucks. That attitude can last a lifetime. "You can do it, you can do it, you can do it!" Say it a hundred times a day. Never stop saying it. Never stop telling your child that there is no obstacle that can't be overcome, someday. Confidence is knowing that you can, even when it seems you can't. The only way to know you can is by achieving, early on in life, some successes that you work hard for. And the best way to get in the habit of working hard is for hard work to be associated with mastery and fun.

7. *Gain skill at the task causing your fear.* Do you remember being afraid to jump off the high-diving board? When I was a boy in Charleston, South Carolina, there was a public swimming pool whose high-diving board seemed to me as if it were a mile above the water. I must have spent a whole summer climbing up to the top of that board and looking down, afraid to jump, until, at last, some feather of fate pushed me off. I jumped! It felt as if I were falling straight from childhood into adulthood in the few seconds it took me to hit the water, sink, and come up for air. Was I proud! I had jumped and survived and even enjoyed the fall. I did it again. I did it again and again. I did it a hundred times more that

summer, I'm sure. I was now a master of the high-dive jump. Mastery dispels fear.

8. *Remember that knowledge can often dispel fear.* Many childhood fears arise due to faulty information. Children have an incredible communications grapevine that is rife with wrong information. Someone told me when I was six that the dentist was going to pull out all my teeth with a rusty jackknife. My mother couldn't understand why I resisted so vehemently going to the dentist that summer. Though I finally broke down and told her, it was all I could do to summon the courage to believe what she, instead of my misinformant, told me.

A friend of mine has a little boy, whom he took to their small local airport to put Grandma on a plane back home. As the plane took off, the boy started to cry. "What's the matter?" his father asked.

"I'm scared for Grandma," the little boy said, sobbing.

"Don't worry," his dad said, "the pilot knows how to fly the plane really well."

"But, Daddy," the little boy protested, sobbing even harder, "the plane keeps getting smaller!" The little boy hadn't seen many planes take off, and wasn't cognitively mature enough to realize that airplanes only appear to get smaller as they get farther away. Grandma wasn't really shrinking.

Many childhood fears are based on simple misinformation. The domain of sexuality is famous for this, but misinformation abounds in all domains of children's lives.

9. *Bear in mind that your child may be right. He or she may know something you don't.* Sometimes our children are afraid because they should be. Sometimes they know of things that are going on that we don't know about. Sometimes they are afraid to tell us, or they don't have the words to tell us, and sometimes we don't listen or believe them when they do tell us.

If your child tells you there's a bear in the cellar, don't automatically assume he's wrong!

10. Eat well, sleep well, and get plenty of exercise. All these combat fear. As I have stressed throughout this book, exercise is one of the best tonics we have for the mind. It is especially good at draining off anxiety and helping one to master fear states. A well-exercised child is less likely to feel overly sensitive or anxious than a sedentary child.

Chapter 9

....

Four Less Common but Important Conditions

The following four conditions are all examples of biologically based problems children may have.

1. Pervasive developmental disorder
2. Trichotillomania
3. Tourette syndrome
4. Fetal alcohol syndrome

The symptoms of these conditions were at one time ascribed to poor parenting, but can now be more fully explained by considering the genetic and neurological views.

PERVASIVE DEVELOPMENTAL DISORDER: WHEN YOUR CHILD IS REMOTE

When Peter was born, his parents knew only that they loved him. He was their first child, and they greeted him with all the new hope and fresh expectations most first-time parents feel.

Lydia and Hank Pickens loved Petey with all their hearts, and they could imagine only bright days ahead.

But what happened to Petey, and to Lydia and Hank, happens to many parents in different ways. Petey wasn't normal. What is "normal"? We don't know, really, but we can usually say when a child isn't. Petey wasn't.

More specifically, he never seemed to get very close to anyone. From the moment he was born, Lydia never felt the warm bond with him she had hoped for. As the months progressed and Petey did not change, she concluded she was doing something wrong. No matter what she did, however, he did not respond like other babies. He was not visibly different; he did not stand out as being abnormal. But Lydia, especially, sensed a distance that bothered her.

For the first two years Lydia and Hank kept the problem to themselves, only vaguely alluding to it with their pediatrician. They thought Petey would grow warmer as time passed. There was no reason not to think this. They read many books on child development, and they tried to stimulate Petey's imagination as much as they could. His room was filled with mobiles and toys and stuffed animals and colors and designs of every sort. He heard music all the time. Lydia held him a great deal, and so did Hank. Both parents followed every bit of advice they could find in the books. But "the problem," as they called it, remained.

They had read about autism, and what they read scared them, but autism seemed much more extreme than what was going on in Petey. The autistic children they read about rocked and banged their heads and never spoke. But this description didn't fit Petey. He spoke. He didn't rock awfully much, and he didn't bang his head. He was just different, much less socially engaging than other toddlers. His parents kept waiting for him to "blossom," but he didn't. He didn't cuddle very much, he didn't smile excitedly when he was happy or rush into his parents' arms when they held their arms out, and he kept to himself much more than other children his age. He was cold, if one can call a toddler cold, and at an age when such coldness deeply disappointed his parents.

Finally, when Petey was three, Lydia and Hank asked the pediatrician if their son was autistic. The pediatrician looked surprised and said, no, but he wondered why the question had come up at all.

When Lydia and Hank described what Petey was like at home, the pediatrician agreed that there might be something wrong, but he was sure it wasn't autism. Petey communicated with others. The pediatrician advised them to watch and wait, and maybe at some point get a neuropsychological evaluation. What was that? Petey's parents asked. He explained that a neuropsychologist specialized in evaluating psychological conditions that had a neurological component, such as autism and learning disabilities. But he predicted that in all likelihood Petey's condition would improve on its own.

However, it didn't. By nursery school Petey was still different from other children. If anything, instead of getting better, his problem was getting worse. He was removed and reserved. He would call out unpredictably, sometimes hitting as he did so. He was emotionally cut off and hard to reach. He seemed smart enough, but he definitely lacked empathy.

What was going on? Lydia and Hank were now quite convinced that they had messed Petey up. They alternately blamed each other and blamed themselves. Lydia accused Hank of not being around enough. Hank accused Lydia of not being warm enough. These accusations hurt. The couple suffered, not knowing what was wrong, lost in guilt and recrimination.

Then Lydia got pregnant again. When Molly, their second child, was born, the parents' hopes focused on her. Petey was able to slide along, attracting less notice.

However, by the time he was in second grade the school had started calling home about his social problems. His first-grade teacher had basically ignored the issue, still going on the pediatrician's reasonable expectation that matters would improve. But:

"He's just not right," his second-grade homeroom teacher told Lydia one fateful day over the telephone. "I don't know how to put it, but I've been teaching second grade for twelve years, and he's just not right."

Something in Lydia snapped, as if a string that had been pulled tighter and tighter ever since Petey was born finally broke. She became enraged. "How dare you say that about my son?" she screeched into the phone. "What degree do you have? Are you a doctor? I think what you have said is totally unprofessional, and I intend to take it up with the principal."

"I'm sorry if I upset you, Mrs. Pickens," the teacher said, "but I was only trying to let you know what is going on."

"Well, we'll just see about that," Lydia spat out. And she hung up.

The next day there was a meeting in the office of the head of the school, Don Armstrong. Lydia and Hank sat on one side of his desk, and Amy Rosenthal, the second-grade teacher, sat on the other, along with me, the school's psychological consultant.

These meetings are never easy, but Don Armstrong is a master at directing them toward a good outcome. Lydia led off with a prepared statement, which she read. It documented her telephone conversation with Amy, quoting the exact words Amy had used, and it presented Lydia's opinion, Hank's opinion, and their lawyer's opinion that these words were outrageous. She wanted disciplinary action taken against Amy immediately, or, she said, she and Hank were going to find another school for Petey and consider legal action against this one. Since Petey's was a private school, a transfer was a viable option, as, of course, was suing.

Don Armstrong listened. After Lydia finished, he stroked his chin and asked her if she had any other concerns. "Not right now," she said. "I just want you to take care of this matter so it will not happen to any other parent."

"It was an upsetting phone call to receive," Don said, looking with concern at Lydia.

"Of course it was," she said briskly. "But what I want to know is, what are you going to do about it?"

"I don't know," Don said. "What do you think I should do?"

"That really is not up to me," Lydia said, "but if you want to know, I'll tell you. I think you should ask Ms. Rosenthal to write me and my husband a letter of apology; then I think you should put a note in her file that she has been warned against diagnosing children over the telephone. And I think you should put her on some kind of probation."

Don sighed. "And you, Hank, you agree?" he asked. Hank, who had been noticeably silent, nodded ever so slightly. "That's a yes?" Don asked.

"Yes," Hank said softly.

Don remained silent for what seemed like an awfully long time. Then he looked at Lydia. "You know, I know this hurts a lot. I know it, I really do. But you've got the wrong culprit here, honestly. You and your lawyer are getting sidetracked from the real issue, which is Petey, don't you think?"

"I thought you might say that, and I resent it," Lydia snapped back. "I only came here as a courtesy to you, since you have been good to us until now, but if you'd prefer to take care of this in court I want you to know I am quite prepared to do so," Lydia said, gathering herself up.

"In *court?*" Don replied, as if in disbelief.

"Yes. In court. You have a teacher who has made a diagnosis without having a license and has slandered my son. I do not take kindly to that, nor, I should think, would you."

"Lydia, please, tell me what is the diagnosis that was made?" Don asked, innocently.

"She said my son is not right," Lydia answered, staring at Amy.

Don paused again. He put his palms together like a church steeple and held them up against his mouth and nose. We all waited. Finally, he asked no one in particular, "Well, *is* he?"

"No, he is not," Hank Pickens spoke up. Lydia shot a look at him. "Honey, let's stop this charade," Hank said to her. "Please, let's stop this now. This isn't our way. You know better than I do that Petey isn't right, and he hasn't been since he was born. Please, honey, these people want to help us. You know that. This whole thing with bringing that lawyer in is for the birds—you know that, and I know that. We're just not that kind of people, are we?"

Lydia heaved an enormous sigh, the kind of sigh that can turn a lifetime around. Slowly, she started to cry. If she hadn't—if she'd dug in instead—a process might have been set in motion that I've seen at many schools, public and private, where a struggle takes over like a disease. The struggle takes on a life of its own. It can last a year, two years, even ten years. I have seen families do battle with schools for their child's entire youth, rather than look at their child's problem. I have also seen schools do battle with families rather than look at the school's problems, and in the process do great disservice to many children.

Lydia was able to break down and cry. She was able to give in. Amy and Don and Hank and I sat with her and we talked for an hour or so about Petey. We talked honestly and openly, and by the end of the meeting Lydia and Hank gave each of us a hug, saying it was the best they had felt since Petey was born. At last, people understood.

But understood what? What was Petey's problem? There are more than a few Peteys out there—children who are socially "off," not able to give affection or receive it nearly as easily as their peers. They are called "weird," or "strange," or "out of it," or they are called "a nerd," or they are just left alone, as if they were of a different makeup, not a member of the pack. Often these children do not seem to mind. They go off into their own worlds. They are able to function well enough to get by socially, but they take no great pleasure in relationships, nor do they give much. One wonders what is going on inside them, but most attempts to find out result in rebuffs or unsatisfying replies. These children are not "sick" enough to be called schizophrenic or autistic, but something is definitely wrong. Their personalities are like a piece of music that keeps on playing, is somehow recognizable, but has no melody.

That day in Don Armstrong's office, Lydia and Hank were able to get off their chests what they had been storing up for years: their feeling that they were to blame for a problem they could not understand except by saying that they had "screwed up."

But they hadn't. Like so many parents in their situation, they felt they had done wrong because wrongdoing was the only explanation they could think of. Most parents and teachers are not aware that there is a group of children who are simply born with a relative lack of emotional availability or reciprocal social skills.

In extreme cases, these children stand out and receive a diagnosis of autism or childhood schizophrenia.* But autism and childhood schizophrenia are both extremely rare. Autism occurs at a rate of about two children in ten thousand, and childhood schizophrenia is even rarer. Much more common is the situation Lydia and Hank Pickens had to deal with: having a child who was remote, not as warm and engaging as he should be.

As a parent I know the importance of the circuit of emotion that resonates between my children and me. The "vibes" between us mean so much; we parents live for them.

But what if the vibes are missing, or only faint? How do you begin to deal with the fact that your child isn't falling in love with you in the same way that you want to fall in love with your child? How do you begin to deal with the disappointment and even hostility you start to feel—emotions that seem so alien to what you had expected parental feelings to be? How

---

* "Childhood schizophrenia" and "autism" used to be used interchangeably. However, now they are not. While the two conditions are both severely disabling and share the symptom of emotional withdrawal and at times bizarre behavior, schizophrenia includes active hallucinations and delusions. In addition, the child who develops schizophrenia may have eight to ten years of normal development, while by definition, the onset of the symptoms of autism is before age three.

can you not look for someone to blame, and who is a more logical target than your spouse? And how can you not blame yourself?

One way to begin to work yourself out of this fix is to know what is going on biologically. In most cases, the child is less responsive because that is how he was born, not because either parent did wrong.

No one had done wrong with Petey. I met with him, and I spoke with Amy Rosenthal and other teachers, and I began to meet with Lydia and Hank to talk in more detail about the past. It turned out that Hank's father had many mannerisms that resembled Petey's, and that he was often reclusive. Hank passed on stories his grandmother used to tell, of what a strange child Hank's father was. The more Hank told us, the more the genetic piece of the puzzle began to seem to fit. I say "seem to" because you seldom know for certain what is causing what in the brain.

But it did seem that whatever was up with Hank's dad we were seeing again in Petey. This was upsetting, on the one hand, because Hank's dad was never much fun but it was reassuring on the other because it helped Lydia and Hank get out of the blame cycle they were stuck in. And we also reminded ourselves that Hank's father had lived a long and productive life. Just because *we* valued sociability and empathy so highly, didn't mean those qualities were prerequisites for good lives.

"Is there a name for whatever this is?" Hank asked me.

"There a several names that we might think of. Probably the best name is simply 'Petey,' " I said, "because all kids are different. We don't know exactly what is going on. But his condition is probably akin to what we call a pervasive developmental disorder, or PDD."

"Egad, what's that?" Lydia asked.

"It is a broad term used to describe children who develop slowly in several ways especially socially."

"Do they catch up?" Lydia asked.

"Some do, some don't," I answered. "In any case Petey doesn't have 'it,' whatever 'it' is, nearly as badly as the children the label was invented for. I'm just saying he is in that constellation."

"Is it due to lack of affection on my part?" Lydia asked, going right after one of her worst fears.

"Absolutely not," I was glad to be able to say. "That much we can say for sure. All the evidence points to a genetic basis for this condition."

"But what *is* 'this condition'?" Hank asked. "You say he doesn't really have whatever it is he has. I'm confused."

"I'm sorry to confuse you. It is just that this diagnosis is so vague. Petey does not have the symptoms of full-blown autism or pervasive developmental disorder. But something is 'off,' as you've known ever since he was born. What I mean when I say he doesn't have the diagnosis is that the way we define it, he doesn't. But he has a little of it. You could say it's like feeling under the weather instead of having the flu."

"Is there a test that could make this more precise?"

"There are psychological tests that can give us a lot of useful information, but there is no definitive diagnostic test. Like most diagnoses in this field, it is a judgment call, what we call a clinical diagnosis. Is this making sense?" I asked.

"Yes, yes it is," Lydia said. "Especially the idea that Petey is like his grandfather. I can really see where he came from."

"Thanks, dear," Hank said with a smile.

"That wasn't a dig," Lydia responded quickly. "It's just helpful in putting it all together to see some precedent."

"Is there treatment?" Hank asked. "How can you teach empathy?"

"You want to try to promote social skills in any way you can, without causing embarrassment. A good school, a good home, maybe a good therapist, lots of love, protection, sometimes medication, and time," I said. "They all can help. Also, change your expectations a little bit. Accept Petey for who is."

"What more can you tell us? Will he be all right?" they asked, urgently.

These questions are always urgent. That is why it is so hard to give the indefinite answers we must give. "It depends what you mean by 'all right.' Chances are he will be somewhat like his grandfather. On the other hand, I doubt his grandfather had a good therapist." Hank shook his head no, and rolled his eyes, as if to say he wished his father *had* had a therapist. "A good therapist can make a big difference," I added.

"Well, will you see him?" Lydia asked.

"I'm not your best bet. I can make a referral to someone who is really gifted with kids like Petey."

The Pickenses took my referral. Six years later, Petey had grown to almost six feet tall. He was in the eighth grade, and he was getting good marks in all his courses. He was still socially awkward, but none of his peers knew anything of his earlier problems. He was accepted in a mainstream school, and he was doing well. I think it was his therapist who, by working with him twice a week for years, taught him how to be more attuned to others. She was a remarkably talented woman. Fortunately, there are more than a few superb therapists around the country.

We use various diagnostic terms, depending upon the exact symptoms the child has, but the unifying theme in children like Petey is a relative lack of empathy and social engagement. In milder cases than Petey's no actual treatment may be needed, just the knowledge that what we're seeing is a result of how the child's brain is put together. The key here is not to make the problem into a more serious one by having parents start blaming themselves and others, or having the school exacerbate the problem by insisting that the child should try harder or shape up. Severe cases, which are beyond the scope of this discussion, require intensive treatment, often in a hospital. These severely affected children are deeply autistic or have a developmental disorder so pervasive that they cannot function socially at all.

There is a subtype of pervasive developmental disorder called Asperger's syndrome. Although it was first described by Hans

Asperger, a Viennese medical student, in 1944, it went unnoticed in this country until the past fifteen years or so. What is striking about children with Asperger's syndrome is that while socially remote, they are verbally very adept. Some people call this the "smart" version of PDD, because language and cognitive development are not impaired; indeed they are often superior.

Children with Asperger's syndrome have circumscribed areas of great knowledge and interest. I once treated a boy (the great majority of these children are boys) with Asperger's syndrome who knew virtually everything there was to know about the Civil War. He had read scores of books on the subject, built models of the various battlefields, could quote from speeches made by Lincoln, Lee, and Jefferson Davis, knew the birthdates of most of the generals and all the dates of all the battles. He could speak on the subject for hours. But he had no friends. He got along all right at home, particularly with his mother, but his social skills outside the home were nil. He did not know to make contact with other people, so he kept to himself.

His coordination was poor, and he was quite clumsy. He was tall and gawky, and he often made funny flapping movements with his hands and arms, so his odd appearance set him apart as well. When I met his father I saw immediately where the son had come from. Dad was an English professor who specialized in Edmund Spenser. He knew everything about *The Faerie Queene,* and he lit into a lecture about Spenser the minute he sat down, virtually ignoring me. I didn't even bother to interrupt; in fact, I learned a lot.

This combination of extreme social isolation everywhere but at home, coupled with a cognitive picture of good verbal skills, high scores on the verbal part of IQ tests with lower scores on the performance part, circumscribed areas of interest and extraordinary knowledge, physical clumsiness, and often a father who fits the profile as well, adds up to Asperger's syndrome.

We still do not know exactly what it is. Fred Volkmar, an expert in the field, says Asperger's "is still a moving target." But all agree that Hans Asperger described something real. As we try to pin down exactly what it is, we continue to learn more.

The reason it's good for parents to know about this diagnosis is, once again, to take the symptoms out of the domain of parental failure and into the domain of neurology. Children with Asperger's syndrome can succeed in life, as long as they aren't emotionally traumatized because of how "strange" they are. Social skills training can help, as well as parent education, and sometimes medication can help too.

Until we know more about the brain, pervasive developmental disorder and Asperger's syndrome will remain descriptive terms. PDD is not common, occurring at a rate of about ten to fifteen children out of every ten thousand. (What Petey had is more common than that, because he had the symptoms only mildly, and he did not have enough of them to qualify for the full-blown diagnosis. Nonetheless, the symptoms caused him trouble and caused his parents great pain.) PDD is not a disease but rather the name of a behavioral syndrome, a collection of symptoms or traits that are gathered together under one heading. As we begin to sort out what is really happening in the brains of these children, PDD will likely turn out to be a collection of different neurological problems all converging on the symptoms of unsociability and inability to communicate effectively with others.

Once you are able to understand the issue as a neurological one, you may be less put off by the symptom of remoteness, and you may see that these children are often deeply interesting. If you try to establish rapport with them wherever they are cognitively, you may find great pleasure in their company. Talk about ideas, if they like ideas. Talk about philosophy. Talk about games. Talk about numbers. Pick a topic that lights the child up. Maybe it's baseball statistics. Maybe it is the history of war. Maybe it's predicting the weather. You never know.

Don't ask these children to be who they can't be. Try to go with them where they are.

TRICHOTILLOMANIA: IF YOUR CHILD PULLS OUT HIS OR HER OWN HAIR

"What?" "I've never heard of such a thing." "You must be kidding." "That's pretty bizarre." "Ugh!"

These are the kinds of responses I usually hear when I describe the phenomenon of a child's pulling out his or her own hair to a person who has never heard of such a thing. But the fact is that this behavior, which is technically called trichotillomania, is not all that rare. Studies indicate that 1 percent to 2 percent of college students currently suffer from it or have done so at some point in their lives. We tend not to hear of it unless we are directly involved, because hair-pulling is an embarrassing symptom, which people don't talk about and which is not greeted with immediate understanding or empathy. Quite the opposite. Imagine if your spouse told you that when she was younger she went through a period of pulling out her eyebrows and eyelashes. In all likelihood, you would not instantly feel empathy. In fact, you would probably think the behavior was quite strange.

However, as we discover that trichotillomania is not so rare, and as we interview people who have it or have had it, we find that although the symptom is unpleasant, the people who have it are not. They are simply ordinary people struggling with a habit that can become a devastating disorder if it is not controlled. Sufferers can become socially cut off and unwilling to go to work out of embarrassment and fear of rejection.

Trichotillomania is a neurological condition. The reason for including it in this book—besides the fact that it is not as rare as was once thought—is that it provides a perfect example of a condition that is still shrouded in shame for many people, even though it is no one's fault. It is not your fault if you get trichotillomania, and you should not suffer blame or humiliation for having it. It does not mean you are a bad, weird, or unseemly person, any more than you are if you develop a rash or a contact dermatitis. To have trichotillomania is to have a treatable neurological condition.

There was a time when anyone who had a tremor was thought to be possessed by evil spirits. Some people were tortured or even put to death simply because they had a tremor. Others were shamed into staying inside, never allowing themselves to be seen in public, because of the stigma attached to their tremor. We now know that tremors are caused by a variety of biologically based conditions such as Parkinson's disease, or abnormal levels of certain ions in the bloodstream, or other metabolic disturbances. Tremors whose cause we cannot ascertain we call idiopathic, which my old teacher in medical school said meant the doctor was an idiot and the patient was pathetic. But at least we don't tell the patient he is possessed by the devil and that his treatment is to be executed! Tremors represent just one of many conditions that we now treat medically but that used to be regarded as evidence of evil or morally infirm character.

We used to think of trichotillomania as exclusively psychologically driven, a form of masochism or self-destruction. These psychological explanations are not too distant from demonic possession. But most attempts to treat trichotillomania with a psychodynamic approach alone have failed. More recently, the addition of behavioral and medication-based approaches has yielded much better results. Only with public education, however, can we begin to remove the unfair shame and stigma young people with trichotillomania usually suffer.

Although we do not know what causes trichotillomania, it seems most likely that there is a genetic predisposition. Often the sufferer has a parent who has a history of tics, various physical habits such as nail-biting or knuckle-cracking, or a range of obsessive-compulsive symptoms. What activates the hair-pulling is not clear. Sometimes the individual feels a sensation similar to an itch beneath the hair. When he pulls the hair out he feels a pleasing relief similar to the feeling of scratching an itch. It is not that he feels driven to pull out his hair in order to comply with some unconscious demand, any more than when any of us scratches an itch he is responding to an unconscious drive. We do not know for sure why these people pull out their hair, but it is helpful to get rid of demonic hypotheses, or suggestions that these people are in some way "bad." They're not bad, any more than someone with an itch that won't go away is bad.

The exact pattern of hair-pulling varies. Hair may be pulled from various parts of the body. One study reported that 67 percent of patients pulled hair from the scalp, 22 percent pulled eyelashes, 8 percent pulled eyebrows, 2 percent pulled facial hair, and 2 percent pulled pubic hair. Most people pulled hair from two or more sites. Often they were unaware of pulling even as they were doing it. Particularly when they were engaged in sedentary activities, such as watching television, reading, talking on the telephone, lying in bed, or driving, the individual might pull hair with only the dimmest awareness of doing it.

Trichotillomania is not the same thing as habitually playing with one's hair, twisting it or curling it or brushing it to the side. That habit is far, far more common and of no great concern. However, trichotillomania is usually accompanied by other minor nervous habits that involve the body, such as knuckle-cracking, nail-biting, or lip-biting.

The person with trichotillomania is unfortunate in that his habit defaces his body somewhat. But it is not a deliberate moral failure, and the sufferer should not be blamed. As we learn more about the brain, no doubt we will understand this condition better. Until then we must rely on treatments that, although not definitive, do help. Several medications have been shown to be helpful in many cases, including clomipramine (Anafranil), fluoxetine (Prozac), and lithium. These medications usually reduce symptoms, but even so the symptoms often recur after the medication has been discontinued.

Nonmedication treatment can include insight-oriented psychotherapy, particularly if there are other problems in the person's life that need attention. More geared toward treating the hair-pulling symptom itself are behavioral therapy or cognitive therapy. Behavioral therapy teaches methods of trying to break the hair-pulling habit. Cognitive therapy, which has been used to treat a wide range of conditions from substance abuse to depression, has been used successfully to treat trichotillomania as well. In cognitive therapy, the patient learns to replace "bad" thoughts with "good" thoughts. By carefully reviewing the kinds of thoughts the patient has at the time of each hair-pulling episode, the patient and her therapist can begin to compose different thoughts, which the patient can train herself to insert in place of the negative thoughts that lead to the hair-pulling. If, for example, the patient reports that she often thinks, "I feel overwhelmed and hurried," just before she starts pulling her hair, she might train herself to replace that thought when it appears, instead telling herself, "Pulling will only embarrass me. I think I'll take a few deep breaths instead."

The general principle of cognitive therapy—learning how to replace negative, damaging thoughts with positive, constructive ones—can be used to treat all kinds of emotional problems. Cognitive therapy is a form of learned optimism, or rehearsed positivity. It may sound forced and contrived; that is because it *is* forced and contrived. But then again, so is most medical treatment. And in the case of cognitive therapy, it is practical and surprisingly effective.

TOURETTE SYNDROME: IF YOUR CHILD HAS TICS OR TWITCHES OR BLURTS THINGS OUT

The telephone rang just as Joan Hubert was sitting down with the morning paper for a few moments' peace. The children had been sent off to school with a maximum of chaos, it seemed, and the dust was only now settling, an hour and a half later. Joan groaned as she reached to answer the phone.

"Mrs. Hubert?"

"Yes?" she replied, immediately detecting tension in the voice on the other end.

"Mrs. Hubert, this is Ben Bailey. I'm afraid we've had quite a serious incident involving Travis."

Joan gasped. "Oh, my God, is he all right? Something's happened to him?"

"Oh, no, I didn't mean that. He's fine, physically. But he has misbehaved quite severely."

"Oh, thank God," Joan said, images of catastrophe fading as fast as they had appeared.

"I beg your pardon?" the somewhat officious principal replied.

"No, I didn't mean thank God he misbehaved, I meant thank God he's all right. You should chose your words more carefully when you call a mother up and tell her something bad has happened." After five children and many school principals, Joan Hubert was not as intimidated by school officials as she once had been.

"Well, I apologize for my choice of words if they upset you, but ironically enough it is Travis's choice of words I'm calling you about."

"Oh?" Joan said, mentally gearing up for whatever she was going to hear next, even as she felt annoyance at Ben Bailey's sense of irony.

"Yes. You see, this morning he called Mrs. Dwyer a bitch. That exact word. Not once, but several times, and not in private but in front of the entire class. I can assure you Mrs. Dwyer was more than mildly upset. The episode was entirely unprovoked, not that there could be any justifiable provocation for the use of such language by a second-grader toward his teacher. Can you come down here, please, to talk about this?"

"He called Mrs. Dwyer . . ." Joan said, squinting in disbelief.

"A bitch. Repeatedly."

"But what had Mrs. Dwyer done?"

"Nothing. Absolutely nothing. She asked Travis to come up and speak to the class about his favorite hobby, and he said, "No, bitch."

Joan burst out laughing. Perhaps it was hearing these words come out of Ben Bailey's mouth, perhaps it was tension release, perhaps it was the devil in her, but whatever the reason, Joan Hubert laughed.

"I'm afraid I fail to see the humor," Mr. Bailey said flatly into the phone.

"Yes, I mean no, I don't think it's funny, either. It's just so unexpected, it caught me off guard. And she's not the warmest lady in the world."

"I *beg* your pardon, Mrs. Hubert. Are you suggesting Travis was *justified* in saying what he said?"

"No, of course not. Of course not. I'll be right down," Joan said, and hung up the phone before she got herself in any deeper. She then called her husband and asked him to come with her.

"He said *what?*" Greg Hubert barked into the phone.

"You heard me, honey. Can I pick you up now?"

"Oh, I guess you better. We must have one PO'd principal on our hands."

The scene in the principal's office was solemn. All heads hung as Ben Bailey recited what had happened and Trudy Dwyer sat by. "I can assure you there was no provocation on my part for what that boy said," Mrs. Dwyer insisted, still shaken. "I have never in all my years of teaching been talked to so offensively and brazenly by a student. It was quite shocking."

"I'm sure it was," Greg Hubert put in before his wife could open her mouth. "I can assure you that we do not condone such language and we will deal with Travis most sternly." There is a kind of drill you go through in the principal's office. Greg was trying to play his role as he was supposed to.

"But it just isn't like Travis," Joan said, having calmed down on the drive in.

"I hope you're not suggesting there's any justification," Mr. Bailey repeated.

"No, absolutely not," Joan said. "It's just that when a child who never swears suddenly calls a teacher a bitch four times in broad daylight with a class full of witnesses, you have to wonder why."

"Well, as long as he apologizes to me and the class," Mrs. Dwyer began.

"And he performs an in-school service, and goes on probation for the term," Mr. Bailey continued.

"That is fine," Joan said. "Whatever punishment you say. But do you have any ideas as to why this happened?"

"I'm afraid I do not," Mr. Bailey replied, adding, "I was hoping you might shed some light on that."

Greg looked at his wife and spoke quickly to intercept her. "Why don't we go home and talk that over with Travis."

"That would be a good idea," Mr. Bailey said.

The matter might have ended there were it not that Travis had a more significant problem than just having had a bad morning. Fortunately, the Huberts' pediatrician had heard of a condition called Tourette syndrome.

In 1885 a French physician, Gilles de la Tourette, described a syndrome that was until recently largely forgotten. However, in the past decade, thanks to the work of the geneticist and physician David Comings, as well as many others, Tourette syndrome has become more widely recognized.

Tourette syndrome is characterized both by involuntary twitching movements, called motor tics, and by involuntary vocal utterances (not necessarily words), called vocal tics. According to Dr. Comings, the most common motor tics seen in Tourette syndrome include, in descending order of frequency, rapid eye-blinking, shoulder-shrugging, absently brushing hair away from one's eyes, repeated mouth-opening, facial grimacing, licking the lips, and eye-rolling. The most common vocal tics include re-peated throat-clearing, grunting, yelling or screaming, sniffing, barking, snorting, coughing, spitting, squeaking, or humming.

The involuntary use of swear words is understandably the most notorious vocal tic associated with Tourette syndrome, but it is, mercifully, relatively rare. In addition to swearing without wanting to, the individual may speak words he would choose to censor if he could. For example, one Sunday there was a man with Tourette syndrome in our church congregation. Right in the middle of the sermon he blurted out, in a loud voice, "Boring! Boring!" He did not want to insult the preacher, but the words leaped out of his mouth.

How is this possible? Isn't this stretching the limits of credulity of even the most gullible? But Tourette syndrome truly is a neurological condition, having nothing to do with a defiant or rude personality. Hard as it may be to believe, neither Travis in the classroom nor the man in my church congregation *wanted* to say what he said. They may have *felt* what they said, but they would have censored the words, as any other person would, if they could have. Listen to Gilles de la Tourette's own description of a female patient from more than a hundred years ago:

> In the midst of an interesting conversation, all of a sudden, *without being able to prevent it,* she interrupts what she is saying or what she is listening to with horrible screams and with words that are even more extraordinary than her screams. All of this contrasts deplorably with her distinguished manners and background. These words are, for the most part, offensive curse words and obscene sayings. These are no less embarrassing for her than for those who have to listen. . . .
>
> Furthermore, nothing changes this vocabulary, neither scolding nor attempts by the patient to substitute these expressions. Perhaps the willpower of the patient can force the obscenities to be momentarily suppressed, but this control is short-lived and usually followed by an exaggerated explosion of obscenities.

While the symptom of swearing attracts the most attention, most people who have Tourette syndrome do not swear. They blink their eyes as if they had an allergy, and they clear their throats as if they had a cold. That is why the diagnosis is so often missed. Even if the doctor has heard of Tourette, he may know only popularized accounts of the extreme version, including barking and swearing. The much milder and more common version may be treated with cold medication instead.

How common is Tourette syndrome? According to Dr. Comings, it affects about one in every hundred boys and one in every eight hundred girls. It is definitely genetically influenced. Neither parents nor teachers cause it. It is usually associated with some other condition, such as attention deficit disorder, obsessive-compulsive disorder, a learning disability, sleep problems, conduct problems, impulsive behaviors, or speech problems. It is *not* associated with low intelligence or poor moral character. The symptoms start in childhood but may persist through adulthood. We have several medications now to treat Tourette syndrome, and usually they can suppress the damaging symptoms effectively.

Even without treatment the tics tend to decrease with age. Unfortunately, as the tics improve other symptoms often develop. These may include depression, obsessive-compulsive disorder, panic attacks, and alcoholism. Early intervention can greatly reduce the severity of these symptoms.

Tourette syndrome is important in its own right, but it is even more important for what it implies. Isn't it remarkable that a symptom as apparently voluntary as swearing at someone can have an involuntary, neurological basis? How many kinds of behavior that we currently ascribe to "badness" of one sort or another might we someday discover to be driven organically instead?

We will never excuse the individual from taking responsibility for the deed. It was up to Travis and his parents, for example, to find a way of controlling his behavior or at least of finding convincing evidence with which to explain his behavior to the school. *One's responsibility for one's actions does not diminish because one understands the cause of them. However, it is almost always true that one is able to take that responsibility most effectively if one understands the root cause.*

FETAL ALCOHOL SYNDROME AND FETAL ALCOHOL EFFECT

One of the most alarming—and potentially helpful—discoveries by substance abuse researchers in recent decades has been the effect of alcohol on the developing fetus during pregnancy. We now know that mothers who drink excessively during pregnancy put their children at risk of being born with fetal alcohol syndrome (FAS) or its milder cousin, fetal alcohol effect (FAE). We do not know exactly how much alcohol it takes to induce FAS or FAE, but regular daily ingestion of more than a glass or two of wine per day appears to be risky. Estimates are that at least 5 percent of American women drink enough during pregnancy to put their children at risk. We must reach these women before they do the irreversible damage to their developing baby that alcohol can inflict.

What is the damage? The most noticeable problems are physical. There is a characteristic set of physical defects in FAS. These include:

1. Small head
2. Flat midface
3. Small eye openings
4. Low-set ears
5. Short, upturned nose
6. Thin upper lip
7. Flat, elongated philtrum (the vertical indentation between the upper lip and the nose)
8. Small chin

In a child with fetal alcohol syndrome these defects are obvious. In fetal alcohol effect, fewer of the physical traits appear, and they are less marked.

But ultimately more pernicious are the invisible mental problems these children develop. Both FAS and the FAE children show various forms of brain dysfunction. They may develop a seizure disorder, which requires treatment with medication to control. They may also have severe conduct problems, leading to a diagnosis of oppositional defiant disorder or another disruptive behavior disorder. Their powers of concentration may be greatly reduced, so that their condition resembles attention deficit disorder, and they may also have major problems with short-term memory as well as with word-finding. Their comprehension is usually impaired, and they have difficulty understanding what is said to them. For example, if given directions, they nod as if they understand what they hear, but then they are unable to follow the directions. They often seem just not to "get" what is going on around them, and they are typically regarded as mentally slow.

The more we follow these children, the more distinct the picture becomes. The problems with word-finding led one child with FAE to state, "Sometimes it's like I have holes in my head." Information spills out, even as it is poured in. These children feel desperate to come up with explanations, as they try to keep up. Sometimes they "confabulate"—make up long, winding stories to explain what they really can't fathom.

Part of the sadness of FAS and FAE is that the mothers who cause it rarely mean to. They drink during pregnancy without knowing how dangerous it can be. Either they do not tell their doctor how much they drink, or their doctor doesn't ask, or they simply do not have access to adequate prenatal care, care that would normally provide them with the information they need to take proper care of their unborn baby.

The key to dealing with FAS and FAE is, obviously, prevention. We must educate the general public, and pregnant women especially, about the potentially harmful effects of alcohol intake during pregnancy. We must be specific about the form this potential harm may take. Most pregnant women would not drink if they knew how severe FAS and FAE can be. Many naively think that the worst that can happen if they drink a lot is that their fetus will sleep more or even "feel high" in utero. They do not know that their drinking can lead to irreversible brain damage in their child. If they did, they would make a greater effort to curtail their drinking while they were pregnant.

FAS and FAE are preventable. Once they occur, they are treatable, with structure, support, and medication, but they are not curable. These children will continue to struggle with their symptoms throughout life, and their mothers will suffer as well. These conditions provide one more example of how important public education is in the prevention of emotional and learning problems in children.

Chapter 10

....

To Medicate or Not to Medicate: How to Decide

The desire to take medicine is perhaps the greatest feature which distinguishes man from animals.

—*Sir William Osler*

One of the most gnawing questions in treating children's emotional or learning problems is the question of whether and when to use medication. Few treatment questions spark debate more quickly. Parents usually balk at the mention of medication. Pediatricians and child psychiatrists often hesitate to suggest medication for fear of the parents' reactions. Sometimes a parent has a hard time just in getting the accurate information needed to make an informed decision.

Most of us feel that the brain is somehow different from our other organs. We use a stricter standard in considering remedies for our brains, our minds. Indeed, this is *because* we see the brain as the tissue of that invisible organ, the mind. While we readily swallow a pill that will make our kidneys flush better, or inhale some vapor that will clear our lungs, we pause at the gate of the brain. Since our knowledge of the brain and its chemistry has lately given us new medications and new physical treatments, we must grapple anew with our feelings about these medications and treatments. Particularly when it comes to applying these treatments to our children, we can never do so without emotion, without fear, without question. Part of the purpose of this book is to answer those questions on the basis of our current knowledge, and also to address the uneasy feelings that so often accompany the questions.

Why is the question of using medication to treat a child's emotional or behavioral problems so sensitive, even controversial? There are three main reasons, in my opinion: side effects; lack of research data; and bad press.

First of all, no parent wants to use a medication of any sort for their child unless it is necessary. All medications have side effects and we do not want to subject our children to side effects without good reason.

Second, the use of medications to treat children for psychological conditions is a relatively new development. While such medications have been used on adults for many decades, it is only over the past fifteen years or so that their use on children has become at all widespread. Therefore we do not have the long-term experience with children that we have with adults, nor do we have a medical-social tradition that makes the medications' use seem routine.

Research in the field is growing all the time, but the data base in the domain of pediatric psychopharmacology is still small compared to what we would like it to be. With the major exception of stimulant medications such as Ritalin, used to treat attention deficit disorder, most of the medications for behavioral or psychological problems in children have been researched for only a few decades. (The stimulants, on the other hand, have been used in this country since 1937; they constitute one class of medications that have been extensively researched in children and found to be extremely safe and effective.) For the most part we are still gathering data about which medications work best in children.

The lack of research data dovetails with the lack of social acceptance of the use of psychiatric medications in children. All treatments must gain not only medical acceptance but also social acceptance to become widespread. Some medical treatments have passed the most rigorous scientific investigations and have established a track record of extraordinary safety and efficacy only to be all but discarded because of bad press. In the field of psychiatry, electroconvulsive therapy (ECT, or shock treatment) is a prime example. Used properly, ECT is painless, quick, safe, and effective; however, because it has a negative press most people think of it as a fearsome remedy. We are quite comfortable with using electricity—or, to use the more provocative word, "shock"—to treat an arrhythmia of the heart. But to apply electricity to the brain—from this we recoil. Our fear is rooted not in scientific fact but in rumor and misinformation.

This is the third reason for the only tentative acceptance of the pediatric use of psychiatric medications: They have an uncertain press. As a result of a lack of information or wrong information, many parents fear such medications as extreme remedies, to be used only as a last resort. Some parents feel almost guilty at the idea of using a medication that affects their child's brain. They feel that they, as parents, should be able to take care of any emotional or behavioral problem their child might have. As one mother said to me, echoing many others, "It's one thing to give him penicillin for strep throat. But to give him a pill for how he behaves? It doesn't seem right. I should be able to take care of that myself."

In his book *Listening to Prozac,* Peter Kramer coined a phrase that is helpful in describing what many of us parents feel regarding the use of psychiatric medications in our children. Kramer referred to "psychopharmacological Calvinism," a tendency to feel that to use medications that affect mood, cognition, or behavior is almost a form of cheating, a kind of immoral act. A pill for a headache, we feel, is all right but a pill for depression is not.

If we feel that way about giving such medication to ourselves, we feel it much more strongly regarding our children. Do not spoil their state of innocence, we say, with mind-altering substances. Do not give them the message that when you feel bad, you take a pill, or when you act up you take a pill, or when you get bad grades you take a pill. Teach them to be responsible for what they do, not learn to rely on medication to do their work for them.

If our children felt bad in some part of their bodies other than their brains, we wouldn't hesitate to treat them with, say, penicillin or aspirin. If their acting up were due to hyperthyroidism, which it easily could be, we wouldn't hesitate to give them medication. Or if their bad grades were due to nearsightedness, we wouldn't hesitate to fit them with eyeglasses; or if they did badly because of a seizure disorder we wouldn't hesitate to give them the right antiseizure medication.

But around certain parts of the brain we draw an imaginary "do not medicate" line. Antiseizure medication, which does indeed target the brain, is acceptable. Headache medication is also acceptable, even though it, too, targets the brain. But medication that affects mood, behavior, cognition, or attention gives most of us pause. Why should this be?

Kramer's "psychopharmacological Calvinism" explains part of it. We feel we should *work* our way out of emotional problems. We should develop self-discipline, get into a good mood, pay rapt attention, or cultivate sound memory *on our own*. While few of us believe we earn a healthy thyroid gland by dint of hard work, most of us believe we earn happiness, achieve self-discipline, train good memory, or focus attention. We believe we do these tasks well in direct proportion to how hard we try.

These attitudes run deep. They are at the core of American values. As a nation we probably believe more in the importance of hard work than in any other single value. We want to pass this value on to our children so that they will lead productive, satisfying lives. We feel it is our duty to teach them that life is not easy. We need to teach them that to succeed they must work hard. We need to teach them not to take the easy way out.

A pill can seem like the easy way out. We are particularly wary of a pill given for a problem that we think is governed by will, and will alone. Such problems might include depression, wandering attention, lack of self-discipline, or shyness.

No one would disagree with parents who want to promote a work ethic among their children. We all endorse the value of hard work, and I would never counsel a parent or a child in any way that would undermine that value.

However, our worry is misplaced if we believe psychiatric medication undermines our children's work ethic, gives them a message that a pill is a cure-all, or provides them with an easy way out. As one child told Priscilla Vail, "I'm not looking for an easy way out. I'm just looking for a way to get in." If the physician prescribing the medication explains carefully what the pill is for and what it is not for, then the medication becomes like eyeglasses—a tool to make one's work more efficient and productive, not an excuse or a license to fail. Medication helps the child take on responsibility more effectively. Medication, like eyeglasses, makes effort more productive. When medication is used properly, it simply evens the playing field so the child can have as good a chance at success as others.

Some parents and children respond, "But I want to do it on my own. I don't want a crutch." But would you say that if you had a broken leg? Would you say, "Let me heal my broken leg on my own. No splint. No cast. No crutch"? Medication for depression is no more a weak way out than a cast is for a broken leg.

Still, it can be difficult to go along with the idea of medication for emotional problems in children. We should never let the medication do what a good parent, teacher, or friend should do. Medication should never be used as a substitute for human contact, but rather to supplement it. Medication can help a child make better use of the human contacts he or she has.

In deciding whether to use medication for your child, consider these five basic guidelines:

1. Keep an open mind. The risk of not using medication, in some cases, may exceed the risk of using it. The risk of not using penicillin for pneumonia, for example, greatly exceeds the risk of using penicillin. We often create an artificial dichotomy between the body and the brain, which leads us unnecessarily to fear medications used for the brain; some medications used to treat the brain, such as Ritalin, are as safe as penicillin, and just as effective.

2. *Learn as much as possible.* Knowledge is the great antidote to prejudice. The field of psychopharmacology is blossoming. Whereas only two decades ago we almost never gave a child medication for an emotionally related problem, we now have many we can consider using. Medication is *never* the whole answer, but we know enough now to use it selectively as a helpful component of a comprehensive treatment plan. For most parents the biggest obstacle to overcome is an emotional obstacle, a feeling that somehow they do not want to use a medication for their child's brain. Before you decide the question of medication on the basis of feelings alone, try to get what medical facts we have.

Where do you go to get those facts? Your pediatrician is a reliable source. Make sure you take enough time to get all your questions answered. Be assertive. Tell your doctor to stay in his or her chair until *you say* your questions are satisfactorily answered! You can always get a second opinion if you're not completely satisfied; no good doctor ever objects to a second opinion.

In addition to physicians, other parents can be excellent sources of information. The only problem is that they can also be unintentional sources of misinformation. As a safeguard, try to talk to more than one parent.

Books abound on medical topics, and on medication in particular. Some are excellent, but many are biased. Try to get a recommendation for a book from someone you trust, like your doctor or a knowledgeable friend, rather than just browsing the bookshelves of your favorite store. You cannot tell a book by its cover!

3. *Identify your own prejudices.* It is impossible to be human and not have prejudices; however, you do not want to base important decisions regarding your children's health on prejudice. It wasn't

so long ago that many intelligent people thought putting fluoride in our drinking water represented a threat to their children; now we recognize that it has spared a generation many cavities.

As with fluoride, sometimes the feeling against medication is most unfortunate because the medication might really help the child. A good example is the use of Ritalin to treat attention deficit disorder. Not a cure by any means, Ritalin is still a highly effective component of treatment for many children. Ritalin does not help all children who have ADD, but for many it makes a dramatic difference in their ability to pay attention and regulate behavior. To deny a child who has severe ADD the chance to benefit from medication is to deny that child the equivalent of eyeglasses. He may get along by squinting, but why should he have to? In the case of attention deficit disorder the risk of not using the medication exceeds the risk of using it. It doesn't always work, but it is worth a try.

4. Discuss your feelings and thoughts about medication with your spouse and child. Open discussion of the issues surrounding medication is a much better idea than keeping the whole topic secret. The idea of giving a child a medication for a psychological problem can be so anxiety-provoking for parents that the topic almost becomes impossible to discuss. The mere mention of it brings a resounding refusal even to consider it. However, many of the medications we now use are very safe and can effectively supplement the nonmedication approaches to certain problems. Remember, taking medication does not exclude using other treatments as well.

5. Talk with other parents who have had direct experience with medication. Your doctor can usually give you some names of parents who have given permission to be contacted, or you may know some parents through your child's school who have had occasion to use medication for one problem or another in their child. Other parents are a great source of information as well as consolation.

One set of parents I know were eager to share their story in the hope that it would be helpful to others. I interviewed them specifically for this book. Let me bring you into the life of Matthew Williams, age ten and a half, and his parents, Lauren and Patrick.

Matthew's story isn't simple. For most of his life, Matthew was troubled by anxiety. Until the end of his first decade, it was assumed the anxiety derived from a traumatic illness he had suffered as a toddler. Usually when children suffer emotionally we can find in their history *some* circumstances that could plausibly explain their suffering. In Matthew's case it was reasonable to assume his life-threatening illness had made him anxious. However, over time his parents grew less and less satisfied with that explanation alone. Matthew himself wasn't sure what was going on.

Let's hear him discuss his life in his own words:

"Matthew," I began, "I'm going to turn on this tape recorder and we're going to talk to the people who will read my book, okay?"

"Yeah, sure," Matthew said, looking at the tape recorder on the couch. "Is it on?"

"Yes," I said.

"This will be in your book?"

"Yes," I said.

"Cool," he said.

"Thank you, Matthew, for being willing to be interviewed for this book," I said, noticing a smile of pride creep across Matthew's face. "I think a lot of children and parents will be interested in what you have to say, and I think you will help them a great deal."

"Gotcha," he said with a smile. He was wearing a Bob Marley T-shirt.

"What grade are you in?" I asked.

"Fifth," he answered.

"And tell me, do you take medication now?"

"Yes, I do."

"Would you tell me a little bit of the story that led up to your taking the medication?"

"Uh, I started taking it in January," he said, sitting back in the couch.

"Why did you start taking it?"

"Because I was always getting stressed out, anxious, like I didn't know what to do. If some little thing happened, I'd blow up about it, saying 'Arrrrrgh!' And I really didn't like doing that."

"I can imagine," I said. "Were you like that all the time?"

"No. Well, mostly I was just really tense and someone just would say, 'Hey, Matthew, why don't you—' and I'd say, 'No, No, *no!*' I'd just blow up at my friends, which I really don't think they liked."

"Were you depressed or sad?" I asked.

"I'd just have these up-and-down spells," Matthew answered. "I'd be feeling great and then I'd be depressed for no reason."

"For no reason at all?"

"No, it would just happen."

"You'd feel . . ."

"Just completely depressed," he said.

"Did you ever want to kill yourself?" I asked.

"No, no, no, never," he replied emphatically.

"You never wanted to hurt yourself?"

"No. Sometimes I'd punch a pillow and sometimes hit myself, but not to hurt myself. I'd just get angry and need to blow off steam."

"And with your friends, what would you be like?" I asked.

"They could just say one thing and completely push me over the edge. So I wasn't great to be around. Like, 'Hey, Matthew, you want to do this?' 'No, I don't.' Or, 'I completely disagree about this,' Just, *'no, no.'* "

"Sort of like—"

"I'd space out," he said glumly.

"So why did you decide to try medication?"

"Well, my dad was taking it, and before he took it he said he was really depressed and couldn't do anything. And he was sort of like me. I talked to the guy I go to, Dr. Bishop, and we considered it for a while."

"Who is Dr. Bishop?" I asked.

"The guy I go to."

"What kind of guy?" I asked.

"Psychologist," Matthew replied.

"You talk to him about . . ."

"Just things," Matthew said.

"These things?" I asked.

"Yeah, uh-huh."

"So I guess you'd been seeing Dr. Bishop for a while before you started the medication?"

"Uh-huh."

"And at some point you talked to him about the medicine?" I asked.

"Yeah, you know, would this help me, why or why not, would I get any side effects, why or why not, do you think this would be good for me, why or why not, and I finally said, 'Okay, how do we give it a try?' So I started taking it. And then I was feeling better. I wasn't going 'Arrrgh!' anymore," Matthew said.

"How did you feel about starting to take the medicine?" I asked. "Were you worried?"

"I said to him, 'I mean, if it'll work for me, that's great,' " Matthew answered.

"So you didn't feel ashamed?"

"No. I said, 'Let me at it!' "

"And what did you notice after you started it?"

"That I had more self-control. I wouldn't blow up over anything. I mean, if someone would really like trash someone, yeah, I'd blow up over that, because everyone blows up."

"Sure," I said.

"But I wouldn't get mad as fast. And I just felt a lot better. I didn't have any up-and-down spells any more. So that was nice."

"You didn't go into any more depressions?" I asked.

"No, no, only if something happened, which is normal. So it's been helping me a lot."

"What is the name of the medicine?"

"Zoloft." Zoloft is an antidepressant similar to Prozac.

"Do you know how much you take?"

"Yeah, twelve and a half milligrams. I used to take twenty-five, but I got sick to my stomach for a while. So we, um, thought the medicine was what was causing it, so we changed how much I took. I'm not getting sick anymore, so we must have been right."

"Does anyone else know that you're taking the Zoloft?" I asked.

"No, just my parents and one relative," he answered, precisely. The one relative was his younger sister.

"And how do you feel about taking it?" I asked.

"I don't care. I mean, it's just something I take."

"It doesn't bother you at all?"

"Nope," Matthew replied positively.

"Not in the slightest?" I asked.

"No, I just take it and that's it."

"What do you think it is doing for you?" I asked.

"I think it's helping me," Matthew answered simply. "It's calming me down, it's bringing out self-control I didn't know I had. It's, um, 'just done wonders.' "

"Whose words are those?" I asked.

"My mom's," he said.

"And would you say so, too?"

"Yes. I'm happier, I can do more things, friends don't get mad at me. Now I don't get mad at my friends, so I don't start losing them."

"Is there a diagnosis for what you have? You know, a name for what's been going on?"

"No, I mean, I don't know what it is, if it's anything," Matthew said.

"But whatever it is it's like what your dad has?"

"I guess so. I mean, I really have no idea of what I have, I just have something. It's just the way my brain is."

"It's no big deal?" I asked, choosing my words on the basis of his tone of voice.

"No, it's not," Matthew agreed. "It's just one of the things I do, get up in the morning and take my Zoloft."

"Then go to school."

"Yup. It's all right."

"Tell me about the rest of your life," I said.

"I like to play sports, I like to read, I like to write, I like to hang out with my friends, go places, typical ten-eleven-year-old things."

"Yeah," I said, suppressing a smile at his assessment of the ten-eleven repertoire. "Tell me about your mom and dad."

"Oh, Dad loves to write music."

"Really? That's great. What kind of work does he do?" I asked.

Matthew paused. "I'm not really sure about the name of it. He buys and sells stocks, I think he's a stockbroker and a consultant about buying stocks. He gets one thing at the end of the year, one check."

"I see. And your mom?"

"My mom's a teacher. She teaches business management. And she likes listening to music, going to restaurants, going places, and being at home."

"And your sister?"

"She likes playing sports and playing with dolls, I mean not Barbie dolls or anything like that. She's seven years old."

"I see. Well, thanks for talking to me, Matthew. We're about finished. What advice would you like to give other kids who're maybe having some of the same problems you were having?"

Matthew paused, then said, "If you have someone like Dr. Bishop, talk to him about it. If you have a doctor, talk to them about it. You don't want to just say, 'Okay, I'm going to start taking this medication.' You really have to get advice about it. If the doctor thinks it is a good idea, then start taking it. Make it like an everyday thing in life."

"What if kids say 'I don't want to take it because it means I'm crazy'?"

"That's not true!" Matthew said vehemently. "You're not crazy if you take it. You just take some medication. I mean, it's not bad or anything. It's not like you're taking something crazy. It's going to help you. If your doctor says you should take it, then take it. I mean, it's not going to do anything bad. It's just going to help you."

"As it's helped you."

"Yes, it has." Then Matthew added, "Except if you get a too-high dosage you might get some stomachaches."

"Well, thanks," I said. "I think what you have said will be very, very helpful to other kids and a lot of moms and dads."

"Okay, cool," Matthew said.

"Anything else you want to say?" I asked.

"No, I just want to say, wow, I've been in a book and I'm happy about it! Okay."

❖

After I spoke with Matthew I met with his parents. Both interviews took place in the Williamses' living room on a sunny Sunday morning.

I turned on the tape recorder as soon as Lauren and Patrick were comfortably settled. "Tell me your experience with Matthew, what led up to your trying medication."

Patrick began. "What was troublesome was the anxiety that would come out of nowhere. Disappointment that was out of proportion to whatever the disappointment was. And a lot of it struck me as being similar to what I went through as a kid, and through my adult life, too. I was more in favor of medication for Matthew than Lauren was, because as a result of my own experience I have become a believer in the biological or chemical sources of emotional distress. I identified what I regarded as characteristics of mine in Matthew, and I became very interested in seeing him not go through what I did."

"How did you know you were not overidentifying with him?" I asked. "How did you know you weren't just seeing yourself in your son?"

"Well, I didn't know that for sure," Patrick answered. "But I do have to go on my own rationality. When I examined Matthew's behavior it was easy for me to see that a lot of his emotions were unbidden and out of proportion to the events that caused them."

"Can you give us some examples?" I asked.

"Sure. He would feel anxious about being away from either one of us. He would feel extreme anxiety about being with other people, I mean friends of his, and extreme anxiety about trying new things and even about things he had done well for years. Every year when we went skiing he would be anxious about it once again, fearing he'd be awful at it, even though he had shown himself and us, over and over, that he was a terrific skier. You could see these as normal kid's anxieties, but if you put them all in a package you'd see Matthew as persistently anxious."

Patrick went on: "My attitude is that anxiety can be a very crippling feeling to have, and to simply say in a Calvinistic way, 'Tough it out, kid'—well, it may take you thirty-five years and you may never tough it out, and in the meantime you have a lot of unfortunate experiences."

I asked Patrick and Lauren if there were any particular stresses in Matthew's life that might have caused such anxiety. They told me about the illness early in Matthew's life. "He had retinoblastoma when he was young," Patrick told me, "and as a consequence of that he eventually lost an eye. He also had a lot of medical treatments, injections, anesthesia, that sort of thing. He was diagnosed with the retinoblastoma at nine months, and he lost his eye when he was three. To this day he continues to have annual checkups. So there is no question that he has reason to be anxious. Much as I had reason to be anxious when I was his age; coming from a highly dysfunctional family, as I did, there were plenty of reasons why I would have been anxious. But there is a difference in the anxiety that most people feel, and an anxiety that comes back and comes back persistently in unrelated circumstances, even when you've given yourself plenty of reasons not to feel anxious. In other words, after you've proven to yourself that you're good in school or good in skiing or that you can deal with people, after you've shown yourself by repetitive behavior that you can do X, Y, and Z, and yet you're *still* anxious about it, then it strikes me that it is more of a medical condition than it is a thing that you can or should get rid of by thinking hard about it. I know that I differ from a lot of people in this, but I think it is wrong to make a child suffer through anxiety that is above and beyond what is normal."

"So what did you do?" I asked.

"Matthew was evaluated by a psychiatrist this year and the doctor agreed that his mood swings were not just the standard ups and downs of life but were more a syndrome or a condition or however you want to put it. He prescribed Zoloft for him on the theory that if it helped me it might help Matthew, because of the genetic factor."

Lauren, who had been more reluctant to give Matthew medication, nodded as Patrick spoke, then added, "I experienced Matthew when he was a very young child as always watching, observing, thinking through situations before he was ready to participate. I saw the moods as he got older, but I also saw him having to take a whole lot more time with things than his peers did. I saw his problem more as a difficulty in participating in life. He started taking skiing lessons; then all of a sudden he would be throwing off his skis and saying he refused to do it. And he'd start running down the hill. Or swimming lessons or just situations at school where he didn't want to participate, didn't know how to make his way into the circle of friends. His kindergarten teacher very astutely said he spent his whole year trying to figure out who he was in the group, and he's done that for all his years of school. Every teacher would say the same thing. That was always the hard piece for Matthew: how to interact with the world. He tended to pull back. I kept seeing over and over in all his eagerness to go forward he would come up to the mark and just not feel he could do it. He'd get to the day of whatever it was and say, 'I just can't do it, Mom.' "

"Why did you decide to try medication," I asked, "instead of trying to help him talk through these issues or just let nature take its course?"

Lauren answered. "It was after spending years with Matthew and having many long conversations with him that I got to the point where I thought something else might be useful to try. I had spent years talking through these experiences with Matthew and with professionals. I think Patrick would say I spent too much time talking to Matthew, explaining and re-explaining and re-going over and relistening, and devoting literally hours and hours to Matthew trying to help him understand himself and help me understand what was going on.

"Early in Matthew's life it was natural to ascribe everything to his illness. But as time went on I just felt there was some missing link. I came to *know* there was. I was frustrated—and, my God, Matthew was frustrated. I didn't know what to do and I found myself constantly on edge with him, anticipating, second-guessing. You know, I wanted to help him avoid situations where I just knew he was going to be unable to manage. Then I started to realize that this was not only bad for him, it was bad for me and all of us. Because he wasn't walking down his own path, it was too controlled by me. I just couldn't do it anymore, I just emotionally couldn't do it anymore."

At this point Patrick took his wife's hand and added, "Part of what you're saying is what I was saying, which is that Matthew's symptoms were so persistent that no amount of conversation or deep thinking or investigation of history or anything else seemed to have any effect on what we called his anxiety. Wouldn't you say that?"

Lauren nodded. She went on, "I do think his situation is not just anxiety. I think that his whole profile goes beyond that. But his problems always seemed to ride on his shoulders. We had a whole psychological test battery done. He came out as an incredibly bright kid with some imbalances in scores."

"Do you remember the numbers?" I asked.

Patrick replied. "Yeah, it was 142 or 143 on the IQ. But we already knew he was smart."

"Did either of you go through a time when you were blaming yourselves?" I asked.

Patrick answered first. "No, I never did, since I have always felt that people are what they are. I was much more concerned with seeing if we could identify what was making him find things diffi-cult rather than assigning blame to it."

Lauren then added, "I didn't blame myself either, but I wasn't as quick to feel that medication would help. But after seeing how useful Zoloft was for Patrick, I started to think it might help Matthew too. I felt—and I suppose I still do feel—more anxious about having children take drugs, when I don't know exactly what kind of harm might come to them as a result."

Patrick started to speak, but Lauren went on, "Just to finish my thought, he'd already been through so much in his life with doctors. I didn't want to turn around twenty years from now and say, 'Gee, I wish I hadn't added another layer on for you.' But I guess the main reason my thinking turned around is that Matthew in his own sweet little way worked around to telling me he wanted to see someone to talk to. He was wondering if someone could help him manage these mood swings. He'd certainly heard a lot about this from Patrick in our conversations."

"But I don't think he was parroting," Patrick injected.

"I was really just saying I was worried. I was concerned as a mother to figure out the best thing for our son. That he might be asking to do this because this was something that Dad did, I had to think about that possibility. Slowly I came over to the idea that Zoloft might be a possibility."

"To me," Patrick added, "anxiety was something that was palpa-ble, and I didn't want him to have to suffer with it."

"But people who don't know the whole story would be shocked that Matthew is taking that medication," Lauren said.

"Why?" I asked.

"You know," she answered, "everyone's taking this or that, and everyone is looking for a quick fix, and everyone seems to want to fall into some category or another. Then you hear people say, 'How can you do this to your child?' It would be one thing for me to take medication, that would be bad enough. But it becomes a few levels worse for your child. It is really perceived as a negative, as a crutch, as a hope for a quick fix. I've had all these kinds of comments come to me, and I find myself sometimes defending the decision to give Matthew medication, but more recently I just let it go. Because there is nothing to defend. I can't change their perception, it's pretty deep in some people."

"It's hurt your feelings?" I asked.

"Yes," Lauren replied. "The negative judgment is so immediate. It's not even, 'Gee, tell me more about that.' People just make an immediate decision. It isn't fair, because they have no idea how much thought and agonizing I put into this decision."

"And yet their judgment hurts," I added.

"Don't get me started on that," Patrick said, shaking his head.

"One of the reasons for writing this book is to help inform people and avoid the kind of prejudice you're talking about," I said. "You've obviously had a positive experience with Matthew going on Zoloft. Since the medication was started, what changes have you seen?"

Lauren and Patrick both sighed and smiled. "He's just so much more even," Patrick volunteered. "He's much more willing to push ahead and go on—for example, go to a basketball practice that he normally would have flipped out about going to because at the last moment he would just become too anxious. Now, if he has a moment of pause he will say, 'Okay, I can do that.' And he goes ahead. This makes him better able to get good at basketball, which for him is a major plus. Or this: In the past he would not call someone up for a play date because he was worried they'd say no; now he'll call them. Sure, he has the occasional anxiety or worry, but these worries no longer grow into nine-headed hydras.

And now he's so much more confident. Now he initiates plans with friends, where he wouldn't before."

"What has Dr. Bishop said?" I asked.

"He doesn't say much to us, because his meetings with Matthew are private, but he says he seems to be more interactive. And, of course, he wants our feedback, which is very positive."

"Dr. Bishop has obviously done a good job here," I said. "What advice would you give to other parents on the basis of your experiences?"

Lauren answered first. "Open your minds and your ears. I really do think that Matthew was saying loudly and clearly that he needed some help. Really listen to your child. Maybe someone on the outside could be helpful. Ask your child, 'Would you like to talk to someone other than Mom and Dad?' It could be really crucial for this to be taken outside the realm of family, because someone else can see things in a whole new light. Consider it as an option."

"And any advice on medication?"

"Find some people to talk to who have had positive experiences, because there will be plenty of people who will tell you the reasons not to do it."

Patrick added, "And most of them will be people who have never tried it."

"So you would say from personal experience that there is a lot of prejudice and misinformation?" I asked.

Patrick went on. "I think most of the negative views of medication are grounded in a sort of morality without much careful looking at where those views come from." He stopped for a minute to look out the window. "I think the main thing is to stop thinking about yourself or your kids as always being good or bad, as if it's always somebody's fault. You or your kids can behave in many ways and have plenty of feelings that are in fact the result of forces beyond their control, chemical forces in the brain."

"I agree," Lauren added. "I do want to say one more thing.

The other day Matthew was in the middle of trying to make a certain computer program work. Suddenly he looked at me and said, 'Mom, before Zoloft I would have trashed this.' He could actually feel the difference. He knew the moment when the medication was helping him. That was thrilling for me."

"I want to say one more thing," Patrick chimed in.

"No, I want to get the last word," Lauren retorted, and laughed.

We all paused. At that very moment Matthew stuck his head into the room and said, "Time's up!" And so it was.

While medication can be very helpful, usually we rely on non-medical interventions. Many of these interventions have been described in this book. From structure to exercise to the right diet and getting a good night's sleep, from reading aloud to using the right computer to talking to a friend to augmenting what I call "connectedness" in your life and your child's, there are many, many ways to redirect your child's life and to bolster both achievement and self-esteem. Medication is just one tool in this very large toolbox.

If you do choose to use medication, I recommend that you tell the school about it. At first you may fear that administrators will label your child or in some unintentional way stigmatize him. However, this concern can be dealt with up front if you are honest. If you are secretive, however, you yourself unintentionally stigmatize your child. Why be secretive, unless there is something shameful to hide? Before you give medication to your child at all, it is best to be totally comfortable with the idea yourself, so that you do not fear telling other people who should know, such as the people at school.

The greatest problems that arise with medications given to children for emotional or learning problems are not the physical side effects, but the psychological ones. You can prevent these invisible side effects only by thoroughly educating yourself and your child as to what the medication is and why it is being prescribed. As long as you or your child is ashamed of it, the medication will not

Children's Emotional or Behavioral Problems for Which Medication May Be Helpful

Problem	Medication(s) Used (*Sometimes* helpful, according to most medical research)
Attention deficit disorder	Stimulants, such as Ritalin; antidepressants, such as Tofranil or Wellbutrin; an antihypertensive, Clonidine
Obsessive-compulsive disorder; perseverative behaviors; ruminations	Antidepressants, such as Anafranil or Prozac (these are from different categories of antidepressants)
Insomnia	Antihistamines, such as Benadryl; various others
Bed-wetting	Antidiuretic hormone analogues, such as Desmopressin; tricyclic antidepressants, such as Tofranil
Impulsive, aggressive behavior; conduct disorder; oppositional defiant disorder; tantrums; rages; acts of physical violence; self-injurious behavior	Beta-blockers, such as Inderal; anxiolytics, such as BuSpar; mood stabilizers, such as such lithium; antiseizure medication such as Tegretol or Depakote; various others and combinations of others

(continued)

Problem *(continued)*	Medication(s) Used
Depression	In general, medication is not nearly as effective in childhood depression as it is in adults, but it sometimes works. Antidepressants from the tricyclic category, such as Tofranil and Elavil; antidepressants from the serotonin reuptake inhibitor category, such as Prozac and Zoloft; rarely, antidepressants from the monoamine oxidase inhibitor category, such as Parnate
Tantrums	Mood stabilizers like lithium or Tegretol
Tourette syndrome	Clonidine; antipsychotic agent, Haldol
Eating disorders	Antidepressants from the serotonin reuptake inhibitor group, such as Prozac and Zoloft; tricyclic antidepressants like Tofranil and Elavil
Post-traumatic stress disorder	Antidepressants in the serotonin reuptake inhibitor category, such as Prozac and Zoloft; tricyclic anti-depressants, such as Tofranil; anxiolytics, such as BuSpar
Psychotic disorders, such as schizophrenia	Antipsychotic medication, such as Haldol and Mellaril

work properly. Shame is at least as toxic a side effect as the more standard ones we usually mention.

Therefore, take the time to talk with your doctor at length about what the medication means to you and to your child. Read about it. Talk to others. Then, when you tell the people at school, take the time to make sure they feel comfortable with the medication as well. A simple note usually won't do. You may have to spend many hours educating others, but it is time well spent.

Chapter 11

·

Where to Look for Help

When you are worried about your child, share that worry with whoever is closest to you. Start there. Then speak to your circle of "consultants": mother, father, in-laws, other parents, extended family, friends.

Beyond this informal network, most parents have access to two experts on child development: the schoolteacher and the pediatrician. Consult with both. Between them, they can probably give you a good idea of whether you need additional help. In addition, if your pediatrician does not know of a specialist he or she would recommend, call the medical school nearest you and ask for the department of child psychiatry. The people there can always point you in a helpful direction.

Also, if you need long-term psychotherapy or other care not covered by your insurance program, as many children do, the hospitals affiliated with medical schools, called "teaching hospitals," can often help you. Long-term therapy is ruled out by many health insurance programs, but certain children, such as children who have pervasive developmental disorder or severe conduct disorder, need long-term therapy. It is extremely shortsighted of insurance programs not to pay for the intervention these children need while the children are young and most able to be helped, because the problems they get into as adults are much more expensive both to the insurance company and society. However, this is the dire situation many parents face: Their child needs the help their insurance company refuses to pay for.

If you cannot afford to pay yourself, try going to a teaching hospital. A fellow in child psychiatry—that is, a child psychiatrist-in-training—can treat your child. This is actually a very good deal. The fee is greatly reduced, but the quality of care is still high. Residents in child psychiatry are closely supervised by their teachers, who are experienced child psychiatrists. You get two doctors for much less than the price of one.

You may also be interested in getting more information on certain topics brought up in this book. One good source is the American Academy of Child and Adolescent Psychiatry. They publish a series of fact sheets for parents, and they can also refer you to a child psychiatrist near you.

American Academy of Child and Adolescent Psychiatry
3615 Wisconsin Ave.
Washington, DC 20016-3007
800-333-7636 or 202-966-7300

For reading and learning problems, the Orton Dyslexia Society is an excellent resource.

Orton Dyslexia Society
Chester Building
Suite 382
8600 LaSalle Rd.
Baltimore, MD 21286-2044
410-296-0232

Also good:

National Center for Learning Disabilities
381 Park Ave. South
Suite 1420
New York, NY 10016
212-545-7510

Learning Disabilities Association of America
4156 Library Rd.
Pittsburgh, PA 15234
412-341-1515

CHADD
(Children and Adults with Attention Deficit Disorder)
499 NW 70th Ave.
Suite 308
Plantation, FL 33317
305-587-3700

In addition, I recommend the following books for more information on selected topics brought up in this book:

GENERAL:
Damasio, Antonio. *Descartes' Error: Emotion, Reason, and the Human Brain.* Grosset/Putnam, New York, 1994.
Erikson, E. H. *Childhood and Society.* W. W. Norton, New York, 1950.
Kagan, Jerome. *The Nature of the Child.* Basic Books, New York, 1984.
Lickona, T. *Raising Good Children.* Bantam Books, New York, 1983.
Strayhorn, J. M. *The Competent Child.* The Guilford Press, New York, 1988.
Turecki, Stanley, M.D. *The Difficult Child.* Bantam, New York, 1985.

Turecki, Stanley, M.D. *The Emotional Problems of Normal Children.* Bantam, New York, 1994.

ATTENTION DEFICIT DISORDER:

Barkley, Russell. *Attention Deficit Hyperactivity Disorder: A Handbook for Diagnosis and Treatment.* Guilford Press, New York, 1990.

Barkley, Russell. *Taking Charge of ADHD: The Complete, Authoritative Guide for Parents.* Guilford Press, New York, 1995

Cahill Fowler, Mary. *Maybe You Know My Kid: A Parent's Guide to Identifying, Understanding, and Helping Your Child with Attention Deficit Disorder.* Birch Lane Press, New York, 1990.

Hallowell, Edward M., M.D. and John J. Ratey, M.D. *Answers to Distraction.* Pantheon, New York, 1995.

Hallowell, Edward M., M.D. and John J. Ratey, *Driven to Distraction.* Pantheon, New York, 1994.

GENERAL LEARNING PROBLEMS:

Armstrong, Thomas. *7 Kinds of Smart: Identifying and Developing Your Many Intelligences.* Plume/Penguin, New York, 1993.

Edwards, Betty. *Drawing on the Right Side of the Brain.* Tarcher/Putnam, New York, 1989.

Gardner, Howard. *Frames of Mind: The Theory of Multiple Intelligences.* Basic Books, New York, 1983.

Levine, Mel, M.D. *Keeping a Head in School.* Educators Publishing Service, Cambridge, Mass. 1991.

Pennington, Bruce. *Diagnosing Learning Disorders: A Neuropsychological Framework.* Guildford Press, New York, 1991.

Pinker, Steven. *The Language Instinct: How the Mind Creates Language.* William Morrow and Company, New York, 1994.

Vail, Priscilla. *Emotion: The On/Off Switch for Learning.* Modern Learning Press, Rosemont, N.J., 1994.

Vail, Priscilla. *Learning Styles: Food for Thought and 130 Practical Tips.* Modern Learning Press, Rosemont, N.J., 1993.

Vail, Priscilla. *Smart Kids with School Problems: Things to Know and Ways to Help.* New American Library, New York, 1987.

CENTRAL AUDITORY PROCESSING DISORDER:

Kelly, Dorothy A. *Central Auditory Processing Disorder: Strategies for Use in Children and Adolescents.* The Psychological Corporation, Tucson, Arizona, 1995.

OBSESSIVE-COMPULSIVE DISORDER:

Rapoport, Judith, M.D. *The Boy Who Couldn't Stop Washing: The Experience and Treatment of Obsessive-Compulsive Disorder.* Dutton, New York, 1989.

TOURETTE SYNDROME:

Comings, David E., M.D. *Tourette Syndrome and Human Behavior.* Hope Press, Duarte, Cal., 1990.

Hearle, Tracy, ed. *Children with Tourette Syndrome: A Parents' Guide.* Woodbine House, Rockville, Md., 1992.

TEMPERAMENT:

Kagan, Jerome. *Galen's Prophecy: Temperament in Human Nature.* Basic Books, New York, 1994.

Chess, Stella, and Alexander Thomas. *Temperament in Clinical Practice.* Guilford Press, New York, 1986.

Afterword

....

When No One Is to Blame

They say best men are molded out of faults,
And, for the most, become much more the better
For being a little bad.

William Shakespeare, Measure for Measure

If I could make a plea to my fellow parents out there it would be this: Please don't give up. *There is always hope for a child.* Look for the best in your child, and don't give up on your own best instincts. Don't get so exasperated by the difficult behavior of your child that you start using "solutions" you know in your heart aren't right. Under stress, all of us sometimes do things we later regret. All parents suffer from stress. The stress of being a parent is particularly difficult because there is no public reward or acclaim for doing the job: There is no salary, no Academy Award or Tony, no affordable assistance or publicly funded vacation time. Parents get little credit for what they do right, and they get lots of blame for what they do wrong. Parents feel the sting of disapproval from all sides—from their own parents, from other parents, from teachers, from spouses, from doctors, from passersby on the street or onlookers in shopping malls; they even feel it from their own children, the very people they are giving up so much time and money to care for and rear.

Being a parent can be a thankless, impossible task. It is no wonder that when children become demanding, parents often reach the end of their rope in a hurry. They begin to look for solutions in places they never would have looked before. They scream and yell a lot, even though they know the more you scream and yell, the less effective they are. They spank or slap, even though they don't think physical punishment is a great idea. They offer bribes, even though they wish they weren't reduced to doing that. All parents do these deeds when stressed.

Even if simple solutions don't work in the long run, it is hard not to opt for them—just because they *are* simple. As parents, we are probably tired, and we are not really expert at what we do. No one trains us, after all. The work is hard and the patience required is great. All we can do is keep trying, and trying to keep up.

We are getting closer and closer to being able to define, in terms of the brain's anatomy, what we mean by character, will, empathy, intent, and many other advanced human functions usually ascribed to undefined forces. Wouldn't it be amazing if we had in the future a test that could assay willpower? Or if we had a brain scan that could measure the depth of one's empathic powers? Or a way of measuring intuition? Or a quantifiable test for initiative? These things will probably happen.

What will all this knowledge do to our sense of individual responsibility? Individual responsibility will be as pivotal and important as ever. As we learn more, we will simply understand it better—what it is and what it isn't. We will understand what it means in neurological terms to take responsibility or to avoid it. Individual responsibility itself will always matter; its importance can never be put to rout. What will be put to rout—what is, mercifully, being put to rout right now by our developing knowledge—is the shaming process of unfair blame.

The child and parent must always take responsibility, but sometimes a problem is still no one's *fault*. No one is to be blamed. There is a difference between taking responsibility and taking blame. I think we are right to insist that parents and children take responsibility, but we do not also have to insist that they suffer blame.

The distinction between responsibility and blame may seem obscure, but it is crucial. We can rightly ask all members of our society to take responsibility for their actions, and in the case of children we can include their parents in that social contract. But we do not have to fold blame into the request.

The history of how we humans have "disciplined" our children is a gruesome horror story full of physical acts of violence and mental cruelty. Children will almost always tell you it wasn't the physical pain of a punishment that hurt; it was the shame that did the damage.

Not only the annals of parenting but also those of education are full of examples of shame as discipline. For centuries, schools have badly mistreated some children, particularly those who learn slowly. These days, when it often seems as if children need more discipline in school, we can easily forget that our tradition is one of schools' overdisciplining children. Probably anyone over the age of thirty can remember public school systems where it was routine for children to be spanked, paddled, or otherwise hit, where it was normal for children to sit in a corner wearing a dunce cap or to be called up in front of class and be ridiculed, where many teachers used public humiliation as a "teaching technique," and where every class contained at least one forlorn child whose lot was to be embarrassed by the teacher on a daily basis. These practices continue today in some schools.

We quickly forget our own childhood. Most of us remember only a few details from our elementary school years. But if you look in the teachers' supply catalogues from those years and see pictures of paddles and leather straps for sale, or if you read written accounts of children who remember being called stupid or an idiot or a dolt on a daily basis, you can imagine how awful those years were for some kids. It didn't have to be that way. It *doesn't* have to be that way.

Think of children. Think of those little faces, those little minds rushing into classrooms. Children's energy: It is the densest distillation of the life force we have. Walk down any elementary school corridor, even one with no children in it, and you will feel that life force emanating from behind the classroom doors, filling the corridor as if with magic light. Look on the bulletin boards at their little projects scrawled in colored pencil: a map of South America looking like Jimmy Durante's nose, or a colored-in bar chart of birthday months in grade two (looking not quite like the annual report of IBM). Look at the row of raincoats hung on hooks on rainy days, red and yellow slickers waiting to be wiggled into.

Just as teachers can criticize or blame children for not being perfect, so can we parents. Nature gives our children traits—a learning problem, or a certain temperament, or even eye color or a dislike of baseball—we sometimes have a hard time accepting. But we do much greater damage by pretending those traits are not there than by doing the often painful work of reconciling ourselves to who our children truly are.

No child is perfect, not even ours. We do our children a great favor by accepting them as they really are rather than insisting upon some impossible, ideal version that can never be. It is the *real* child who needs our love, not the imagined, perfect child. (The real child soon becomes much better than merely perfect.)

The distinction to be made here is between loyalty, which every child needs, and denial, which can prevent a child from getting help he or she might also need. Sometimes the best form of loyalty is a parent's willingness to see that his or her child is troubled or in some way imperfect.

What is so hard for us parents to grasp is that the perfect child is our invention, and we love that invention to satisfy ourselves rather than to help our child. As it carries us closer to some fantasized, ideal version of our child, denial carries us far away from our real child. No child is perfect. Not mine, not yours. We do not have to announce this fact in public, and we can still go on sticking up for our children even if they're wrong, but we should acknowledge to ourselves that they are not perfect. As long as we know what we see, and as long as we see what is there, we can, and perhaps should, pretend to the rest of the world that we have a perfect child. But we need to know deep inside that our child, like all children, is imperfect.

To use a simple example, if proud Dad thinks six-year-old son is a professional-caliber ballplayer, Dad will never accept that his son maybe can't field ground balls, and he won't teach him how, or forgive him for not being able to.

When a parent will love only the idealized child, the made-up, Hollywood version, this is selfish love. It isn't really even love, but rather narcissism, because what the parent is looking for is self-gratification rather than the child's well-being.

What happens in these situations can be cruel. The child senses from an early age that Mom or Dad or both don't really love him as much as they say they do. The child knows that despite all their protestations he just doesn't measure up the way his siblings do. He wonders what is wrong with him. However, because no one tells him what is wrong—in fact, they tell him they think he is wonderful and all his feelings to the contrary are absurd—he feels defective and confused.

A child can sense when he is not totally accepted. When this lack of acceptance permeates his childhood, he takes it in and it becomes part of who he is. He begins to reject himself. If you bathe in a certain water, your skin takes in the water's salts. How does the transition occur—from being done to, to doing it to yourself? How does a child go from being subtly rejected to rejecting himself? I think it is like hearing a song. If you hear it often enough and long enough you begin to whistle it yourself. Even if you hate the song—as in the case of many advertising jingles—you can't stop yourself from humming it as you travel through your day.

So it is with how we treat our children. Love from us can seep into their minds and set off a happy song they whistle, but a subtle reluctance to love can trigger a sad song that lasts forever. All we really need to do is accept the child we have.

You may find that the real child who steps out of the haze is more wonderful than any child you had ever conceived of. You may find that the child standing there in the dirt driveway looking hopefully up at you with the sun at his back is in fact the child you have wanted to love all along. You may find that the perfect child was a burden on you, as much as on your child. Perfection was just another achievement you had to get. The perfect child was just another trophy.

Our children should be who they are. That is what we want for them, to be comfortable being themselves. I don't think we parents are ever better than when we love our children for who they truly are.

After all is said and done, this is what we parents can do for our children: We can love them. You never know how much that love means while you're giving it, especially because—like all real love —it's messy, full of anger and frustration and worry as well as sweetness and light. But that love means the world. A famous man was once asked how he had achieved so much in his life. He replied, "In my mother's eyes I only saw smiles." For your children, you provide those eyes and those smiles.

Acknowledgments

. . . .

Many professionals and friends helped me create this book. Drs. Joseph Coyle, Jerome Kagan, Judith Rapaport, and Neal Ryan, all major experts in their fields, generously gave of their time and knowledge. My friend Peter Metz, head of the department of child psychiatry at the University of Massachusetts, offered many bits of advice along the way. My colleague, two-time coauthor, and squash partner, John Ratey, was most encouraging. Two colleagues, Dr. Edward Khantzian and Dr. Charles Magraw, gave of their time and their wisdom like the old-fashioned doctors they both are. My friend Jonathan Galassi and his wife, Susan, both read my work and, as always, tactfully steered me along. Michael Thompson, another colleague, coauthor, and dear friend, offered encouragement and reassurances before and after our weekly tennis games. Jeffrey Sutton, a squash partner and brilliant neuroscientist and psychiatrist, helped with his spontaneous comments all along the way. Fred Hills, my editor at Simon & Schuster, defines excellence in his field. He shaped this book from the beginning to the end. His assistant, Hilary Black, answered questions whenever I had them and gave me reassurances

Acknowledgements

along the way for which I cannot thank her too much. The copy editor who worked on the manuscript, Jolanta Benal, did a superb job. As a writer I know how much painstaking work goes into considering the shape of each sentence, the choice of each word. Ms. Benal reviewed every word and sentence with care and incredible attention to detail. What mistakes remain are my fault, no one else's.

My extended family, as always, supported and challenged my ideas, giving me hope at every turn. My cousin Jamie, and Josselyn and Tom Bliss and their children, as well as my brothers, Ben and John, have always given me their best. I thank them last, but never least.

Index

Index

About the Author

. . . .

EDWARD HALLOWELL, M.D., a child and adult psychiatrist, is the founder and director of The Hallowell Center for Cognitive and Emotional Health, an outpatient diagnosis and treatment center for children and adults located in Concord, Massachusetts, just outside Boston. Dr. Hallowell is on the faculty of the Harvard Medical School and is also in private practice. He is a consultant at numerous schools, lectures widely on topics related to children's emotional health and learning disabilities, and is frequently cited as an expert by various media, including *Time, Newsweek, The New York Times, The Boston Globe, The Boston Herald, Wired* magazine, *Inc.* magazine, the *Los Angeles Times, Child* magazine, and *Parent* magazine. Dr. Hallowell is married to Sue George Hallowell, a psychiatric social worker; they have three children and live in Arlington, Massachusetts.